Surfing Hawaii

Help Us Keep This Guide Up to Date

Every effort has been made by the author and editors to make this guide as accurate and useful as possible. However, many things can change after a guide is published—regulations change, techniques evolve, organizations come under new management, and so on.

We would love to hear from you concerning your experiences with this guide and how you feel it could be improved and kept up to date. While we may not be able to respond to all comments and suggestions, we'll take them to heart and we'll also make certain to share them with the author. Please send your comments and suggestions to the following address:

The Globe Pequot Press
Reader Response/Editorial Department
P.O. Box 480
Guilford, CT 06437

Or you may e-mail us at:

editorial@GlobePequot.com

Thanks for your input.

Surfing Hawaii

A Complete Guide to the Hawaiian Islands' Best Breaks

Rod Sumpter

FALCONGUIDE®

GUILFORD, CONNECTICUT
HELENA, MONTANA

AN IMPRINT OF THE GLOBE PEQUOT PRESS

To buy books in quantity for corporate use or incentives, call **(800) 962–0973, ext. 4551,** or e-mail **premiums@GlobePequot.com.**

The author and The Globe Pequot Press assume no liability for accidents happening to, or injuries sustained by, readers who engage in the activities described in this book.

Contents

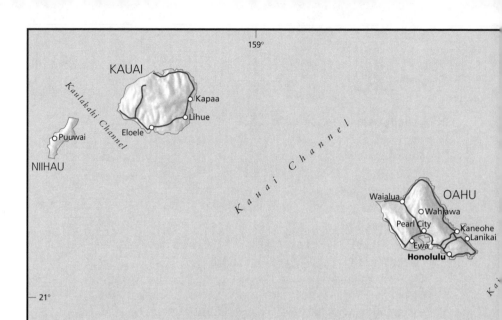

159°

KAUAI

Kaulakahi Channel

○ Kapaa
○ Lihue
Eloele ○

○ Puuwai

NIIHAU

Kauai Channel

Waialua ○ ○ Wahiawa
Pearl City ○ ○ Kaneohe
○ Ewa ○ Lanikai
Honolulu ○

OAHU

Kai

— 21°

Kai

PACIFIC OCEAN

HAWAIIAN ISLANDS

SCALE RF 1 : 2,500,000

0　　Kilometers　　100

0　　Miles　　50

— 19°

159°

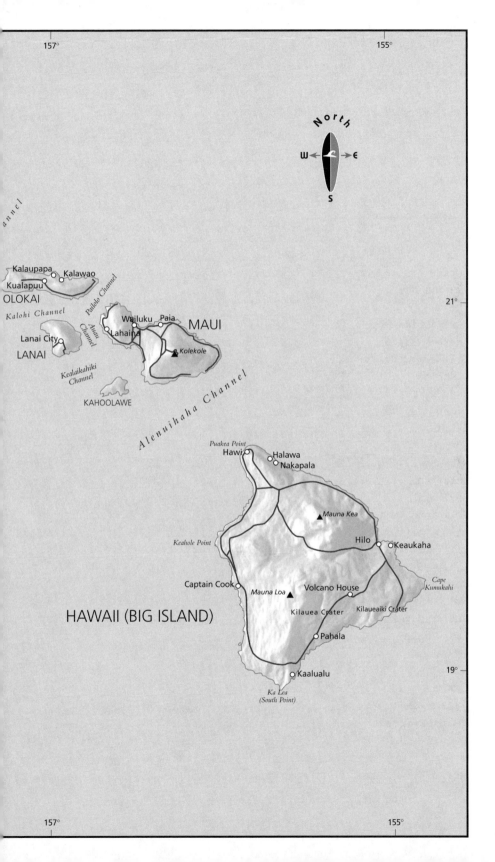

157°

155°

North

W ← → E

S

Kalaupapa Kalawao
Kualapuu
OLOKAI

Kalohi Channel

Pailolo Channel

Auau Channel

Wailuku Paia
Lanai City Lahaina MAUI
LANAI ▲ *Kolekole*

Kealaikahiki Channel

KAHOOLAWE

Alenuihaha Channel

21°

Puakea Point
Hawi ○ ○ Halawa
○ Nakapala

▲ *Mauna Kea*

Keahole Point
Hilo ○ Keaukaha

Cape Kumukahi

Captain Cook ○ Volcano House ○
Mauna Loa ▲
HAWAII (BIG ISLAND) *Kilauea Crater* Kilaueaiki Crater

○ Pahala

19°

○ Kaalualu
Ka Lea (South Point)

Acknowledgments

This book would not have been possible without the support, help, and enthusiasm of my wife, Valerie, who endlessly checked the manuscript. Thanks to my son John for his imaginative surfing at Backdoor, and to my daughter-in-law Sarah and baby Ben for their support. To Chris and Liz for travel advice, Mark and Clare for wave awareness, Colin and Diana, and to Mom, who was always there.

Thanks to Scott Adams, Laura Jorstod, and Lynn Zelem for help and guidance. Thanks also to the surfers Gerald Hurd, Eland Gray, William Kereawi, Bully Kapahulehue—who gave invaluable insight on Kauai—and to the *Waimea Gazette Kauai*.

On Maui much appreciation goes to Bob Olsen, who met me in 1963 at LAX for the premiere of the *Endless Summer* film and willingly gave concise surf formation. To Gavin Campbell, Franpenco Drusendi, also to John Chiu and Jenna Silisaiva.

On Molokai thanks to Fred Saunders and to the Department of Business, Economic Development & Tourism. On Lanai to Meg Smith and the Department of Business, Economic Development & Tourism.

On the Big Island I could not have had a better expert or more knowledgeable surfer than Chris Boward, whose inspired surfing and island knowledge gave me so much information.

On Oahu much appreciation goes to John Perry and BK, who made our Sunset boards. To Chris "Bommie" Beacham, Mick Mabbott, Johnny McAroy, Chris Kennings, Eddie Manning, Tony Bradley, Kim Bradley, Davey Jones, John Penn, John Dunn, Anthony Morby, and Dick Van Straland; and to Johnny Brocksema for saving my life when I got knocked out by my board and went butt-up. To the Avalon crew for inspiring me to go live the dream. I take them everywhere in my thoughts and remember those formative years filled with unwritten pledges made by the campfire after a heavy day's surfing that fired the imagination in all things surfing (stoked). And it was the first Hawaiian surf movies at Avalon Surf Life Saving Clubs and the Windansea Surf Club that showed the wildest backwash air and huge Makaha point-surf footage that still stands today as some of the most inspiring imagery ever shot.

To the great surfers I met and learned so much from: Billy and Laird Hamilton, Mike Doyle, Margo Godfrey (Oberg), Barry Kanaiaupuni, Thor Svenson (the Hawaii team manager when I won the Banzai Pipeline junior Windansea Expression Session), and Duke Kahanamoku. The writing and research of this book have been a fun experience.

The first seeds were sown many years ago in the history lessons at school detailing the exploits of Captain James Cook, who first documented surfboards and surfing in 1778 on the Big Island. And when I met the great Duke Kahanamoku surfing in the Makaha International Championships of 1964—and came in seventeenth in the juniors—the process of creating this guide was started.

In 1970 I was making the surfing film *Oceans* based around the Hawaiian Islands while showing my film *Freeform* at Haleiwa and Honolulu University. I have since worked and lived ten winter seasons on the north shore of Oahu and traveled to all the islands; I guess you could say I am endlessly stoked by the Aloha State. I hope you enjoy this guide and I wish to thank all those who helped along the way—and those I have surely forgotten to mention.

Introduction

"You know, there are so many waves coming in all the time, you don't have to worry about that. Just take your time— waves come. Let the other guys go; catch another wave."

—Duke Kahanamoku

Surfing Hawaii

The United States is blessed with waves of all kinds, from the best in the world to the world's most difficult. To find the best of the best of these waves, you need only go to Hawaii, where some of the world's leading waves thunder in for prime surfing. Today there are more famous surf spots per mile in the Hawaiian Islands than anyplace else on earth.

Comprising eight major islands in the central Pacific Ocean, Hawaii stands alone as the world's first and foremost surfing mecca. This is the place where surfing began and where today's best surfers come to test their skills against nature's toughest waves. Among these islands, Oahu and Maui stand apart, offering up some of the Aloha State's finest surf. Warm waters, blue-turquoise seas, and mountainous groundswells from the Pacific give Hawaii its legendary surf.

It is the North Shore of Oahu where surfing is at its peak. From December to March you can see 30-foot-plus surf at Waimea Bay and Kaena Point. Maui does quite well on its own, with places like Jaws, which may break at 60 feet, and Honolua Bay often offering surfers the perfect wave. Overall, what's on offer at most of Hawaii's breaks are short, fast, vertical, and powerful waves with hard sand or sharp coral waiting to break a leg. Hawaii is not for the fainthearted. Many a surfer has grown up, grown older, and grown wiser at the hands of the most gripping waves in the world at places like Sunset Beach, with its bigger-than-life peak; Banzai Pipeline, ready to maim; and Chuns Reef, ready to give longboarders the best fun of an entire trip.

And there's so much more. Sandy Beach pounds out bodyboards like it's a stamp machine. Waikiki's outrigger canoeists surf Diamond Head alongside longboarders. And Hawaiian surfing legend Buffalo Keaulana's Big Board Surfing Contest is held every February at Makaha. In Hawaii surfing is epic.

With perfect swells from tropical weather systems originating in the Aleutians and Alaska, long-distance groundswells provide powerful winter surf to these islands from November to March. Of the eight islands, Oahu, Maui, Kauai, the Big Island (Hawaii), Molokai, and Lanai can be surfed, while Ni`ihau and Kaho`olawe are off-limits. There are also twenty-nine atolls on what is called the Northwest Hawaiian Islands; these are open to ocean surfing, tow-in surfing, and extreme launch-ins from boats. There is plenty to discover in these Hawaiian Islands if you have the will and respect the local traditions, peoples, and their way of life. You also need to respect Mother Ocean—your life will depend on it.

How to Use This Guide

Surfing Hawaii starts with the notion that every wave is different. The reasons for this are very complicated, as you'll see in the sections that follow. Put simply, however, if you'd like to have a full wave repertoire and a continually rewarding surfing experience, you must travel and challenge all kinds of conditions. To surf well you need to visualize your movements. And so a surfer's dream wave develops as a vision out of advancing ability and technique. The only real way to satisfy a craving for progress is by surfing different and better breaks on the other side of the hill.

This book is a guide for the beginner and the expert alike. It accommodates the needs of all grades of surfer and describes every location comprehensively with the facts you need to know. All the best and named longboarding, shortboarding, bodyboarding, and bodysurfing locations in the Hawaiian Islands are covered. The book is organized in the order of the islands as the sun rises and sets across them from east to west, beginning with the Big Island and ending with Kauai.

All the surf spots in this book, both featured and secondary spots, are arranged in geographical order and are listed counterclockwise from the north side of each island. Names of featured spots appear in boldfaced type in the contents and on the maps. The featured spot listings contain directions, detailed information, and surfer ratings, which include beginner, novice, learner, intermediate, experienced, expert, advanced, and big-wave rider. Thumbnail surfing photos indicate secondary spot listings, which contain short descriptions and useful facts.

How Waves Are Formed

The most common cause of waves is wind action in the open ocean. Earthquakes and volcanic eruptions beneath the ocean can cause seismic sea waves, but these surging, killing walls of water are rare. Storms in the open ocean, on the other hand, are quite common. They provide the sport of surfing with ridable waves as a result of variations in air pressure that force gusty winds upon the ocean's surface. If the wind is strong and steady enough, it will form chop over a large area referred to as a *sea* or *wind fetch*. As these wind waves are blown downwind, they become longer, smoother, and more organized and take the form of what is known as a *groundswell* or *wave trains.* A swell is what we recognize as the marching *lines* of energy that travel across the open ocean; they're called *corduroy* upon reaching a shore. Swells can travel thousands of miles without losing much energy until they hit shallow water on our shores to form a breaking wave. Hawaii's huge surf is a result of long-distance groundswells and wave trains from faraway storms.

North and northwest swells or wave trains are produced by storms in the North Pacific in winter months and are the largest and most powerful.

West swells are created by storms in the West Pacific and are most common in fall and spring.

South and southwest swells are generated by storms in the South Pacific in our summer months and can also result in overhead good-size waves.

Wind swell is a term used to refer to less consistent and usually smaller waves that are produced by storms or strong winds within a couple of hundred miles of the coast.

Waves generated by the wind may range in height from less than an inch to as much as 60 feet. Ocean wave size is determined by the wind velocity, the fetch, the length of the area affected by the wind, and the length of time the wind blows. Big surf is made by large, long-lasting storms with strong winds far out at sea. Surf forecasters today can precisely determine when large waves will hit a particular spot on the coast by using weather data and computer models.

> The Hawaiian Islands are grouped closely together, with each island casting a swell shadow across its neighbors. Only those coasts open to the direct swell path receive wave trains or the full force of the waves; blocked or shadowed islands receive waves of smaller size, or they may even be flat.

Wave Parts

The highest part of a wave is called the *crest* or *peak*. The lowest part is called the *trough* or *pit*. The front of the wave is called the *face,* and the back of the wave is generally referred to as simply the *back*. The *curl* is the part of the wave that is breaking. The *lip* is a term used to describe the very tip of a cresting wave that curls or plunges down. The *wall* is a general term used to refer to the area of the face that has yet to break. A *section* is a portion or an area of break wave. The *pocket* or *barrel* is the section of the wall just ahead of the breaking curl. It's usually the steepest and fastest part of the wave and the most desirable place to surf. The *shoulder* or *flats* is the less steep section of the green part of wave face, away from the breaking part.

Wave Measurement

Some folks measure waves from the face, while others, especially in Hawaii, measure from the back. Waves are dynamic and change in width, height, and shape as they approach shore. To complicate things further, wave size differs depending on the angle of the observer. Regardless of your choice of measurement while in the water, it's important to understand how it's done in surf predictions. Satellites combine wind speed, length and duration of fetch, and direction to predict a surf height for a surf zone. Ocean buoys measure the up-and-down height and period between swells for its location. Vessel reports use instruments and oberservation to measure the rise and fall of swells. Meteorologists use all the above data as well as live location reports to compile forecasts—and they've become very accurate at predicting surf. Surf reports usually describe what direction the swell is traveling, the time interval between waves, and the wave height from the front. *Wave height* is determined by measuring the vertical distance between the crest and trough. *Wave length* is the distance between two successive wave crests.

Wave Shape

Wave shape can vary drastically from day to day at the same spot. Swell size, speed and direction, tides, currents, curve and shape of the shore, and kelp and wind conditions all affect shape. Every surf spot has a unique set of variables that will affect wave shape.

Among surfers, beginners generally head straight to shore for the shortest ride. Once you have progressed past the beginner stage, however, cornering with a peeling wave is the accepted way to surf; it gives greater length of ride and speed.

Areas with long, gradual rises from deep to shallow water at land points and coral reefs usually result in what's known as a peeling wave. A peeling wave breaks easily down its face, spilling or toppling over. It appears to crumble or peel in a curling motion along its length and is generally the most forgiving type of wave.

Breaks with a more abrupt change from deep to shallow water usually result in what's known as a *tubing* wave. A tubing wave breaks from top to bottom, because the swell peaks more quickly and pitches the crest down the wave face. This type of wave creates a hollow *tube* or *barrel* section. The term *hollow* is used to describe this concave and steep wave face shape. The term *sucky* is also used to describe wave conditions that are hollow and breaking in shallow water. And when waves break all at once along their entire face, they are referred to as being *closed out*.

Tides

Tides are related to the moon's cycles and occur in all bodies of water, but they're more prominent along the coast. In most places the tide rises and falls twice a day. The maximum and minimum levels of the rise and fall are called *high* and *low tide,* respectively. It takes roughly six hours for rising water to reach high tide and approximately another six to reach low tide again. This sequence is called the *tidal cycle* and is repeated every twelve hours and twenty-five minutes. The amount of change in the water level during the cycle is known as the *tidal range.* During the first and last quarter of the moon's cycle, called a *neap tide,* there is minimal difference between high and low tides. When there's a full or new moon cycle, known as a *spring tide,* there's a bigger difference between high and low tides.

Most surf shops can provide you with a book listing the times that high and low tide will occur each day for the entire year; they also sell tidal wristwatches, which showing high and low tides in an LCD display. Both can help you plan your surfing session, because changes in water depth at the points where waves break can significantly alter the shape of the wave. Most waves increase in height from the period of low tide to the high-tide mark.

Wind Conditions

The direction the wind is blowing can greatly affect wave shape. In the morning or evening, there tends to be little or no wind and the surf is more likely to be *glassy*—a phenomenon known as the *morning* or *evening glassoff,* in reference to the incredibly smooth appearance of the water.

An *onshore* wind is one that blows from the ocean and is usually the least favorable direction. Strong onshore winds often result in *blown-out* surf. Blown-out surf is the condition of waves that have been made bumpy, flattened, confused, or blown apart by the wind. This type of surf is also referred to as *mush.*

A *sideshore* wind blows across the swell. Although it's better than an onshore wind, it can also lead to deteriorating conditions.

An *offshore* wind blows from the shore into the surf and will enhance wave shape. An offshore wind helps hold up the incoming waves, giving them cleaner faces to ride.

If you hear a surf report saying, "It's 6 feet and going off, and it's pumping," you can be sure there's an offshore wind and a new swell, more than head high, with good waves.

Types of Breaks

Surf spots are also called breaks, in reference to an area where waves that can be surfed form. Wave energy will break differently depending on the tide, the swell direction, and, just as importantly, the characteristics of the shore bottom.

- *Beach Breaks* are left- and right-hand breaking waves. Often, such breaks will create a gradual sloping sand, stone, or pebble beach where some of the best beginner's surf rolls in softly.

- *Sand Bottom Breaks* are areas where waves break over a sandbar. These breaks can be altered, because sand shifts and can look very different from time to time. Sand breaks are usually found relatively close to shore. Winter tides and currents change the sandbars more frequently, sometimes turning sand-bottomed breaks into rock-bottomed breaks until the sand is returned, usually in spring.

- *Reef Breaks* are areas where waves break over a coral or rocky reef. Coral reef breaks tend to occur in shallow water and can create some of the most spectacular barrels in the world. The majority of the famous island breaks in the world are coral reef breaks.

- *Point Breaks* are areas where waves break at a part of the shore that extends outward. These breaks tend to be larger and more consistent than other breaks because they are the first areas of shallow water that the swell hits. Often, a swell will wrap around a point. There are left point breaks and right point breaks where rides switch into a beach break.

- *Outside Breaks* are areas of somewhat shallow water where waves break farther from shore. These breaks can create some of the largest and most powerful waves. Because the water is deeper than inside breaks, outside breaks usually require a bigger groundswell in order for waves to form.

- *Cloud Breaks* are distant offshore breaks—more than 0.5 mile out. They're usually surfed by tow-in Jet Ski teams.

- *Avalanche, Bombora's,* and *Open-Ocean Reefs* are all terms referring to big-wave surfing spots where waves are formed above reefs or rocks sometimes 80 feet deep.

- *River Mouth Breaks* feature waves breaking over sand or rock at the mouth of a river. These can be dangerous due to their strong currents; the murky water can be a feeding ground for sharks.

- *Lefts* are waves that break from the peak to the surfer's left.
- *Rights* are waves that break from the peak to the surfer's right.
- *Peaks* are waves consistently forming in the same place breaking and peeling to the left or right.
- *Wedges* are waves formed when a side or deflected swell comes across an incoming swell (usually due to nearby rocks or a cliff face).
- *Breakwaters* are human-made structures that can create most of the above types of waves.

Learning to Surf

You can learn to surf on all the Hawaiian Islands, but there are huge differences between a mobile surf school that takes you around an island, finding the best spot in the given conditions, and a fixed surf school. Below are the main beginner spots, but by no means are these the only locations on each island:

- Canoes break at Waikiki, Oahu.
- Ka`anapali Point, Maui.
- Keauhou Point, Kona, the Big Island.
- Poipu, Kauai.
- Manele Bay, Lanai.
- Kepuhi Beach, Molokai.

There are other places to learn to surf. Contact information for surf lessons can be found in the resources sections.

Surfing Terms

Tow-In. Working as a team, you and a partner use a Jet Ski and rope to tow you onto the swell just when the wave is about to break. This saves you the task of paddling out to the break and onto a wave.

Natural Foot or **Regular Foot** refers to surfers who stand with their left foot forward of the right.

Goofy Foot refers to surfers who stand with their right foot forward of the left.

Big-Wave Surfing

World-famous surf spots in the Hawaiian Islands litter this book like a Who's Who of destinations, ranging from Second Reef Banzai Pipeline to Waimea Bay and Sunset Beach. Here big-wave surfers come to tackle the most challenging and powerful waves Hawaii has to offer. Below are the most amazing surf locations on planet earth:

- Jaws, Maui.
- Waimea Bay, Oahu.
- Kaena Point, Oahu.
- Sunset Beach, Oahu.
- Phantoms, Oahu.
- Outer Log Cabins, Oahu.
- Second Reef Banzai Pipeline, Oahu.

Coming to Hawaii

Do as much of your trip planning as possible before you leave home. Given today's heavy tourist pressure and travel-related headaches, you'll have a lot of logistics to deal with. You don't want them to bite into your leisure time and maybe cost you the best waves of your vacation!

Which island should you visit? Probably the best way to decide is to look at this guide's information. But very generally speaking:

- Oahu is for the very beginner and the advanced to big-wave rider.
- Maui is for the intermediate to expert and big-wave rider.
- Kauai is for the novice and expert.
- The Big Island is for the novice and expert.
- Lanai is for the expert.
- Molokai is for the expert.

Winter is the best time to come—between November and March. Stay as long as you can. Remember that south swells come in winter as well as northerly swells. Summer can have the very best south swells and generally the most consistent surf. Still, whatever the season, Hawaii will blow your mind with pure wave power, blue clear water, and refreshing aloha spirit.

Getting Around on the Hawaiian Islands

By Air

Nearly every surfer coming to Hawaii will arrive by air to either Maui or Oahu International Airport and fly among the four main islands via either Aloha Airlines or Hawaiian Airlines. Interisland flights are frequent and reliable to Oahu, Maui, Kauai, and the Big Island.

Air travel among the four main islands runs from $70 to $100 per flight each way. Expect the same luggage security scans and long lines here as you'll find at any airport around the world. Long ticket queues are possible, as is lost luggage, so it's wise to arrive at the airport two hours before departure. (The airlines advise arriving one hour ahead, but from my own experience, this is cutting things close.) You never want to miss a flight—it will cost you the price of a new ticket *and* the waiting-around time till you're able to board the next flight (all the while dreaming of those perfect waves going to waste). Flights depart approximately every two hours in daylight and are usually at capacity in the winter season. Locals will tell you about the days—only a few years ago—when you could arrive ten minutes before your flight and get on and go. Those days are long gone.

Aloha Airlines Baggage Offices:

- Honolulu, Oahu (808–837–6816).
- Lihue, Kauai (808–245–6618).
- Maui (808–877–5614).
- Kona, Big Island (west coast) (808–329–1651).

Localism is these days a worldwide response to the sheer volume of tourists. It shows up in Hawaii in different ways. Respect is the key word to carry with you everywhere. And if you take the time to learn as much Hawaiian (see the sidebar on page 13) as you can, it will put you in good stead to be given waves, welcomed in most locations, and given the aloha treatment. I have pointed out places in this book where localism is known to run strong. Still, the warmth and friendship you'll be met with throughout our state far outweigh whatever localism you may experience at certain spots.

By Bus

Buses make good sense and are a great way to meet people. See:

- Oahu (around the island): www.thebus.org
- Kauai: www.kauai.hawaii.gov/Default.aspx?tabid=208
- Maui (Lahaina to Kahului): www.wanderplanet.com or www.akinatours.com/maui_shuttle.htm
- Big Island: www.co.hawaii.hi.us/mass_transit/heleonbus.html

Molokai and Lanai have no bus service.

By Car

Renting a car is the popular and best way to see the islands; if you split the cost among four people, it's an affordable option. Don't forget to bring soft roof racks and rope for the boards.

Alamo
(800) 327–9633

Avis
(800) 321–3712

Budget
(800) 527–0700

Dollar Rent a Car
(800) 800–4000

Enterprise
(800) 325–8007

Hertz
(800) 654–3011

National
(800) 227–7368

Thrifty
(800) 367–2277 or (800) 767–9603

Driving in Paradise

- Don't honk. It's considered poor manners to honk your horn in traffic in Hawaii. You don't honk in surf paradise!
- Right turns at stoplights and stop signs are permitted after a stop.
- Watch for surfboard trailers being towed behind bikes, or boards wedged into welded forks on the sides. Surf bike riders tend to get blown about in the wind and surf in the bike lane.
- Look for the red and yellow markers in the shape of Hawaiian warriors along the roads. These indicate historical landmarks and points of interest.
- When you see a whale or the perfect wave, pull over carefully to the side of the road. Don't just jam on your brakes.

If you're going to be in the islands for more than a month, then it's worth looking into buying a used car and selling it at the end of your trip. A good way is to rent a car for a couple of days while you check out the supermarket notice boards at the key surf spots like Haleiwa, Oahu; Hanalei, Kauai; Lahaina, Maui; and Kailua Kona on the Big Island. (This is not an option on Lanai and Molokai.) You can sell your car when you return home in the same way; allow two weeks before your departure to find a buyer. This option does take a chunk out of your surfing time, but it can also save you big bucks—and if you have a mechanic surf buddy with you to check out the used car, you can get into the driver's seat safely while putting those dollars aside for future trips.

Molokai and Lanai

Molokai and Lanai are smaller than the major Hawaiian Islands and present a special case for travelers. To reach these islands by plane, **Paragon Air** (866–946–4744) offers service from Maui. Paragon is an unscheduled on-demand air carrier; its flights are subject to aircraft availability and prior bookings. It doesn't take surfboards, which you'll have to ship separately; call **Hawaii Cartage Inc.** on Maui (808–877–7997).

You can also travel by charter yacht. Contact **Lahaina Princess Cruises** (808–667–6165) or **Molokai Charters** (808–553–5852).

You can travel by ferry from Lahania, Maui, and take your surfboard for $25 with no hassle. By ferry from Lahaina, it's forty-five minutes to Lanai (808–661–3756) and an hour and a half to Molokai (**Maui Ferry,** 866–307–6524).

Getting Around with Your Surfboard

Should you bring your own surfboard, or rent or buy in the islands? Here are some thoughts to consider:

- Beginners can rent a board at the beach. If you attend a surf school, board rental will be part of the package.

- Novice surfers do best renting for short periods at the beach or from a surf shop.

- Intermediate to expert surfers should bring their own or buy a new or used board from a surf shop. Most shops offer buy-back plans, often with very favorable terms. This ensures that you'll get a good amount of your purchase price back at the end of your trip, if you sustain only regular wear and tear to the board. It's a much cheaper option than renting a board by the day. *Note:* Don't forget the receipt when you return the board; losing this will make the deal null and void and cost you big bucks. And when you set up a purchase, get the seller to spell out the buy-back option on the receipt before you hand over any money.

- Advanced to big-wave riders will want to bring their own specially shaped boards.

Left-baggage departments at the airports have all been closed indefinitely, so leaving your boards there is not an option. If you bring your boards along with the idea of selling them at the end of the trip, putting a card up on the supermarket notice boards

Pounders, Kokololio Beach Park, Oahu. PHOTO ROD SUMPTER

or in your car window can work well. Surf shops, unfortunately, will offer you very little money—unless your board is Hawaiian or a nice longboard. Even then, however, don't expect a good price.

How do you choose a board—knowing that your life depends on it? Generally your best bet is to rent a couple of boards, test out a few breaks, and get the feel of a particular model. As your skills evolve, you'll probably edge away from performance surfing and start to feel the need for speed. Then buy the biggest fastest gun or rocket launcher you've ever dreamed of, and go.

Surfing Organizations

Hawaiian Longboard Federation
P.O. Box 61303
Honolulu, HI 96822
(808) 988–1726 (phone and fax)
E-mail: HLFHawaii@aol.com

For information on the **National Scholastic Surfing Association,** you may contact the national or regional directors:

Janice Aragon (National Office)
P.O. Box 495
Huntington Beach, CA 92648
(714) 536–0445
Fax: (714) 964–5232
E-mail: jaragon@nssa.org

Gayline Clifford (Southwest/Hawaii Conference)
P.O. Box 495
Huntington Beach, CA 92648
(714) 536–0445
Fax: (714) 964–5232
E-mail: gclifford@nssa.org

Bobbi Parker
P.O. Box 427
Kahuku, HI 96731
(808) 456–7873
Fax: (808) 638–9136
E-mail: nssahawaii@hotmail.com

Speaking Hawaiian

The Hawaiian language has only twelve letters: five vowels (a, e, i, o, and u) and seven consonants (h, k, l, m, n, p, and w). All the consonants are pronounced as in English, with the exception of the w, which is pronouced v after after an i or e.

Vowels are pronounced:

A = ah as in hurrah   I = ee as in tee   U = oo as in look
E = ay as in tray   O = o as in pole

Hawaiian Word	English Meaning
ali`i	royalty
aloha	love, hello, good-bye
bruddah, brah	friend
calabash	bowl
da kine	describes anything
ha`ole	non-Hawaiian
he`ealu	surfing, wave sliding
lanai	porch
lei	flower garland
mahalo	thank you
mana	power
nalu	waves
pau	finished
keiki	child
kane	man
wahine	woman
mauna	mountain
moana	ocean
kaukau	food, meal
ho`olaule`a	street party, festival

MAP LEGEND

Accommodations	♠	Highways		═══(H1)═══
Airport	✈	Major Roads		──(78)──
Gate	•−•	Trail		....
Overlook	◘	Rivers / Creek		∼∼∼
Point of Interest	★	Park Boundary		▢▢▢▢
Structure	■			
Towns / Cities	○			
Waterfall	⟍			
Peaks	▲			
Campsites	⋀			
Craters	◉			

CHAPTER 1

Big Island

S tart your journey on the Big Island by landing at Keahole Kona International Airport on the western coast (leeward side). This is the best side of the island for surf.

Indeed, in ancient times many kings made their home here due to the excellent weather, good water, and consistent waves. Later, missionaries built churches and residences, turning the tiny fishing village of Kawaihae Harbor into a small seaport and reducing the size of this classic surf spot.

The best surf is nestled at the bottom of the Hualalai Volcano, where a west swell creates a dozen or more classic breaks. When you're gliding in to land and peering out at swell sweeping in evenly around jet-black lava, you know you're in for some tasty waves—waves that break in the same spot time and time again. It doesn't take long for you to realize that the Big Island of Hawaii is *big* in every sense of the word. Driving time to the North Shore or to the east coast from the Kona airport is three to four hours.

The surf on the Big Island is fickle. It's blocked from the main source of northwest winter swells because it's in the shadow of the other islands' swell-window. The big winter surf on the North Shore of Oahu may never reach the Big Island; still, a swell will get through from time to time. You may find it breaking at one spot, yet half a mile on either side is flat even though the underwater topography is similar. This amazing phenomenon is still a mystery and the talk of many surfers on their first visit here. It may be that

Regional Map

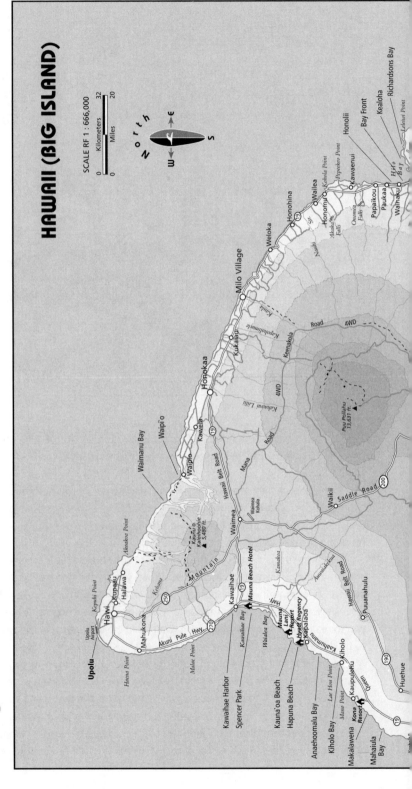

HAWAII (BIG ISLAND)

SCALE RF 1 : 666,000

Kilometers 0 — 32
Miles 0 — 20

North
N
W E
S

Upolu
Upolu Airport
Hawi
Kapaau
Halaava
Kapulei Point
Hoookena Point
Mahukona
Akuni Pule Hwy
Haena Point
Malae Point
250
270
Kawaihae Harbor
Spencer Park
Kauna'oa Beach
Hapuna Beach
Anaehoomalu Bay
Kiholo Bay
Makalawena
Mahaiula Bay
Kona Resort
Kaupulehu
Huehue
Kiholo
Kaahumanu
Kapalaoa
Hyatt Regency
Mauna Lani Resort
Mauna Beach Hotel
Kawaihae
Kawaihae Bay
Waialea Bay
Hwy
19
Waimea
Waimea Kohala
Waikii
Saddle Road
200
190
Lae Hou Point
Mano Point
Queen
Puuanahulu
Hawaii Belt Road
Auwaiakeua
Kamakoa
Kohala
Mountain
Kaunu o Kaleihoohie 5,480 ft.
Kalana
Waimanu Bay
Waipi'o
Waipio
Kaweia
Honokaa
Hawaii Belt Road
Mana Road
Kahawai Iuiu
4WD
Keamotola
4WD
Kapohomuele
Road
Kukaiau
Kauha
Milo Village
Weloka
19
Honohina
Wailea
Honomu
Honomu
Kolala Point
Kolala
Pepeekeo Point
Onomea Falls
Akaka Falls
Nanli
St.
Pou Pohaku 13,631 ft.
Kawaenui
Honolii
Papaikou
Paukaa
Waihuku
Hilo Bay
Bay Front
Kealoha
Richardsons Bay
Leleiwi Point

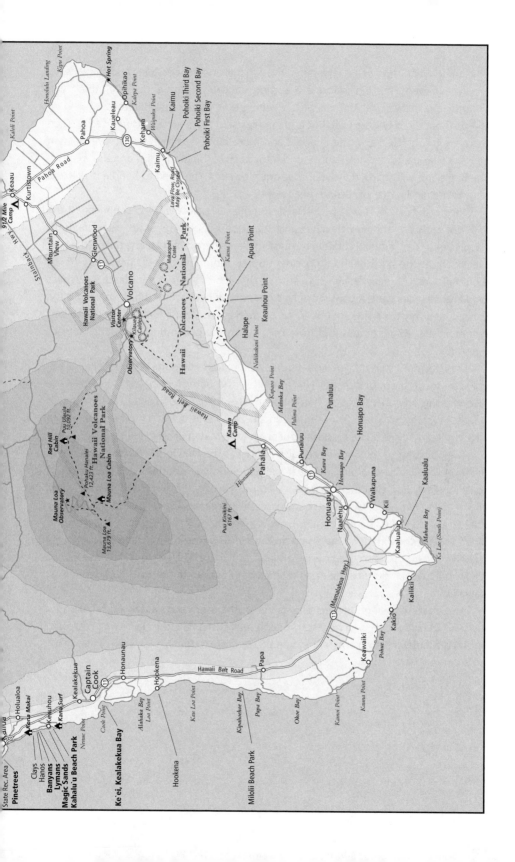

State Rec. Area
Pinetrees
Clays
Hanos
Banyans
Lymans
Magic Sands
Kahalu'u Beach Park

Ke'ei, Kealakekua Bay

Kailua
Holualoa
Kona Makai
Keauhou
Kona Surf
Kealakekua
Captain Cook
Honaunau
Hookena
Hopkena
Milolii Beach Park

Nonoe Point
Cook Point
Alahaka Bay
Loa Point
Kau Loa Point
Kipahoehoe Bay
Papa Bay
Okoe Bay
Kauna Point
Kamoa Point

Hawaii Belt Road
Papa

Keawaiki
Kakio
Kailikii

Kaalualu
Mahana Bay
Ka Lae (South Point)

Naalehu
Walkapuna
Kii

Honuapu
Honuapo Bay

Pahala
Punaluu
Kawa Bay
Punaluu
Honuapo
Punaluu

11 (Mamalahoa Hwy.)

Hawaii Belt Road

Kaava Camp
Hinamoa

Mauna Loa
13,679 ft.
Puu Kulua
13,677 ft.
Puu Ulaula
10,092 ft.
Red Hill Cabin
Pohaku Hanalei
13,423 ft.
Mauna Loa Cabin
Mauna Loa Observatory
Puu Kinikini
6167 ft.

Hawaii Volcanoes National Park

Kapuuo Point
Mahuka Bay
Palima Point

Apua Point
Keauhou Point
Halape
Naliikakani Point
Kaena Point

Observatory
Kilauea Caldera
Visitor Center

Hawaii Volcanoes National Park

Hawaii Volcanoes National Park

Volcano
Glenwood
Mountain View
Makaopuhi Crater

Lava Flow, Road May Be Closed

11

9 1/2 Mile Camp
HWY. 11
Keaau
Kurtistown
Stainback

Pahoa Road
Pahoa
130
Kaueleau
Kehana
Kaimu
Kaimu

Pohoiki Third Bay
Pohoiki Second Bay
Pohoiki First Bay
Waipuku Point

Opihikao
Hot Spring
Kalepa Point

Honolulu Landing
Kijju Point
Kaloli Point

it's created when the swell is channeled though underwater passages and canyons.

In any event, the Big Island is a surfing education. Just about everything you thought you knew about surf will puzzle you here, at least at first. Barefoot walking on sharp, smooth, and twisted lava (boots are rarely used) takes some getting used to. Then there are tan, black, and white beaches and more black lava than you've ever seen in your life. Day in and day out, you are under the spell of the mountains and the weather. The Big Island will sharpen up your thought processes. You need to handle it as locals do—as part and parcel of surfing great waves.

The north coast of Hawaii hosts classic remote surf below valleys; far beneath these 200-foot cliffs lie stunning beaches and seascape beauty. The south coast features Hawaii Volcanoes National Park. On the east coast—where it rains all the time—the best breaks are at the base of the long, slow-sloping mountain called Mauna Loa ("long mountain," 13,679 feet), which lies near the geographic center of the island. Sixty miles long and 30 miles wide, it consists of lava often described as "iron-hard," making it the densest and most massive mountain on earth. Nearby, Mauna Kea, the world's tallest mountain (33,467 feet measured from its base on the ocean floor), stretches toward the stars.

From its frigid summit, powerful telescopes are trained on the outer reaches of the universe. You'll surf under its spell where it enters the water; look back to land from the takeoff spot, and the scene is breathtaking. The whole mood is ever-changing as weather systems circulate from the mountain peaks and down to the sea, heralding new swells and storms. Depressions appear, and the march of swell lines grows.

The grandeur of the Big Island—also known as the Orchid Isle—includes some of the world's tallest mountains, deepest valleys, plunging waterfalls, and 266 miles of coastline. With long, straight highways, it's a driver's dream, for the most part well signed and boasting high-quality, sealed roads. At 95 miles long and 80 miles wide, the island's total land area is 4,038 square miles—more than the other three major islands combined. Indeed, the Big Island makes up more than 63 percent of the land area of *all* the Hawaiian Islands. It's also the youngest island, at a mere 500,000 to 800,000 years old. (Only Lo`ihi, a seamount to the east that hasn't yet broken the surface, is younger than Hawaii.)

And it's still growing. Kilauea Crater on its southeastern end has flowed actively into the sea and taken and given new surf spots. It seems that Pele, the Hawaiian goddess of fire, is constantly creating and re-creating this magical spot.

Upolu

When you arrive at this great surf spot, you'll see black sand and thundering peaks far below you, while waves line up, dash against the cliff, and peel. This remote black-sand beach has a right-hand point break and collects a raw northwest, north, and northeast swell in winter—often triple overhead. It's a big-wave rider spot most of the time. On small days you'll need hiking and climbing experience to get in and out. Park at Upolu Lookout and hike down a difficult 300-foot path through rivers and streams to the beach.

Best Tides: Low.

Best Swell Direction: North.

Best Wave Size: Waist to double overhead.

Bottom: Sand.

Type of Break: Left and right.

Skill Level: Expert to big-wave rider.

Best Boards: Shortboard and gun.

Best Seasons: Fall and winter.

Crowds: Never crowded.

Water Quality: Clean.

Hazards: The hike in is steep and difficult.

Fees and Permits: No fee or permits are required.

Schedule: Public access 24/7.

Finding the Break

Turn left out of the airport onto Queen Ka`ahumanu Highway (Hawaii Route 19); at Kawahae, turn left again onto Hawaii Route 270 and continue to the end of the road. When you park and look out over the ocean, you'll see the trail down to the beach. It's 61.7 miles from the Kona airport.

Surf Description

Big, deep, heavy waves are the order of the day as a strong north swell hits. It's 10 feet plus and one of the biggest ridable beach breaks on the island. The dark to black sand, high hills, and remoteness—it's like Jurassic Park here—will all put you in a time warp. It's you and the waves and nature and nothing else.

Situated at the end of Upolu Valley Lookout, the scenery in this spot is amazing: 300-foot sheer mountain cliffs plummet into the sea for 30 miles. The hike is for the experienced hiker-surfer only. It'll take you an hour on the trail, crossing lagoons and streams and navigating difficult overgrown paths. Once you reach the black-sand beach, you'll have it all to yourself. The waves are often powerful, with long, sloping crests and thick backs ideal for a 7-foot, 10-inch mini gun. There's bounce off the cliff, so the takeoff can be a lurch up to double overhead on a 6- to 8-foot day.

A few teams of surfers have hired a helicopter and pilot to fly them in during the morning, then airlift them out in the afternoon. Six surfers sharing the cost make this a viable option. This could apply to many other remote beaches around the island.

Upolu, Big Island. PHOTO ROD SUMPTER

Upolu is an ideal spot for advanced surfers to test their mettle as well as their survival and surf planning skills. For the rest of us, however, it's suitable only as a place to watch the experts from the fabulous viewing platform of the Upolu Valley Lookout.

Local Events/Attractions

Kamehameha I Birthsite State Monument. Drive 1.6 miles southwest of the Upolu airport on the Kawaihae–Mahukona Highway (HI 270). Turn off onto the Upolu Airport Road, then onto a coastal dirt road to find the memorial. The boulders within the site are thought to be the great king's birthstones.

Kawaihae Harbor is a left-hand reef break off breakwater; it's best in winter and needs a big northwest swell. Kawaihae was a royal center where Ka`ahumanu—King Kamehameha's favorite wife—was known to have ridden the waves. It remained Kamehameha's residence from about 1790 to 1794 while he planned the invasion of the other Hawaiian Islands.

Spencer Park. A mostly flat, bodyboarding spot with the occasional shortboard wave, this fickle area misses all the north swells, but it likes a south swell with a lot of west in it to create a fun wave. The shallow-water offshore coral reef does pick up the odd swell. You'll also find lots of marine wildlife, showers, restrooms, pavilions, electricity, picnic tables, tennis courts, and tent/trailer camping (with a county permit).

**Kauna`oa Beach** (Mauna Kea) is a hot winter bodyboarding spot best in a west-to-southwest swell. Kauna`oa unfolds like a white crescent sand dune and is 200 yards wide. Hotel-owned bodyboard rentals are available. Public parking places are limited—it's first come, first served. Enter through the gate to the Mauna Kea Beach Resort, off Hawaii Route 19.

Hapuna Beach. A popular beach and park, this white sandy stretch of paradise has beach, reef, and point surf in the winter, but it's a fickle place to get on. Lifeguard year-round; hot bodyboarding when there's surf. It's found off Queen Ka`ahumanu Highway at mile marker 19.

Anaehoomalu Bay (pronounced *a na-ay ho-o mah-loo*) is adjacent to the Royal Waikoloan Hotel. A windsurfing and bodyboarding spot, it's a postcard-perfect white-sand beach with a sky-blue lagoon and groves of coconut trees. Also known as A-Bay, it's the first beach after nearly 30 miles of the blackness of Kohala's lava flows. Off Queen Ka`ahumanu Highway, between mile markers 76 and 77, a well-marked access road leads to the bay.

Kiholo Bay. Reef breaks and a mixture of salt and fresh water with a rocky lava islands and black-pebble beaches give this surf spot a surreal beauty. It's surrounded by private property, but there is public access to the beach. Turn off Hawaii Route 19 at mile marker 82 for a panorama of the bay. To go in, you have to hike from the highway down a long road to the ocean.

Makalawena is a bodyboarding beach break with a white-sand crescent beach. Turn off at mile marker 88 and park; to reach the beach you'll need either a twenty-minute walk or four-wheel drive. No facilities.

Mahaiula Bay, Kona Coast Park. This is a right-hand break with a neat wall from a peak over a sand-and-lava bottom. It also goes left into the rocks—not recommended! The paddle out is tough, although the long lulls between sets will help. A beach launch is easy but takes ten minutes because of the distance. This is a good spot for bodyboards, shortboards, and longboards on the right day; best with a northwest-to-north swell. The park's gate is off Hawaii Route 1 between mile markers 90 and 91, at a sign that reads KONA COAST STATE PARK. Drive in, stop about 100 yards before the boat-launch parking lot, and take the lava trail to the right. The park opens at 9:00 A.M.

Old Airport State Recreation Area. A break in the outer reef here may offer a wave when everywhere else is flat. Hot waves to double overhead, and steep rights and lefts; be sure to wear beach booties when entering the water to avoid cutting yourself on the rocky bottom. To reach the beach, follow the shoreline north from King Kamehameha's Kona Beach Hotel for a few hundred yards. Camping is not technically allowed at Old Kona Airport, but many choose to pitch their tents anyway. The beach's gates close at 8:00 P.M.

Pinetrees

An ideal reef and beach break in tropical surroundings with magical waves, Pinetrees is a narrow crescent white-sand beach known as a swell magnet, producing waves when most spots are flat. Reefs just offshore give both left- and right-hand waves. Beside Kaloko Point, this break has sloping lava formations running into the sea and offshore reefs that produce some classic peaks. Ideal longboarding waves. Breaks year-round, best in southwest and west swells.

Best Tides: Low.

Best Swell Direction: Southwest to big west.

Best Wave Size: Waist high to overhead.

Bottom: Coral, sand, and reef.

Type of Break: Left- and right-hand reef break.

Skill Level: Beginners on small days; experienced surfers when it's over 4 feet.

Best Boards: Short- and longboards.

Best Seasons: Summer, fall, and winter.

Crowds: Crowded.

Water Quality: Clean.

Hazards: Sharks and localism.

Fees and Permits: A parking fee of $4.50 per day is charged.

Schedule: Public access 7:00 A.M.–7:00 P.M. Camping is allowed with a permit.

Finding the Break

From the Kona airport, turn right onto Hawaii Route 19 for 0.5 mile. Turn right at a sign that reads WAWAIOLI BEACH PARK, and again at the NATURAL ENERGY LAB sign; it's 1 mile (down a very bumpy dirt road) to the beach. Pinetrees is situated at the far end of the Natural Energy Lab beach, past the makeshift homes. Note that as of this writing, Pinetrees Beach is scheduled to be made into a beach park with a five-star hotel set 1,000 yards back from the ocean. Public access along the seafront and along a sealed road access from HI 19 will be available.

Surf Description

The mighty waves on this pearly white-sand beach are a breath of fresh air. Take off and drive your deepest backhand turn left into a short wall, then carve a right-hander into the face and back into a 6-foot grinding hook. Do this until you're surfed out and end up on the beach, having gone right-hand as much as left. Stand facing the awesome volcanic beach scene and wonder at it all. Watch the wave faces curl, roll, and spray into the distant Energy Lab reefs. Cold water is pumped down to where the natural energy heats it, and is then piped to hundreds of homes on the Big Island.

This wide, narrow bay picks up any swell going. Not many surf spots can claim a swell-window as wide as this—it picks up swell from both the southwest and northwest.

Pinetrees, Big Island. PHOTO ROD SUMPTER

Local Events/Attractions

Kaloko-Honokohau National Historic Park. You'll find 1,300 acres of petroglyphs, heiau (temples), archaeological sites, and an ancient Hawaiian fishing pond at this park located 3 miles north of Kailua-Kona. It's not well marked, so call for directions (808–329–6881). Open daily, 8:00 A.M.–4:00 P.M.

Camping

Beach camping is limited to seven days at a time; $15 per person. Apply at the gate only. No advance booking.

Clays is a Kailua rock-ledge reef break. There's no beach. Locals shred at this crowded spot.

Hanos, Kailua. Very consistent year-round breaks. Park at Ali`i Drive and walk through lush vegetation to the break.

Banyans

This exciting reef breaks mostly right, but the lefts are good, too. It's a big peak fading to nothing at the edge of the reef. There are, in fact, several reefs close to each other that all break on different-angled swell directions and different-size swells, to give wave trains on three takeoff areas; it's possible to judge where to be, if you're alert and quick at spying a set. Fabulous hot surf spot for the expert with shallow reefs, urchins, and locals.

Best Tides: Low to medium.

Best Swell Direction: Southwest to northwest.

Best Wave Size: Chest high to triple overhead.

Bottom: Sand and reef.

Type of Break: Left- and right-hand reef break.

Skill Level: Expert.

Best Boards: Shortboard, bodyboard, and longboard.

Best Seasons: Summer, fall, and winter.

Crowds: Crowded.

Water Quality: Average to clean.

Hazards: Localism is fierce here.

Fees and Permits: No fees or permits are required.

Schedule: Public access 24/7.

Finding the Break

From the Kona airport, turn right onto Hawaii Route 19 and go 4 miles; the road becomes the Queen Ka`ahumanu Highway. Continue south through the lights at Lako Street and turn right onto the Kamehameha Highway (Hawaii Route 111), winding down down until you reach the Ali`i Drive lights. Turn right and travel 2.9 miles to the Banyans break on your left, with limited roadside parking under banyan trees. You'll see old bikes, chairs, and broken surfboards in the area.

Surf Description

On an early-morning wave before the crowds, you drop in and break a rail free to go left and bury your tip under green through a shower of falling curl, then pull up and arch on the corner turns with dignity . . . this is the only way to surf here. It's that full-on. It's a wave that gets thrown up quickly by the reef and is very short shouldered, with only the main peak's face to carve. But consistency and positioning make this a performance wave where everything happens in a predictable pattern, and you have the chance to rip better and better on each successive wave.

Situated near Kailua-Kona, Banyans is best in summer, but with access to a winter swell-window, there are a lot of surfers watching from apartments for the sight of a new swell. Being in first isn't easy; the crowds get thick enough to make takeoff on a wave impossible. This is a locals-only spot when it's good and on weekends. You'll see what the latest talent can do and watch some outrageous maneuvers. A testing ground for the hotties, and a hot spot for surfers at all stages and grades. The tiny-pebble black-

Banyans, Big Island. PHOTO ROD SUMPTER

sand beach and rock cove is overhung by banyan trees—hence the name—and is the hangout place for surf-watching. It's full of worn-out travel equipment and surf gear, as well as all manner of pushbikes, board trolleys, and street art. It's a place to picnic and hang out in the cool of the trees at midday and see the surfing, rock pools, splash-ups, and distant swell action.

Local Events/Attractions

- The **Volcom Stones Pufferfish** surf contest series is held at Banyans in February.
- The **Kona Marathon & Family Fun Run,** along the Kona coast, offers beautiful views of the Pacific Ocean and lush Hawaiian rain forests. Events include a marathon, half marathon, and 10K and 5K runs, all starting from Kona Surf Resort Kailua-Kona.

Lymans

This long left-hand reef break is best in a southwest swell. It's a perfect hot-dog wave below head high. On waist-high days it's soft friendly fun with a good atmosphere; on big days the vibe is still good, but the competitive nature of good surfing on fine waves takes control. A long left peeling off reef and rock ledges below a lush cliff, it needs a strong southwest swell to go off. Best overhead in summer.

Lymans, Big Island. PHOTO ROD SUMPTER

Best Tides: Medium.

Best Swell Direction: Southwest to northwest.

Best Wave Size: Chest high to overhead.

Bottom: Lava and rock reef.

Type of Break: Left-hand point break.

Skill Level: Beginner to expert.

Best Boards: Short- and longboard.

Best Seasons: Summer.

Crowds: Crowded.

Water Quality: Clean.

Hazards: A rock sticks out of the water when the wave sucks up. Locals sit inside and get barreled off it. Locals are hardcore, but show respect and you will get waves.

Fees and Permits: No fees or permits are required.

Schedule: Public access 24/7.

Finding the Break

From the Kona airport, turn right onto Hawaii Route 19 and continue for 4 miles. Here the road becomes the Queen Ka`ahumanu Highway. Head south on Hawaii Route 11 through the lights at Lako Street, then turn right onto Hawaii Route 111, winding down down until you reach the Ali`i Drive lights. Turn right and travel 2.2 miles to the Lymans break on your left, with limited roadside parking.

Park along the road beside the benches. Walk toward the house on the left of the bay as you look out to sea; a narrow path will take you to a little pebble beach.

Surf Description

The sound of breaking waves wakes you, and you're the first to paddle out. A new swell has hit, with 4- to 6-foot wave faces. You slip into the barrel of the day, then another . . .

Situated 2 miles south of Kailua-Kona, Lymans is the most crowded spot on the island—and at times the best. (You have to beat the crowds, though.) Raw swell acts upon shallow reef to make a near-perfect left-hand point break. It's more fun at 3 feet than perfect, but as the swell grows to 6 feet, this is a wave like Rincon in reverse, and way more attractive. The lefts jack up as a walling, hooking wave and then back off on the shoulder to become a steep roundhouse cutback with a lot of face to turn on. Then a section breaks, collapsing from 10 yards ahead. The green below the curl is full, allowing an all-around-the-section drive, then it's up into the curl as it tubes a short while and out to more shoulder that backs off for a cutback into the pit. On and on this wave goes, and by the time you've surfed 300 yards to the very shore and kicked out in the channel, you're stoked. The beach and shade of the trees and the special basin cove of the coast face southwest, so when the south swells start, this is the spot to be, to see the lines trail back to the horizon and touch the first piece of glass on a windless day.

Local Events/Attractions

This area offers snorkeling, in-line skating, soccer at the Old Airport, fishing, and theater at Hualalai and World Square.

Magic Sands

This superhot beach is a fast, hard-hitting shore break; it takes skill to handle the punishment these waves dish out. From 2 to 4 feet and above, it starts to peel off better, and on big days of 6 feet plus, the left-hand reef break will pump. Bodyboarding grinders barrel into the beach shore break. Fun waves, lifeguards, and left point when the swell is over 6 to 8 feet. Clear blue waves break hard and fast at this prime performance bodybodying spot. Barbecues, picnic tables, restrooms, and showers. Best in winter with a west swell, the spot is also known as "Disappearing Sands" because the sand can disappear in the strong currents; it returns in summer.

Best Tides: Low to medium.	**Best Boards:** Short and gun.
Best Swell Direction: West.	**Best Seasons:** Fall and winter.
Best Wave Size: Chest high to triple overhead.	**Crowds:** Crowded.
	Water Quality: Clean.
Bottom: Sand.	**Hazards:** Localism.
Type of Break: Left and right.	**Fees and Permits:** No fees or permits are required.
Skill Level: Beginner if it's 1 or 2 feet; expert at 3 to 4 feet.	**Schedule:** Public access 24/7.

Magic Sands, Big Island. PHOTO ROD SUMPTER

Finding the Break

From the Kona airport, turn right onto Hawaii Route 19 and continue for 4 miles. The road becomes the Queen Ka`ahumanu Highway. Head south on Hawaii Route 11 through the lights at Lako Street and turn right onto Hawaii Route 111, winding down until you reach the Ali`i Drive lights. Turn right and travel 1.8 miles to Magic Sands; look for a small parking lot on your left. The beach and lifeguard tower are 400 yards away.

If you're coming from Kailua-Kona, Magic Sands is 4 miles south on Ali`i Drive.

Surf Description

Magic Sands is one of the few beach breaks on the Big Island with really good body-boarding and bodysurfing waves. Like many classic beach breaks, this ride is short—between 10 and 25 yards. It's a peak barrel to nothing, as locals say, or a peak to nowhere. Still, down the line in the barrel and into a wipeout can be great fun.

Situated 4 miles south of Kona International Airport, this white-sand beach loses its sand every winter and gets it back every summer, which is why it's sometimes called Disappearing Sands. No one knows where the sand goes or exactly how it comes back year after year—most of the nearby shoreline is rocky, and the closest beach with white sands is the Pines, 3 miles north. But the pounding shorebreak and powerful rip currents make all the beautiful white sand disappear during periods of high surf in winter, leaving lava bedrock exposed. What's really interesting is the speed at which the entire beach can vanish—literally overnight during a winter storm!

On big days, game beginners ride the rapidly moving whitewater swatch of the broken waves up the beach face on boogieboards. The trick is to stay in very shallow water so that you aren't swept back out to sea. The fast wedgy takeoffs can make shortboarding a speed trip with amazing wipeouts.

Magic Sands is an inviting beach for water recreation. This small pocket beach is backed by a coconut grove, which provides welcome shade and a full range of park facilities. An offshore sandbar and gently sloping beach provide excellent conditions for swimming and bodysurfing on average 2- to 3-foot days. The outer left rock reef gets a fantastic left-hand wave in a big south swell and is ideal for shortboards and bodyboards.

Local Events/Attractions

This is a good shore snorkeling and diving area, with depths ranging from 2 to 60 feet as well as caverns and lava tubes. The entry is 100 yards south at the white coral beach.

Kahalu`u Beach Park

This tiny, sheltered, rocky bay with a dark tan strip of beach has three layers of surf stretching out over reefs and lagoons. The farther out you go, the bigger the waves get. Just past the snorkeling lagoon is the first wave—with small surf, this is a beginner's wave. Then intermediate surfers can enjoy a variety of peaks and sections over more reefs that tube and peel. When overhead, the outer reef is a dream longboarding peak, long and sloping. Rarely hollow, all the breaks are full faced and fun.

Best Tides: Medium to high.

Best Swell Direction: Southwest to northwest.

Best Wave Size: Chest high to overhead.

Bottom: Reef and rock.

Type of Break: Left- and right-hand reef break.

Skill Level: Beginner to intermediate.

Best Boards: Short- and longboard.

Best Seasons: Summer.

Crowds: Crowded.

Water Quality: Clean.

Hazards: Localism and rocks.

Fees and Permits: No fee or permits required.

Schedule: Public access 24/7. Lifeguard year-round.

Finding the Break

Turn right out of the Kona airport onto Queen Ka`ahumanu Highway (Hawaii Route 19). Go south, turning right (west) onto Palani Road then left (south) onto Ali`i Drive. Parking is available in the park, which is 5.5 miles from the airport. You'll find a lifeguard tower and rentals on the beach.

Kahalu'u Beach Park, Big Island. PHOTO ROD SUMPTER

Surf Description

Waves fold into curls and the heavens shout thunder while cracking waves swell and sets pile in. As you view the bay from above, a little voice tells you it's time to go surfing.

Rock-hop an easy path out across the stones and lava grid. Paddle with ease between the sets, glide into some hefty walls, and enjoy cruise surfing and the excitement of smooth, clean waves.

Kahalu'u Beach Park is one big reef with a tiny beach in a shore of dark sand. Waves form a 2- to 10-foot break on the outer reef on every new swell, giving clean takeoffs and smooth rides. If it's flat elsewhere and there's any chance of a swell, this is the place to be. By morning the waves are up and it's pumping across the bay.

Situated 4 miles south of Kailua-Kona, this is one of the most popular beaches on the Big Island. A good reef wave for beginner to intermediate surfers and bodyboarders, Kahalu'u breaks in deeper water on the outer reef and peels into little channels and gullies. It picks up any southwest-to-west swell and is best in summer. You'll also find the added attraction of a large coral reef in the bay, which makes for predictably calm waters, ideal snorkeling, and a whole sea full of fish and *honu* (turtles). The outer reef is rarely over 8 feet; when it's bigger, the incoming sets feather to break, and break much farther out on cloud-break reefs.

The positioning and scrambling that take place are reminiscent of Sunset Beach in the west peak. But the late takeoffs are great, a big drop to fly walling and rail hugging; fin slips are all part of the fun when it's well overhead. The middle reefs are nice, picking up the re-formed swell and breaking right and left slowly and cleanly. Some waves do close out, so the choice of set wave is all-important.

This spot is ideal for intermediate surfers most of the time.

Local Events/Attractions

In addition to surfing, this area offers bird-watching, boating, canoeing, fishing, golfing, hiking trails, horseback riding, lifeguard services, cool showers, telephones, and excellent picnic spots. Kahalu`u Beach Park is a good spot for beginners interested in snorkeling.

Ke`ei, Kealakekua Bay

At this huge, mile-wide bay deep below the mountain, the best waves are at the southern end, Ke`ei—mostly a left-hand reef break, with several peaks that join up on a good day into one 400-yard ride that really pumps and jacks up double overhead to produce a steep, fast-barreling wave. But there are also hair-raising rights into a deep pit, and a hard paddle back out for those who venture. Kealakekua Bay State Historical Park in the middle is a left point break (called Manini Point) that peels off in a big southwest or west swell.

Best Tides: Low to medium.

Best Swell Direction: South.

Best Wave Size: Chest high to double overhead.

Bottom: Reef.

Type of Break: Left- and right-hand reef break.

Skill Level: Intermediate to expert.

Best Boards: Short- and longboard.

Best Seasons: Summer, fall, and winter.

Crowds: Crowded.

Water Quality: Clean.

Hazards: Sharks and localism.

Fees and Permits: No fees or permits are required.

Schedule: Public access 24/7, but little parking; respect the residents' property.

Finding the Break

From the Kona International Airport, take Hawaii Route 11 south. Drive for about half an hour, through Kona and Kealakekua, to the Kealakekua Bay turnoff; this is on your right just after you pass a Chevron gas station (on the left). Turn right onto Napo Road, heading down and around many curves. Halfway down, you'll pass the middle Ke`ei turnoff (which goes to Painted Church); turn left on the third dirt road, a very bumpy track that leads to the coast. Park where you can. Remember not to park in someone's driveway in your eagerness to hit the waves! The tall trees and bush canopies make a neat beach commune atmosphere here.

Ke'ei, Kealakekua Bay, Big Island. PHOTO ROD SUMPTER

Surf Description

Take a look around at some of the finest scenery in Hawaii . . . then wax up and stand on the coral platform ledge to wait for a lull before sliding out through the channel to the point. This supersteep left-hander with the occasional right wave will pull you into the pit and fling hollow walling waves over sharp coral at you, just 500 yards out from traditional wooden houses fronting straight on the beach. This is where lava ledges and shelves stretch out to meet a west swell and produce classic waves. At times it's the best wave on the Big Island, picking up south and west swells in summer and winter.

Situated 1 mile south of Kealakekua Bay on the south side, this famous left-hand reef break has several peaks that join up on a good day into one long 400-yard ride. Steeped in history, this is the place where Captain James Cook was killed. The monument at Cook's landing point on the east side doesn't actually have waves to ride, but the first left point (Manini Point) peels off 0.5 mile west. The Kealakekua Bay shore break is a bodysurfing and bodyboarding spot. A thousand yards farther to the left is Ke`ei, the perfect left reef break, sometimes called Shark Point. It's the best-lined-up barreling wave and most consistently well-shaped wave in Hawaii, ideal for the experienced to expert surfer.

Local Events/Attractions

- **Captain Cook Monument.** The spot where Captain Cook first landed in the islands, in Kealakekua Bay near Napoopoo, is marked by a submerged plaque that can be read through the water. The best views are offered by boats, kayak, and surfboard. An above-water white monument can be easily seen from the opposite shore.

- **Big Island Kayak.** This firm offers daily guided natural history tours of the beautiful Kona and Kohala coasts, which both feature a rugged lava shore punctuated by sea caves and arches. Snorkel in the world's largest saltwater aquarium and view tropical fish and coral in remarkably clear and warm ocean waters. For more information, contact Big Island Kayak at 81-6367 Mamalahoa Highway, Kealakekua, HI 96750; (808) 323–3005 or (888) 371–6035 (toll-free).

Hookena. With black-sand beaches and an old fishing village, Hookena is a favorite spot for local boogieboarders and body-surfers when there are waves.

Milolii Beach Park offers a series of protected tide pools and snorkeling. The reef out back here creates quality peaks; body-boarding can be excellent, and there's nice longboard fun. Picnic table and restrooms.

Kaalualu. Reef-break surfing, tide pool fishing, no crowds, and epic scenery.

Honuapo Bay. Surf on lava rocks; point. There's a pavilion and camping here, but no water. It's a fickle spot, located between Naalehu (the southernmost town in the United States) and Punaluu Beach Park.

Punaluu. This narrow black-sand beach is a good bodyboarding wave in a southeast swell and northwest winds; thin, hollow waves. It's located off Hawaii Route 11.

Halape beach and reef break has a pavilion, restroom, food concession, drinking water, and lifeguard services. No tent camping; six A-frame shelters only. It's off Queen Ka`ahumanu Highway (Hawaii Route 19) 2.3 miles south of Kawaihae.

Keauhou Point. This remote reef and point break, which faces southeast, picks up southeast wraparound swell. It often goes off in the early morning with no wind. It's a long left, and the paddle out is for expert surfers only. Dynamic scenery makes this a memorable spot, especially on a perfect day with 6- to 8-foot swell.

Apua Point. This black-sand oasis on the south coast of Hawaii Volcanoes National Park is a fun beach and reef break requiring an east, southeast, or south swell. Apua Point is 10 miles from Kilauea, the world's most active volcano. The only place you can surf, camp, and view bona fide eruptions, it's also the southernmost point in the United States.

Pohoiki First Bay, Second Bay, and **Third Bay,** all within walking distance of each other, give a variety of waves in an east-of-south swell. These breaks are for experienced surfers only. You'll also find access to the active lava flow that buried Kalapana Village from 1986 to 1992; it's still flowing into the ocean with spectacular fury.

Kaimu. Where else in the world might your view include a volcanic eruption? In late 1990 the ongoing eruption of Kilauea's Kupaianaha vent covered the famous black-sand beach and reef break at Kaimu Bay. At the same time, a new beach was created a short distance away. From Kaimu, if lava is flowing into the ocean, you can see a plume of steam rising high in the air. At night you may view lava descend into the sea. It's found off Hawaii Route 130 south from Pahoa. When it dead-ends at Hawaii Route 137 (near mile marker 11), turn right.

Richardsons Bay. This explosive outer reef off Richards Park gives heavy lefts and rights for the expert surfer. Rocky entry is difficult in a big swell; it's best at 4 to 6 feet. Fantastic snorkel pools and ponds, plus plenty of facilities.

Kealoha. James Kealoha Park (also known as Four Mile) offers well-rounded surfing. Scout Island, a good camping ground, is located just offshore. The island derives its name from the frequent Boy Scout camping trips held there. Located east of Onekahakaha Beach County Park, along Kalanianaole Avenue, the spot was originally used by the ancient Hawaiians as a fishing ground.

Bay Front is characterized by gray sand. It's a hot bodyboarding spot.

Honolii. At the mouth of the Hilo River. Fantastic long rides right and left—300 yards on a good day; three separate reefs; good waves in an east swell. This is a very popular surf-watching spot on big days. Take Hawaii Route 19 a little way out of Hilo; when you see a cemetery on your left, take the next road to your right, then turn left into the parking lot.

**Waipi`o.** A black-sand beach with good bodyboarding. The Waipi`o Valley on the north shore of the Big Island is a succession of valleys and steep cliffs tumbling into the sea. The long, sweeping, soft black-sand beach that lines almost the entire valley mouth is hemmed in on either side by steep cliffs, both with waterfalls falling right into the sea. At Hawaii Route 19, go northeast to Honoka. Then take Hawaii Route 280 east and follow the signs to Waipi`o Valley.

Waimanu Bay boasts good longboarding and bodyboarding with awesome scenery. A thousand feet deep, a mile across, and 6 miles long, the Waipi`o Valley is the most spectacular of the series of amphitheater valleys in the Kohala Mountains. The hike in and out is very steep: 25 percent grade. You'll walk between ferns and elephant-ear plants and past African tulip trees aflame with red blossoms until you reach the black-sand beach.

Big Island Resources

Hawaii Activities Offices
Aloha Tower, 5th Floor
1 Aloha Tower Drive
Honolulu, Oahu 96813
(877) 877–1222 or (808) 524-0008
Fax: (808) 599–3778
www.hawaiiactivities.com

Aloha Airlines Baggage Offices
Kona, Big Island (west coast)
(808) 329–1651

Bus Service

www.co.hawaii.hi.us/mass_transit/heleonbus.html
E-mail: heleonbus1@go.com

Hawaii County Parks

Department of Parks and Recreation
101 Pauahi Street, Suite 6
Hilo, HI 96720
(808) 961–8311
Online camping permits: www.hawaii-county.com/parks/parks.htm
Hours: 7:45 A.M.–4:30 P.M. Monday through Friday; closed weekends and holidays

Camping permits are required for all of the county parks and camping sites, with fees of $5.00 per day for adults and $.50 a day for children ages 13 through 17 (kids under 12 are free). Campers can stay up to one week in summer months and two weeks during the rest of the year. Some sites have showers, restrooms, and drinking water. At some of these parks—especially Spencer Beach and Mahukona—you *will* be checked daily for your permit. If you don't have one, you will likely be escorted out of the park.

Surf Shops

A` Ama Surf & Sport
75-5741 Kuakini Highway
Kailua-Kona, HI 96740
(North Kona District)
(808) 326–7890
Surfboards, surfwear, and surfgear.

Big Island Surf Company
Prince Kuhio Plaza
111 East Puainako Street
Kawailani, HI 96720
(South Hilo District)
(808) 959–2472
Surfboards, surfwear, and surfgear.

C&S Cycle and Surf
64-1066 Mamalahoa Highway
Kamuela, HI 96743
(North Kohala District)
(808) 885–5005
Surfboard rentals.

H₂O Action Surf Shop
Lanihau Center
75-5595 Palani Road
Kailua-Kona, HI 96740
(North Kona District)
(808) 329–8962
Surfboards, surfwear, and surfgear.

Honolua Surf Company
Kona Inn Shopping Village
75-5744 Ali`i Drive
Kailua-Kona, HI 96740
(North Kona District)
(808) 329–1001
Board rentals.

Local Style
Prince Kuhio Plaza
111 East Puainako Street
Kawailani, HI 96720
(South Hilo District)
(808) 959–6121
Surfboards, surfwear.

Ocean Sports Waikoloa
69-275 Waikoloa Beach Drive
Waikoloa, HI 96738
(South Kohala District)
(808) 886–6666; (808) 885–5555;
or (888) SAIL–345
Fax: (808) 886–9407
E-mail: information@hawaiiocean
sports.com

Orchid Land Surf Shop
262 Kamehameha Avenue
Hilo, HI 96720
(Downtown Hilo District)
(808) 935–1533
Custom surfboards.

Pacific Vibrations
75-5702 Likana Lane
Kailua-Kona, HI 96740
(North Kona District)
(808) 329–4140
Board rentals.

Slick Surf Designs
P.O. Box 39
Kurtistown, HI 96760
(Puna District)
(808) 966–7328
Custom high-performance surf-
boards.

Surf Lessons

Hawaiian Lifeguard Surf Instructors
P.O. Box 390664
Keauhou, HI 96739
Beach house: (808) 324–0442
Fax: (808) 324–0332

CHAPTER 2
Maui

aui holds the most, and the best, longboarder surf spots of all the Hawaiian Islands. Add this to the island's easygoing lifestyle and laid-back approach to surfing, and you've got a very fun place to be. Many say it's the best place on earth and consider it a paradise. From a surfing point of view, I think they're right—and judging by the number of famous surfers (including Jerry Lopez and Laird Hamilton) who've moved here, there's no question Maui has everything a surfer could want.

Maui is famous for having waves to suit all grades of surfers. Its west and northwest corners pick up winter swells from November to March and summer swells from April to September. The town of Lahaina on the northwest coast is a true surf town: Lazy-day surf breaks off the Harbor Reef fire in great green-blue waves that range from small to three times overhead, making it a dream destination. The North Shore is another matter; its heavy, pounding winter surf is for experts only, and the shortboard rules at places like Ho`okipa and the big-wave spot of Jaws, where crews of Jet Skiers tow in surfers to ride 40- to 60-foot monsters. Summer surf sees Ma`alaea fire in the fastest right-hander, and a host of spots go off to pump alert signals and indicators when the swell is up. It's a hot trail on a blazing coast as good as any on the planet.

Regional Map

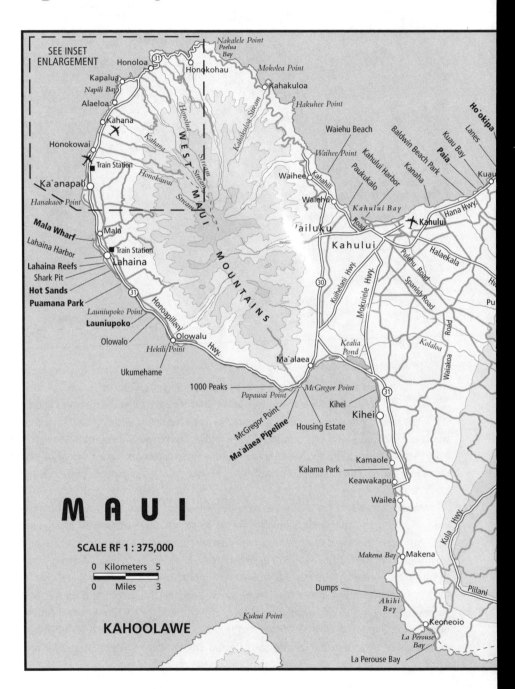

SEE INSET
ENLARGEMENT

Nakalele Point
Poelua Bay
Honoloa
31
Honokohau
Mokolea Point
Kapalua
Napili Bay
Kahakuloa
Alaeloa
Hakuhee Point
Ho'okipa
Kahana
Waiehu Beach
Lanes
Kuau Bay
Baldwin Beach Park
Pa'ia
Honokowai
Waihee Point
Kahului Harbor
Kanaha
Kuau
Train Station
Waihee
Kahahili
Paukukalo
Ka'anapali
Kahulai
Hanakaoo Point
Wailuku
Kahului Bay
Kahului
Hana Hwy.
Mala Wharf
Mala
Lahaina Harbor
Wailuku
Road
Kahului
Halaekala
Lahaina Reefs
Train Station
Kahului
Puuhu Road
Shark Pit
Lahaina
Hot Sands
Kuihelani Hwy.
Spanish Road
Hwy.
Puamana Park
31
30
Mokuiele Hwy.
Pu
Honoapiilani Hwy.
Launiupoko Point
Launiupoko
Olowalu
Kealia Pond
Kolaloa
Road
Olowalu
Hekili Point
Hwy.
Waiakoa
Ukumehame
Ma'alaea
1000 Peaks
Papawai Point
McGregor Point
31
McGregor Point
Kihei
McGregor Point
Kihei
Ma'alaea Pipeline
Housing Estate
Kamaole
Kalama Park
Keawakapu
Wailea
Kula Hwy.

MAUI

SCALE RF 1 : 375,000

0   Kilometers   5

0   Miles   3

Makena Bay
Makena

Dumps
Ahihi Bay
Piilani
Keoneoio
Kukui Point
La Perouse Bay

KAHOOLAWE

La Perouse Bay

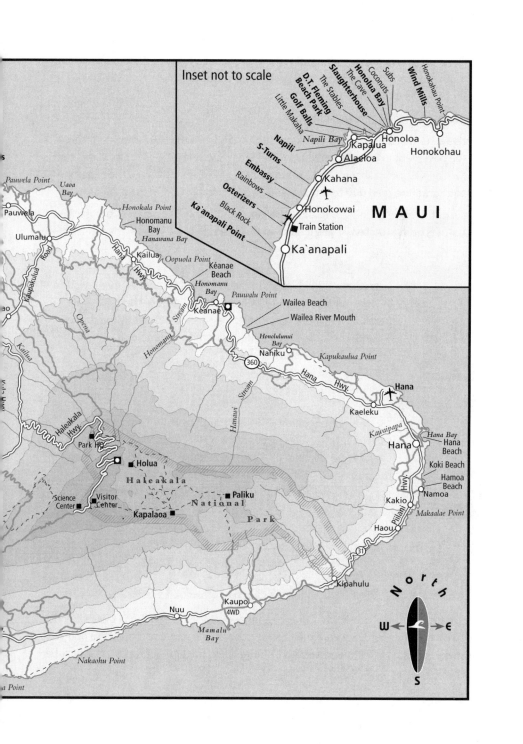

Inset not to scale

Wind Mills
Honokahau Point
Subs
Coconuts
Honolua Bay
The Cave
Slaughterhouse
D.T. Fleming
The Stables
Beach Park
Golf Balls
Little Makaha
Napili Bay
Honoloa
Honokohau
Kapalua
Napili
S-Turns
Alaeloa
Embassy
Kahana
Rainbows
Osterizers
Honokowai
Black Rock
Ka`anapali Point
Train Station
Ka`anapali

MAUI

Pauwela Point
Uaoa Bay
Honokala Point
Pauwela
Honomanu Bay
Ulumalu
Hanawana Bay
Kaupakulua Road
Hana Hwy
Kailua
Oopuola Point
Kéanae Beach
Keanae
Honomanu Bay
Pauwalu Point
Wailea Beach
Wailea River Mouth
Opeua
Honolulunui Bay
Nahiku
Kapukaulua Point
360
Hana Hwy
Kailua
Hana
Hana Hwy
Kaeleku
Haleakala Hwy
Park HQ
Kawaipapa
Hana Bay
Hana Beach
Holua
Hana
Koki Beach
Haleakala
Hamoa Beach
Namoa
Science Center
Visitor Center
National
Paliku
Kapalaoa
Park
Kakio
Makaalae Point
Piilani Hwy
Haou
Kipahulu
31

North

Kaupo
4WD
Nuu
Mamalu Bay

W — E

S

Nakaohu Point

a Point

Driving on Maui

See the Introduction for tips on driving the islands in general. On Maui:

- Get used to hearing directions with the terms *mauka* (toward the mountain) and *makai* (toward the sea) rather than north and south. (Example: Alio Street is *mauka* of Front Street.)

- Avoid driving in the bike lanes on Maui.

- Use extreme caution when checking the surf and beaches just a few feet from the pavement in places like Olowalu and Kihei. I wish I had a dollar for every car I've seen stuck in what looked like trustworthy sand. And it's often tricky getting back onto the road due to the sometimes heavy traffic flow in these areas.

- Do not ride the brakes going down Haleakala. Shift into a lower gear before the car gets going too fast or you'll burn up the brakes!

Subs is a right-hander with a steep takeoff and long curving wall in front of Honolua Bay Point. Situated below the pineapple fields, it offers no access; the easiest way to reach it is to paddle around from Honolua Bay. Best when it's overhead at Honolua, and best for the expert in all sizes of surf.

Coconuts (often called Outside Honolua Bay). This right point wave is a fast-walling wave with a swell line stretching across the bay and beyond. You're not able to surf all the way through to inner Honolua Bay on one wave, but 100 yards of perfection is a gas and will leave you with memories that last for years.

Honolua Bay

This right-hand point break with an exceptional performance wall has been a world-famous break since 1961. Speed, a super bowl arena on the inside section, and a 600-yard ride make this a classic all-time wave. With its long rides and reputation as a fantastic tube, it's a must-see surf spot.

Best Tides: Low to medium.

Best Swell Direction: West-northwest.

Best Wave Size: Chest high to double overhead.

Bottom: Reef.

Type of Break: Right-hand point break.

Skill Level: Intermediate to advanced, depending on the size and speed.

Best Boards: Shortboards, up to 7-foot, 10-inch pintails.

Best Seasons: Fall and winter.

Crowds: Crowded.

Water Quality: Clean.

Hazards: You'll have a steep walk to the small rock-and-coral beach area. Big waves, dangerous rip currents, and a shallow reef. The inside section closes out hard to all sizes of waves.

Fees and Permits: No fee or permits are required, but remember that this is private land intended for the production of pineapples. Access is to the public is on a goodwill basis—please respect this.

Schedule: Public access 24/7.

Finding the Break

Starting from the Kahului Airport, head south out along Dairy Road (Hawaii Route 380), passing several stoplights. Continue past major shopping centers until you reach the Mokulele Highway (Hawaii Route 35C). Continue straight through this light; you'll be on a long, straight road through sugarcane fields.

After several miles you'll reach a stoplight at Honoapi`ilani Highway (Hawaii Route 30). Turn left and follow this road straight through the town of Ma`alaea. It will bend off to the right, passing the Maui Ocean Center. The road follows the coast, with the ocean on your left, for about 10 miles, taking you straight into Lahaina. In Lahaina, head north on HI 30. Honolua Bay is 5 miles north past Kapalua. Look for the small road that dips steeply to your left. Park on HI 30 unless you have four-wheel drive. The bay is 200 yards down the small roadway.

If you're just looking for a good view of the waves, drive a little farther along the road and park along pineapple trails that skirt the cliff where the road reaches the top and bends away.

Surf Description

When push comes to shove, there's no better place to be than Honolua Bay waiting for the wave with your name on it—the one that says, *I'm yours*. Then you go, and the ride of a lifetime begins. This fast, awesome point wave is so long and neat that the swell lines are like dark-blue-flecked marble in a light blue sea. The curling barrel is a white-green cavern. Hang on in there and bite the bullet. On takeoff, it's bombs away. The explosion behind you hammers your tail. The oncoming wall curls, and then gracefully breaks clean over your head. Now its pumping curl lines tube by the second, and you feel your feet lift up and fly.

The quintessential surf bay, Honolua Bay is situated 12 miles from Lahaina on the northwest coast, and is famous for its perfect point surf breaking off the headland. One of the most scenic bays in the Hawaiian Island chain, it's well known for its world-class surfing from November to March. The waves march in around Lipoa Point, building up

Honolua Bay, Maui. PHOTO ROD SUMPTER

to a takeoff that's near vertical. The wave breaks fast, hollowing out and pitching a curl next to a long shoulder, which curves around to face you as the "Bowl" nears. The focus of this wave is unique to Honolua Bay, as the wave's outer swell bends inward into a horseshoe shape, forcing you left toward the cliff and a steepening fast section. While the wave stretches out in front of you, it doubles in height. This is what locals call the Bowl. And it's amazing.

Honolua Bay is a symbol of surf perfection, a bay steeped in wave-riding tradition since the time of the Hawaiian kings. The island of Maui is just twenty minutes' flying time from the Honolulu International Airport, and just five hours from the U.S. mainland. The local airport, Kahului, is named for the capital of Maui. The lush vegetation, trees, and vines make this an exceptional beauty spot.

When summer brings flat water, the snorkeling is very good here. But leave the fishing spear at home, as this is one of Hawaii's Fish Conservation Areas. Since there are no lifeguards here on Honolua Bay, you'll be surfing entirely at your own risk. Some beach breaks do, however, have lifeguards, so check notice boards and follow the warnings. Surf alerts will be announced on the radio station's weather bulletins.

Local Events/Attractions

- Perhaps Maui's most famous landmark is the mighty **Haleakala** to the east of the island. This massive dormant volcano is 10,023 feet high and capped with thick snow in winter. The central spine connecting Haleakala with the **West Maui Mountains** is Maui's prime agricultural region. It was created when lava flows from the Haleakala volcano filled in the gap between it and the much older West Maui volcano, above Honolua Bay. The West Maui Mountains run close to 6,000 feet high and are surrounded by prime farming land, cattle ranches, and sugar and pineapple plantations.

- **Roxy Pro Ladies Championships** take place in January.
- **Honolua Surf Co. Legends of the Bay** is held on February 7.

Local Surf Shops

Just take a walk along Front Street from Lahaina Harbor for several stores filled with all the best brands of surf clothing and accessories.

The Cave is a dangerous barrel section inside Honolua Bay next to the reef cliff. On crowded days it's best to take off on any empty wave, and the Cave is always tempting—often putting you in the driver's seat of a barrel that's about to close.

Slaughterhouse

A huge left-hand barrel on a big west swell in winter can make this an epic spot. On smaller days the beach break provides secluded neat waves sheltered from strong trade winds. A tiny beach break beneath 100-foot cliffs.

Best Tides: Low to medium.

Best Swell Direction: North.

Best Wave Size: Chest high to triple overhead.

Bottom: Sand.

Type of Break: Left and right.

Skill Level: Intermediate to advanced.

Best Boards: Shortboards and guns.

Best Seasons: Fall and winter.

Crowds: Rarely crowded.

Water Quality: Clean.

Hazards: Localism.

Fees and Permits: No fee or permits are required.

Schedule: Public access 24/7.

Finding the Break

Starting from the Kahului Airport, head south out along Dairy Road (Hawaii Route 380), passing several stoplights. Continue past major shopping centers until you reach the Mokulele Highway (Hawaii Route 35C). Continue straight through this light; you'll be on a long, straight road through sugarcane fields.

Looking through the fence at Slaughterhouse, Maui. PHOTO ROD SUMPTER

After several miles you'll reach a stoplight at Honoapi`ilani Highway (Hawaii Route 30). Turn left and follow this road straight through the town of Ma`alaea. It will bend off to the right, passing the Maui Ocean Center. The road follows the coast, with the ocean on your left, for about 10 miles, taking you straight into Lahaina. In Lahaina, head north on HI 30. Slaughterhouse is 4.5 miles north past Kapalua: Look for the wire fences, windy road, and roadside stops, or park at the foot of Honolua Bay before the bridge and walk.

Surf Description

One of the most treasured and respected breaks on the North Shore, this wave goes to five times overhead with good shape, but it's rarely ridden more than triple overhead because of the closeness of the cliffs. If it's low tide and the waves break on the beach just short of the rocks, it's okay.

Situated 0.5 mile south of Honolua Bay and 6 miles north of Ka`anapali, this left-hand reef and beach break is sheltered from all but northwest winds by 100-foot cliffs. It's a haven for bodyboarders when it's small and big-wave riders when it's big.

Mokuleia Beach's big winter-time waves make it a favorite spot for bodysurfing and big-wave riders alike, but it is hazardous. Still, that's not why it's called Slaughterhouse.

This entire area has been designated a Marine Life Conservation District, and its waters are home to a wide variety of exotic fish. The snorkeling is fantastic in summer.

There actually was a slaughterhouse here once; it was torn down in the 1960s, but the name stuck.

Winding around the sealed but narrow two-way Honoapi`ilani Highway, you pass a wire fence 20 feet tall on the left (seaward) side. This partially blocks the view of the ocean, with trees masking it further. When you stop at the roadside and peer down at the left-hand wave reeling off, you'll feel as if you're in jail, looking out the bars at perfection.

A dangerous beauty, Slaughterhouse's many moods set it apart as one of the world's great little bays—but one that protects itself by being hard to get to.

The Stables is a long right-hander on a big swell or a short reef peak on 4- to 6-foot conditions. This is an out-of-control break to see pumping December to March on a big northwest swell and raging storm conditions—one of the epic Hawaiian spots to see breaking. Pull off the windy road 0.5 mile before Honolua.

D. T. Fleming Beach Park

Everything a good beach break should be and more on the right day, D. T. Fleming Beach Park is always crowded with good longboarders, bodyboards zipping around, and radical shortboard surfing. It's a real competitive surf zone.

Best Tides: Medium.

Best Swell Direction: North.

Best Wave Size: Chest high to overhead.

Bottom: Sand.

Type of Break: Left- and right-hand beach break.

Skill Level: Beginner to expert, depending on wave height.

Best Boards: Bodyboards, shortboards, and longboards.

Best Seasons: Fall and winter.

Crowds: Crowded.

Water Quality: Average to clean.

Hazards: This is a steep shelving beach with a heavy high-tide shorebreak.

Fees and Permits: No fee or permits are required.

Schedule: Public access 24/7.

Finding the Break

Starting from the Kahului Airport, head south out along Dairy Road (Hawaii Route 380), passing several stoplights. Continue past major shopping centers until you reach the Mokulele Highway (Hawaii Route 35C). Continue straight through this light; you'll be on a long, straight road through sugarcane fields.

D. T. Fleming Beach Park, Maui. PHOTO ROD SUMPTER

After several miles you'll reach a stoplight at Honoapi`ilani Highway (Hawaii Route 30). Turn left and follow this road straight through the town of Ma`alaea. It will bend off to the right, passing the Maui Ocean Center. The road follows the coast, with the ocean on your left, for about 10 miles, taking you straight into Lahaina. In Lahaina, head north on HI 30. Go 4.7 miles from the Ka`anapali light; just past the Ritz-Carlton hotel, turn left into the park.

Surf Description

Solid waves push in off solid sandbars and produce epic lefts and rights. But it's the right-hand reef that's the real star wave here. It swings around from Honolua Bay and provides classic barrels.

This seriously fun beach break has a right-hand reef that peels into the beach lineup and only adds to what is an epic wave. D. T. Fleming Park Bay pushes up the swell like a row of soldiers arriving, and surfers rip the lineup to make the drop, paddle over, or dive for cover. The waves line up and spread across the beach, catching the right reef first and sending a perfect barrel into the sandbars. To the west, left and right peaks form in front of the picnic tables that line the shorebreak to the lifeguard tower.

Situated 2 miles west of Honolua Bay and 5 miles east of Lahaina, this is one of the best beaches on Maui. Very popular in winter, the consistent high-quality surf attracts all the hardcore and expert crew, who put on an unrivaled display of grace and powerful surfing. Bodyboarders wipe out regularly, finding the speed too much and the angle required to go down the line too flat. The left side of the beach is a heavy semi-closeout where a huge sandbar stretches for 100 yards. Here the best bodysurfers ride for a split second, enjoying the tuck under and out the backdrop.

Local Events/Attractions

D. T. Fleming Beach Park is one of the most popular beaches on the western end of Maui. This mile-long crescent attracts not only surfers but also droves of sunbathers and swimmers. Families come to picnic in the shadow of the trees. There are showers, restrooms, picnic facilities, and grills.

Golf Balls

This fickle left-hand break needs just the right northwest swell to work—but then its epic wedge-shaped barrel will amaze you. Take off inside the rock point, just inside the cliff rock.

Best Tides: Low to medium.

Best Swell Direction: Northwest.

Best Wave Size: Chest high to triple overhead.

Bottom: Sand.

Type of Break: Left and right.

Skill Level: Expert to advanced, due to the tricky paddle-out.

Best Boards: Shortboards and guns.

Best Seasons: Fall and winter.

Crowds: Rarely crowded.

Water Quality: Clean.

Hazards: This is a steep shelving beach with a heavy high-tide shorebreak.

Fees and Permits: No fee or permits are required.

Schedule: Public access 24/7.

Finding the Break

Starting from the Kahului Airport, head south out along Dairy Road (Hawaii Route 380), passing several stoplights. Continue past major shopping centers until you reach the Mokulele Highway (Hawaii Route 35C). Continue straight through this light; you'll be on a long, straight road through sugarcane fields.

After several miles you'll reach a stoplight at Honoapi`ilani Highway (Hawaii Route 30). Turn left and follow this road straight through the town of Ma`alaea. It will bend off to the right, passing the Maui Ocean Center. The road follows the coast, with the ocean on your left, for about 10 miles, taking you straight into Lahaina. In Lahaina, head north on HI 30. Go 4.7 miles from the Ka`anapali light; just past the Ritz-Carlton hotel, turn left into the park. Golf Balls is 600 yards to your left.

Surf Description

This is an awesome wave with a history of spectacular near misses caused by golf balls landing in the water—wayward shots from the ninth green of the Kapalua golf course,

Golf Balls, Maui. PHOTO ROD SUMPTER

just feet away. Fickle by nature, it's an epic wave needing just the right wraparound north swell to appear.

Golf Balls is situated on the left side of D. T. Fleming Beach Park, 2 miles south of Honolua Bay. The wave is almost a wedge-shaped swell as it pushes in against the cliff, and the rebound and next swell meet to wedge a fast vertical takeoff. Underfoot, the speed is double that of a single wave. On big days surfers reach 25 miles an hour on or after takeoff. Ideal for the expert when it's breaking.

Little Makaha. The famous Little Makaha reef break is immediately offshore from the base of the cove. Various peaks in this small bay offer short, steep rides, best in a northwest-to-west swell. There's a rocky shoreline and a small beach with super-clear water and good snorkeling on flat days. A small, sandy cove makes water access safe and easy under normal ocean conditions. Best reef breaks 3 to 5 feet, with steep wave faces.

Napili

This predominantly left-hand reef is one of the island's best walling waves, with a sting in the tail. You either connect on big sets to surf waves around the rock slap-bang in the middle of the beach, or you slip inside to cruise to the grinding beach break—although you may end up with bruising body blows as it crunches you up on dry sand!

Best Tides: High tide.
Best Swell Direction: Northwest.
Best Wave Size: Waist high to overhead.
Bottom: Sand.
Type of Break: Left.
Skill Level: If it's big, it's for the expert, but on small days intermediates will find the slow waves great fun.
Best Boards: Shortboards up to 8 feet.
Best Seasons: Fall and winter.

Crowds: Crowded on weekends and at vacation time.
Water Quality: Clean.
Hazards: A unique coral rock slab here bars beach entry and causes strange wave shapes, re-forming the inside waves before the shorebreak.
Fees and Permits: No fee or permits are required.
Schedule: Public access 24/7.

Finding the Break

From the Kahului Airport, take Hawaii Route 380 west to Lahaina. At the intersection of Honoapi`ilani Highway, head left to Lahaina. Continue through Lahaina, going north past the exits for Ka`anapali, Honokowai, and Kahana. After Kahana, take the next exit—Napili. Turn left on Napilihau Street at Napili Plaza. Continue to the stop sign at the Lower Honoapi`ilani Road intersection. Turn right at stop sign, heading north, and look for Gazebo's restaurant. You can park in the two dozen small spaces available and walk down the beach path to the waves.

Surf Description

A terrifically visual beach with pure white sand and a lava reef break that boggles the mind when you first turn the bend under the palm trees. Distant turquoise swells fill the horizon as you look out over the 20-foot cave-filled drop to a pounding shorebreak.

Napili is 2 miles south of Honolua Bay and 4 miles north of Lahaina. The end section here is one of the scariest anywhere—given the rock in the middle of the beach—but no matter what, it's an adventure and a barrel of fun. On small days (under 3 feet), small-wave riders have a lot of boogieboard fun.

When bodyboarders and bodysurfers ride the shorebreak and skimboarders are riding the slope to the face of the next wave, it can be dangerous here—a solid swell with swimmers and surf inflatables, especially on a Sunday afternoon. The backwash resembles the famous Makaha backwash, throwing bodies 10 feet in the air at high tide.

Napili, Maui. PHOTO ROD SUMPTER

Places to Eat

Banyan Tree
1 Ritz-Carlton Drive
Kapalua, Maui
(808) 669–6200

S-Turns

This epic spot—two reefs side by side—gives both rights and lefts. On a good day, it's an all-time classic wave setup. It's possible to alternate between S-Turns north (rights) and south (lefts) on successive waves. This super break stands head and shoulders above the rest for ease of access, easy paddle-out, and, above all, epic left walls and pitching sections. And did I mention the right-hand wave that's more of an A-frame peak, with roundhouse cutback turns that enable you to keep turning until the lagoon fills and fades it to zilch?

Best Tides: Low to medium.

Best Swell Direction: North.

Best Wave Size: Chest high to overhead.

Bottom: Sand, rock, and reef.

Type of Break: Left- and right-hand reef break.

Skill Level: Intermediate to advanced.

Best Boards: Longboards and short-boards.

S-Turns, Maui. PHOTO ROD SUMPTER

Best Seasons: Fall and winter.

Crowds: Crowded.

Water Quality: Average to clean.

Hazards: When the outer reef break, the main reef rights can range from a hot-dog wave to one that spells dynamite—a crushing bowl section, steep vertical peak, big waves, and dangerous rip currents.

Fees and Permits: No fee or permits are required.

Schedule: Public access 24/7.

Finding the Break

Exit the Kahului Airport on Keolani Place and proceed for 1 mile. Stay in the middle lane and continue onto Dairy Road (Hawaii Route 380), which becomes Kuihelani Highway (still HI 380) at the intersection with Pu`unene Avenue. Continue straight on HI 380 for 5 miles until it ends. Turn left onto Honoapi`ilani Highway (Hawaii Route 30) and proceed 22 miles. After passing Lahaina and Ka`anapali, turn left onto Lower Honoapi`ilani Highway and proceed 0.25 mile until you see the pink tower of the Embassy Hotel.

Surf Description

With overhead or double-overhead wave faces, this is a place for deep turns, carving fast to run down the wave face and escape its falling curl. At head high it's a place to perform slower, longer, sweeping turns. The two reefs need different swell directions.

S-Turns is like kryptonite: two reefs facing each other with beautiful waves peeling off into an overlapping channel, which gives the choice of a good ride length to connect up and surf the other. In fact, you could ride a wave on the rights and then the lefts all day long.

Situated 3 miles south of Honalua Bay, this super spot is considered the best break in Maui by many surfers. It boasts easy access, an easy paddle-out, and, above all, epic left walls with perfect shape and pitching sections on the left reef, plus equally good waves on the right reef.

Wax up on the grass in front of the 25-foot rocky drop, take the path, and wind down to a strip of beach and flat coral ledges before you and look out out in awe at the lagoon to paddle over before the break. Paddle out in the lagoon, avoiding the shallow sections here and there, and move into the deeper currents heading out.

Embassy

Out in front of the Embassy Hotel is a fast right in wintertime that's often overhead on a northwest swell, and a left in summer when it's small. This reef break off a strip of sand is the ideal spot when all the breaks farther north are either blown out, too big, or just not lined up well. This is one of the first spots that goes clean during a giant 20-foot-plus north swell. When the winds switch from onshore to northeast trade winds, a classic long, fast, hooky barrel forms.

Best Tides: Low to medium.

Best Swell Direction: North.

Best Wave Size: Chest high to triple over-head.

Bottom: Sand and coral reef.

Type of Break: Left-hand reef break with occasional rights.

Skill Level: Intermediate to advanced, due to a tricky paddle-out.

Best Boards: Shortboards, longboards, and guns.

Best Seasons: Fall, winter, and summer.

Crowds: Crowded.

Water Quality: Clean.

Hazards: Localism.

Fees and Permits: No fee or permits required.

Schedule: Public access 24/7.

Finding the Break

Exit the Kahului Airport on Keolani Place and proceed for 1 mile. Stay in the middle lane and continue onto Dairy Road (Hawaii Route 380), which becomes Kuihelani Highway (still HI 380) at the intersection with Pu`unene Avenue. Continue straight on HI 380 for 5 miles until it ends. Turn left onto Honoapi`ilani Highway (Hawaii Route 30) and proceed 22 miles. After passing Lahaina and Ka`anapali, turn left onto Lower Honoapi`ilani Highway and proceed 0.25 mile until you see the pink tower of the Embassy Hotel a mile away. Turn left onto Ka`anapali Shores Place and proceed 0.3 mile to a small public parking lot, where you can wonder how crowded it would be here on a Sunday.

Embassy, Maui. PHOTO ROD SUMPTER

Surf Description

When a sweeping north swell pours in between Lanai and Maui, you can be sure this heart-stopping surf spot will light a fire to paddle out and try your luck. It's a very fast-dropping wave, and one that runs seemingly downhill past hotels and apartment balconies, where the residents will snap a picture, drink a toast, or ignore your passing performance only 100 yards out from shore.

Situated 3 miles north of Lahaina and 4 miles south of Honalua Bay, the waves run at 45 degrees to the coast. A classic but difficult takeoff, the waves weave in a shifting pattern; takeoff at the farther point is sometimes a mirage, disappearing as inside waves only. Lines partly close out, with only the reef on the inside pushing the envelope to break and cause this furious fast right-hander to work.

Rainbows. This fickle spot is best in a big wraparound north swell in winter. A right-hander, Rainbows can have exceptionally long lulls and wave periods due to the wraparound swell. Unusual swell patterns form a fun longboard wave with long nose-riding possibilities. Watch out for sneaker sets that cream everybody inside.

Osterizers

A kind of limestone and lava ledge 200 yards out produces a big right with a big drop takeoff; the reef takes swell of 10 to 15 feet. A big-wave spot when everywhere else is closed out. It's an easy paddle-out from white sand over flat coral, if you time things right between sets. Strong drift current left toward Lahaina. This fast right-hand reef break doesn't work until a big north or northeast swell is wrapping around the coast. When it does, it stops traffic and most of Maui will be in surf frenzy. A big storm is likely to get this break working.

Best Tides: Low to medium.

Best Swell Direction: North.

Best Wave Size: Chest high to triple over-head.

Bottom: Sand and lava.

Type of Break: Left- and right-hand reef break.

Skill Level: Intermediate to advanced.

Best Boards: Shortboards and rhino guns.

Best Seasons: Fall and winter.

Crowds: Crowded when it's good.

Water Quality: Average to clean.

Hazards: Localism, rips, rocks, and under-tow.

Fees and Permits: No fee or permits are required.

Schedule: Public access 24/7, but limited public parking at hotels.

Finding the Break

Exit the Kahului Airport on Keolani Place and proceed for 1 mile. Stay in the middle lane and continue onto Dairy Road (Hawaii Route 380), which becomes Kuihelani Highway (still HI 380) at the intersection with Pu`unene Avenue. Continue straight on HI 380 for 5 miles until it ends. Turn left onto Honoapi`ilani Highway (Hawaii Route 30) and proceed 22 miles. After passing Lahaina and Ka`anapali, turn left onto Lower Honoapi`ilani Highway and proceed 0.25 mile until you see the pink tower of the Embassy Hotel a mile away. Turn left onto Ka`anapali Shores Place, go 0.25 mile, park in the small public parking lot, and take the coast path to the beach.

Surf Description

Power is nothing until you've tasted and felt it at Osterizers. This heavy, howling loud wave sweeps in from the horizon like a three-story building with an avalanche peak about to topple as you take off—it's amazing. The run starts like this and just gets faster; you have to make it or be crushed. It's a long, sloping, graceful wave with all the size and muscle of a giant killer. From shore you're surfing just a stone's throw out from the apartments and hotels on the beach. It doesn't break very good very often. The wave lines up stretching 100 yards in front of you, and you know a pitching barrel and the thick lip are hammering behind you, hitting thin air inches from your head.

Osterizers, Maui. PHOTO ROD SUMPTER

Situated 2 miles north of Lahaina, this fickle spot needs a big north swell or an extreme wraparound northeast swell to swing into the northwest-facing coast and fire in great waves with really outrageous surfing possibilities. If the swell is northwest, it's blocked by the island of Lanai. Although it can be fun small surf in these conditions, it's not spectacular and has an onshore angle that then favors lefts. This is one of the most respected surf spots on Maui, partly because it breaks so rarely and partly because the rip current and wave can be mean. Ideal for the advanced surfer.

Black Rock. At the north end of Ka`anapali Beach, a small rock cape gives a short right-hand point wave—one of Maui's unique small capes. It needs a massive swell, upon which it will fire fast rights up to and over 10 feet on takeoff. The wave walls into a flying swell stretching across the beach area in deep water and angles slowly to the beach. There's a possible connection to the thundering beach break and heavy barrels. Sheltered for strong trade winds, and worth check out on big swells.

Ka`anapali Point

This beach and coral point's surf is unusual. It's a sand-lava point underpinned by rock, and nice left and right wedges peel off in the right conditions. It's a fun wave most of the time, without much length of ride until the right swell comes along—and then it's magic. There's always some kind of ridable wave here on a north or south swell. The beach setup is fantastic: A pinnacle or spit of sand and coral stretches out toward Lanai, and the lefts and rights just crank perfectly. In summer, the lefts are the best; in winter, the rights.

Best Tides: Low to medium.

Best Swell Direction: North in winter, south in summer.

Best Wave Size: Chest-high-plus.

Bottom: Sand and coral.

Type of Break: Left and right point break.

Skill Level: Beginner to intermediate.

Best Boards: Longboards and short-boards.

Best Seasons: Fall, winter, and summer.

Crowds: Crowded.

Water Quality: Clean.

Hazards: Beginners dropping in.

Fees and Permits: No fee or permits are required.

Schedule: Public access 24/7.

Finding the Break

Exit the Kahului Airport on Keolani Place and proceed for 1 mile. Stay in the middle lane and continue onto Dairy Road (Hawaii Route 380), which becomes Kuihelani Highway (still HI 380) at the intersection with Pu`unene Avenue. Continue straight on HI 380 for 5 miles until it ends. Turn left onto Honoapi`ilani Highway (Hawaii Route 30) and proceed for approximately 20 miles. Just after passing through Lahaina town, the entrance to Ka`anapali Resort will be on your left. Make a left turn onto Ka`anapali Parkway. Ka`anapali Golf Course is located immediately on the right. After about 0.5 mile, park near Ka`anapali Resort. Public parking can be hard to find, but does exist next to all the resorts; keep an eye out for BEACH PARKING signs. Follow signs for beach and look for the sand point sticking out into the ocean.

From Ka`anapali Parkway and the HI 30/Honoapi`ilani Highway lights, it's 0.6 mile.

Surf Description

Ka`anapali Point is positioned where the coast forms a right angle at a left-hand turn to form a sand spit. Here the Pacific swells drift and bend to produce some great rights and lefts. With Lanai Island in the background, this is a scenic surf spot that gets consistent waves. At takeoff, the set-on choice wave could be a left or a right, and you won't know till the last second which way to go for the maximum barrel length; one way will wedge and push, while the other fades out. Most of the time this fun wave is best on a south

Ka`anapali Point, Maui. PHOTO ROD SUMPTER

swell for the long left and in a north swell for the rights. But given the fact that it picks up any swell around, it's a consistent reef off a sandy beach with plenty of facilities. The perfect swell might be tomorrow.

Situated 2 miles south of the Embassy Hotel and 2 miles north of Lahaina, this tourist-packed beach is best when the surf is over head high and the crowds retreat to the shore. It's then that the wedgy, glassy peaks with walls that change angles really fire, and you can direct your power and mind to some inspired surfing. Your surfing goes into overdrive fun, and awkward moments of difficulty become great rewarding rides.

Local Events/Attractions

- Named for a Maui king, **Kahekili** is the newest beach park in the area, offering picnic facilities and a pavilion. You can access it off Kai Ala Drive. The beach here is sometimes used for scuba lessons.
- **Absolute Sportfishing,** Ka`anapali Beach, Napili; (808) 669–1449
- **Aerial Sportfishing Charters,** Lahaina Harbor; (808) 667–9089
- **Ka`anapali Golf Courses,** North Course: (808) 661–3691; South Course: (808) 661–3691
- **Maui Marathon**—Kahului to Ka`anapali; (808) 871–6441

Places to Eat

Basil Tomatoes
2780 Keka`a Drive
Lahaina, Maui
(808) 662–3210

Mala Wharf

A longboarder's dream wave on the right day, Mala Wharf is a fickle spot best in summer (April to September). A long left-hand reef coral shelf makes the wave jack up and peel fast. There are winter rights in a northwest swell. Shallow low-tide reefs 1 to 2 feet deep and urchins make entering via the next available gully the best way out—or use the boat ramp. This was called the best wave in the Hawaiian Islands by 1960s longboarders, who found the sheltered reefs perfect for long nose rides and stylish turns a la Johnny Fain of Malibu fame. Today it still pumps great clean waves, but the gilt has gone from the area. Neglected by investors, the neighborhood reflects the mood but not the quality of the waves, a new surf karma rarely rivaled anywhere in the world.

Best Tides: Low to medium.

Best Swell Direction: South.

Best Wave Size: Chest high to overhead.

Bottom: Reef and rock.

Type of Break: Left- and right-handers on a south swell, rights on a north swell.

Skill Level: Experienced due to a tricky paddle-out.

Best Boards: Longboards and shortboards.

Best Seasons: Fall and winter.

Crowds: Crowded; on weekends, ultra-crowded.

Water Quality: Average to clean.

Hazards: Sharks, localism, urchins, rips, and rocks.

Fees and Permits: No fee or permits are required.

Schedule: Public access 24/7.

Finding the Break

Starting from the Kahului Airport, head south out along Dairy Road (Hawaii Route 380), passing several stoplights. Continue past major shopping centers until you reach the Mokulele Highway (Hawaii Route 35C). Continue straight through this light; you'll be on a long, straight road through sugarcane fields.

After several miles you'll reach a stoplight at Honoapi`ilani Highway (Hawaii Route 30). Turn left and follow this road straight through the town of Ma`alaea. It will bend off to the right, passing the Maui Ocean Center. The road follows the coast, with the ocean on your left, for about 10 miles, taking you straight into Lahaina. Make a left anywhere to the seafront (Front Street) and follow the coast for 1.9 miles from Lahaina Harbor. Mala Wharf is signposted and offers plenty of parking.

Mala Wharf, Maui. PHOTO ROD SUMPTER

Surf Description

At 4 to 8 feet, Mala is incomparable. A mouthwatering long left-hander that has speed, hollowness, a wall to fire on all six, and a right to kill for—this is a great break.

There's a time to wait and a time to go surfing, and Mala Wharf doesn't play about. When it's good, it's very good, and when it's off, it just doesn't happen. It's flat. Predicting Mala is impossible—it's about as fickle a break as any on Maui.

Situated 2 miles north of Lahaina, this is mostly a summer left. Tucked up under the old pier on the leeward side, a sharp V, A-frame right-hander forms to perfection off a flat reef ledge that runs out 100 yards 2 feet deep from the shore and drops away quickly at the start of the break. This a blast of a place to surf—a reminder of times past as the pier crumbles away. The ghostly neglect of the area is a little spooky on an evening sunset barrel when your leash breaks and you swim to the beach.

Mala Wharf can be entered by the boat slipway or from the beach, depending on wave height; anything over 6 feet is best tackled by a paddle-out through the harbor from the slipway. The channel takes you around to the takeoff with ease.

This old part of Lahaina has a long, flat reef stretching 100 yards offshore to a coral drop-off where good waves pipe in on a good day. Surrounded by a beach, old wharf, and captains launching boats from the slipway, this is the way out if it's over 6 to 8 feet. There's a deep harbor and entrance out through the reef. The sweep pulls you into the lineup just seconds past the wharf, near the point of the cemetery.

Local Events/Attractions

Opposite Mala Wharf, **Jodo Mission Cultural Park** sits on a point of land known as Pu`unoa Point, "the hill freed from taboo." The area was once a small village fronting the royal grove of coconut trees planted by the governor of Maui's wife, Hoapiliwahine. The area was called Mala ("garden"); the adjacent wharf still bears the name.

The largest Buddha outside Japan sits majestically and serenely in Jodo Park, commemorating the arrival of the first Japanese immigrants in 1868. The compound includes the temple shrine and an extensive outdoor meeting area. The grounds of the church are used for the annual Obon celebration and community functions.

Lahaina Harbor. Located in front of the moored tall ship and north of the quay for trips to Lanai and Molokai, the harbor offers the best summer waves in Lahaina; from April through September this place cranks.

Lahaina Reefs

An epic wave in front of the yacht harbor, Lahaina Reefs (sometimes called Breakwall) is the best winter break on Maui. When there's a big northwest swell, it will be a superhot long barreling left-hander, while in summer it's both a left- and right-hander with a short vertical wall over shallow reefs. Best when it's overhead-plus, this is the famed fast turquoise left that holds up for perfect nose rides and walls for 100 yards. Shallow reefs make the waves zip.

Best Tides: Low to medium.

Best Swell Direction: South.

Best Wave Size: Chest high to double overhead.

Bottom: Lava.

Type of Break: Left- and right-hand reef break.

Skill Level: Expert if bigger than 6 feet.

Best Boards: Shortboards and longboards on small days.

Best Seasons: Fall, winter, and summer.

Crowds: Crowded.

Water Quality: Clean.

Hazards: Sharks and localism.

Fees and Permits: No fee or permits.

Schedule: Public access 24/7. There's limited town parking near the harbor.

Lahaina Reefs, Maui. PHOTO ROD SUMPTER

Finding the Break

Starting from the Kahului Airport, head south out along Dairy Road (Hawaii Route 380), passing several stoplights. Continue past major shopping centers until you reach the Mokulele Highway (Hawaii Route 35C). Continue straight through this light; you'll be on a long, straight road through sugarcane fields.

After several miles you'll reach a stoplight at Honoapi`ilani Highway (Hawaii Route 30). Turn left and follow this road straight through the town of Ma`alaea. It will bend off to the right, passing the Maui Ocean Center. The road follows the coast, with the ocean on your left, for about 10 miles, taking you straight into Lahaina. The harbor is signposted.

Surf Description

You'll find more barrels on a good day here than on most of the other Islands' breaks put together. It's a fast, friendly swell that just begs surf me on every wave—and it's in the heart of Lahaina, where the intersection of art, surf shops, and tropical life inspires creative surfing. The locals here are red hot, and the wave is so rippable that a lot of top surfers rate it the best in Maui. On a day of pumping groundswell, the waves appear out of the light blue reef as fast as the fetch is short from the deeper dark blue reef. Every sense in your body will tingle through the steep takeoff, and you'll drop like a fly descending a glass wall as the swell picks up speed and the lip throws you a kiss. It's that good.

Situated in the center of Lahaina, this left- and right-hander goes from one extreme to another. On small days it's the neatest longboard wave, and mainly left in a south swell. On 4- to 8-foot days, the sweetness turns into speed and hovering walls, while the poky fun sections thrill like no other all the way to Shark Pit. It's best in a south swell but can be good in a southwest-to-west—and a big north swell can be the best. It's a dream break with a great layout of reefs and takeoff areas. Ideal for the beginner on 2-foot days and experts at head high and over.

Local Events/Attractions

- The **Honolua Wahine Surf Classic,** a women's contest, takes place July 17 in Lahaina Harbor.
- **Big Brothers/Big Sisters 5K/10K Fun Run/Walk,** Lahaina Chart House. Call (808) 661–0937.
- **Banyan Tree Birthday Party,** Front Street, Lahaina; (808) 667–9175.
- **Maui County Ag Trade Show and Sampling** is held at the Ulupalakua Ranch and Tedeschi Winery; (808) 242–6989.
- **Slack Key and Ukulele Festival,** Lahaina Cannery Mall. Call (808) 661–5304.

Places to Eat

Bale Sandwiches
Lahaina Cannery Mall
1221 Honoapi`ilani Highway
Lahaina, Maui
(808) 661–5566

BJ's Chicago Pizzeria
730 Front Street
Lahaina, Maui
(808) 661–0700

Shark Pit. South of Lahaina's Front Street, this popular local spot has a channel carved through a reef, producing lefts and rights. On big days it gets 15 feet plus, usually stormy but ridable; on small days it's a clean-gas wave for performance and an excellent longboarding wave when there's swell.

Hot Sands

A magical break in a 6- to 8-foot-plus swell, Hot Sands has a heavy right-hand peak and strong falling curtain that's about as good as it gets. It needs a big swell and light trade winds. There isn't much beach—just a strip of white and tan sand. Loads of low lava knobs, rocks, and gaps make the paddle-out tricky at low tide. With steep takeoffs and faces with lots of bottom, it's an ideal big performance wave.

Best Tides: Medium.	**Best Boards:** Shortboards.
Best Swell Direction: South and big winter swell.	**Best Seasons:** Summer.
	Crowds: Crowded.
Best Wave Size: Waist high to overhead.	**Water Quality:** Clean.
Bottom: Sand and reef.	**Hazards:** Sharks and localism.
Type of Break: Mostly a right-hand reef break.	**Fees and Permits:** No fee or permits required.
Skill Level: Experienced.	**Schedule:** Public access 24/7.

Finding the Break

Starting from the Kahului Airport, head south out along Dairy Road (Hawaii Route 380), passing several stoplights. Continue past major shopping centers until you reach the Mokulele Highway (Hawaii Route 35C). Continue straight through this light; you'll be on a long, straight road through sugarcane fields.

After several miles you'll reach a stoplight at Honoapi`ilani Highway (Hawaii Route 30). Turn left and follow this road straight through the town of Ma`alaea. It will bend off to the right, passing the Maui Ocean Center. The road follows the coast, with the ocean on your left, for about 10 miles, taking you straight into Lahaina. Turn left onto Shaw Street then left again onto Front Street; park where you can. Take the path to the coast beside Lahaina Shores Beach Resort. If it's breaking, you'll see the best spot to be.

Surf Description

A fast right reef break in winter and a left-hander in summer off a south swell, this is a classic break when it's big. The biggest swells are the winter northerly wraparound swells that pound the North Shore and these make Hot Sands really fire.

Situated just 1 mile south of Lahaina Harbor, Hot Sands gets its name from the hot white ribbon of sand that faces due west and catches all the afternoon sun. The wave is a thick moving swell until it hits the reef. There the face pulls up sharply to make a steep takeoff and wave face with lots of bottom—ideal for big performance turns.

There is a barrel but it's more a head-dip barrel—a short and round curved shoulder that folds over, running right along the coast, past all the foreshore houses, gardens, and trees with Kahalawai Mountain in the background. The paddle-out is easy but the

Hot Sands, Maui. PHOTO ROD SUMPTER

side-sweep current is strong when it's overhead, and runs from north to south. The favorite parking, picnic, and paddle-out area for this spot is the Puamana Beach Park. Although there are other shaded places to park, Puamana looks up into a north swell as the teeth of the barrels pour in. You can walk the coast from either above or below Hot Sands to reach the narrow coral-and-sand beach. It's at its best in a huge north swell— which may happen only twice a year, if at all. When the lineup sets run the length of the Honoapi`ilani Highway and the beat of the surf rings in the air, the town of Lahaina sings to the tune of surf. Idea for the expert surfer when it's overhead and for the inter- mediate below chest high.

Puamana Park

Puamana Park: summer surf, sunset and barbecues, longboarding heaven, and a neat small-wave spot for most of the year. It breaks off a line of reef 200 yards out and goes very shallow at low tide; it can take a big swell from the southwest, west, and northwest as well. Gentle in most conditions, the wave turns hard hitting in a 6-foot-plus swell.

Puamana Park, Maui. PHOTO ROD SUMPTER

Best Tides: Low to medium.	**Best Seasons: Summer, fall, and winter.**
Best Swell Direction: South.	**Crowds: Crowded.**
Best Wave Size: Overhead.	**Water Quality: Clean.**
Bottom: Sand and reef.	**Hazards: Sharks and localism.**
Type of Break: Left and right.	**Fees and Permits: No fee or permits are**
Skill Level: Beginner to expert.	**required.**
Best Boards: Shortboards, longboards, and bodyboards.	**Schedule: Public access 24/7.**

Finding the Break

Starting from the Kahului Airport, head south out along Dairy Road (Hawaii Route 380), passing several stoplights. Continue past major shopping centers until you reach the Mokulele Highway (Hawaii Route 35C). Continue straight through this light; you'll be on a long, straight road through sugarcane fields.

HI 380 ends at the intersection of Hawaii Route 30 (Honoapi`ilani Highway). Make a left at this light and follow HI 30 for 18 miles. Puamana State Park is on your left 2 miles before Lahaina.

Surf Description

Hop on the nose and hang five or ten and spend some time there on the tip before cruising back to the tail; then drop a knee, swing a roundhouse cutback, and trim and lock in. This is longboarding heaven on a 2- to 3-foot day. This close-to-shore wave breaks fast and short with a barreling end section when conditions are right. It's a place to race the curl and either turn straight and prone out, or kick out and get a little air, or go for the cover-up and crash in the pocket.

Situated 3 miles south of Lahaina, the park is shaded and ideal for watching the waves of Hot Sands. Access is easy along the 5-foot strip of white-sand beach where coral and reef pinnacles dot the coast. It's a family surf spot with picnic tables and a soft longboard wave most of the time. Often flat for months, it comes alive in a south swell in summer or the big north swells in winter. Just off the Honoapi`ilani Highway, Puamana Beach Park is a tradition in surfing Maui, a place where waves have always been ridden; when the surf's up, every passing car gets the word spread throughout Lahaina within hours of a new swell. Park and watch waves for an hour and choose the right time to surf sweet perfection—it's all in a day's surfing on Maui. Ideal as a beginner's spot and good for the intermediate and expert longboarders when bigger.

Local Events/Attractions

The small, quaint, traditional **Puamana State Wayside Park** offers awesome views and shade. It's good for picnics, for snorkeling on flat days, and for just plain relaxing.

Launiupoko

Like Waikiki, Launiupoko is one of the great fun beginner spots—easy, well lined up, and fun. A must-surf spot both for fun and to appreciate its history. This is one of Maui's traditional surf spots, where surfing redwood boards is an art form. It has great-quality lefts and rights, surfable down to 2 feet and up to 12 feet. It suits all grades, and there's also good shade, parking, grass, barbecues, and showers.

Best Tides: Low to medium.

Best Swell Direction: Big winter north swell or summer south swell.

Best Wave Size: Knee to head high.

Bottom: Sand, rock, and reef.

Type of Break: Left- and right-hand reef break.

Skill Level: Beginner to expert.

Best Boards: Shortboards and longboards.

Best Seasons: Summer, fall, and winter.

Crowds: Crowded.

Water Quality: Clean.

Hazards: Sharks and localism.

Fees and Permits: No fee or permits are required.

Schedule: Public access 24/7.

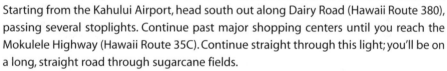

Starting from the Kahului Airport, head south out along Dairy Road (Hawaii Route 380), passing several stoplights. Continue past major shopping centers until you reach the Mokulele Highway (Hawaii Route 35C). Continue straight through this light; you'll be on a long, straight road through sugarcane fields.

After several miles you'll reach a stoplight at Honoapi`ilani Highway (Hawaii Route 30). Turn left and follow this road straight through the town of Ma`alaea. It will bend off to the right, passing the Maui Ocean Center. The road follows the coast, with the ocean on your left, taking you straight into Launiupoko State Park (3 miles before Lahaina) on your left. Pull into the park and check the waves.

Surf Description

If you remember your first wave standing up, you will remember the thrill of small-wave surfing. It's like that on most days here when a small south swell pushes through and the place becomes a beehive of activity. On big north swells, it's pumping overhead waves with long lefts perfect for nose riding. This is a great fun park that gives both old and young a chance to chat and learn about surfing before modern foam boards or talk about the latest outer reefs just surfed—a kind of newsroom beach for surfing. This can be the best beginner, novice, and expert wave on the coast; it all depends on the direction and size of the swell.

Located 3 miles south of Lahaina, this is a great place to relax on most of the south and north swells that swing in down between Lanai and Maui and give this break such consistent fun. It's a hot-dog wave with class, and it's a mean and gnarly barreling wave on big-swell days. Blessed with beautiful surroundings and facilities, it's the site of the annual redwood board meet, where only boards made before 1940 are displayed and ridden, just like the surfing heroes Tom Blake and Duke Kahanamoku used to do. Riding the nose on these boards may not be possible but you can still trim close to the tube, stand on your head, and do spinners, one-leg balances, and tandem tricks. Ideal for beginners and experienced alike, this spot offers a wide catchment of swells and wave shapes.

Local Events/Attractions

- In addition to surfing, **Launiupoko** offers a nice grassy lawn with picnic facilities and restrooms. Swimming is best when the tide is high; a breakwall provides a safe swimming spot for children. There are no lifeguards on duty.

- The annual **pre-1940s surfboard festival** takes place here each February. See how redwood boards influenced a surfing style and how they used to be ridden.

Olowalo is a fickle spot best May to September. It's right on the highway, so if you see it working, stop and go in now—the waves won't last, due to tide changes, and winds will blow in and out quickly. Crowds form very fast. It's found south of Lahaina at mile marker 14.

Ukumehame. Radical outer reefs with long rights into the bay and lefts across a white-sand beach that has one shower and an emergency callbox. The best longboarding is in a small swell, when it's fun and easy; it goes off over 6 feet as a fierce right. Ukumehame is found at mile marker 11 on the Honoapi`ilani Highway.

1000 Peaks is located at the east end of Papalua Beach near the highway tunnel. When there's a swell wrapping in, the wave peaks in a thousand places; just paddle out and wait where you are. A wave with your name on it will come.

McGregor Point. This is a serious right-hand point break under McGregor Look and Lighthouse, found close to the solid cliff wall and 40 feet below. The wave runs into deep water. In a big south swell, it's an epic wave; you'll ride very close to cliff and rocks.

Ma`alaea Pipeline

Found in Ma`alaea Bay on the west coast of Maui, Ma`alaea Pipeline is known as one of the fastest waves in the world. This reef-break right-hander works in a south swell and is the hairiest summer surf spot on Maui.

Best Tides: Low.

Best Swell Direction: South.

Best Wave Size: Waist high to overhead.

Bottom: Sand and coral.

Type of Break: Right-hand reef break.

Skill Level: Expert to advanced.

Best Boards: Shortboards to mini guns.

Best Seasons: Spring and summer.

Crowds: Crowded when it's good.

Water Quality: Average to clean.

Hazards: Shallow reef, hollow waves, rip currents, and localism.

Fees and Permits: No fee or permits are required.

Schedule: Public access 24/7.

Finding the Break

Starting from the Kahului Airport, head south out along Dairy Road (Hawaii Route 380), passing several stoplights. Continue past major shopping centers until you reach the Mokulele Highway (Hawaii Route 35C). Continue straight through this light; you'll be on a long, straight road through sugarcane fields.

After several miles you'll reach a stoplight at Honoapi`ilani Highway (Hawaii Route 30). Turn left and follow this road for 1 mile, then turn left onto Ma`alaea Road at the MA`ALAEA VILLAGE sign. Turn left again onto Hauoli Street. Ma`alaea Banyans (190 Hauoli Street) is on the right. Public access to the break is from the Maui Ocean Center, a short walk to the east side of the harbor.

Surf Description

Take a big chance and paddle out. Look at the speed, the fall line of the curl, the thickness of the lip, and the reverse curve in the wave face. Then tell yourself, *Go for it!* That's the attitude you need to ride one of the fastest waves in the world. Just sit back, watch, wait, and wax up until the first signs of the reef turn to a boiling white. This signals the start of an epic voyage.

Ma'alaea Pipeline, Maui. PHOTO ROD SUMPTER

Situated 15 miles south of Lahaina near Kihai, the Ma`alaea Pipeline in Ma`alaea Bay on Maui's west coast is known for its superfine, very fast surf. Here the seabed is made of sharp coral and lava rock, angled at just the right degree to produce fine waves. When it's a 6-foot day and the surf is really pumping, lots of experience is needed to handle the takeoff. Once you're off, you need even more experience to handle the speed of the Racetrack. The Racetrack, just about halfway through the ride, is so called for being the fastest section of the pipeline. Length of ride can be between 150 and 300 yards on a good day. Ma`alaea requires a swell of 3 to 5 feet before it will work. However, it can hold waves of 12 feet or higher when a south swell and a southeast wind create the ideal conditions.

Crowded surf conditions prevail here when the surf's up—and the word will spread quickly. Surfing by yourself is very unlikely when the waves are incoming.

Local Events/Attractions

Maui Ocean Center
192 Ma`alaea Road
Wailuku, Maui
(808) 270–7000

Places to Eat

Buzz's Wharf Restaurant
Ma`alaea Harbor, Maui
(808) 244–5426

Housing Estate, at the far end of Ma`alaea at the end of the Ocean Center parking lot. This summer break, popular with locals, needs the right conditions for a fast right slide that can mimic the break of Ma`alaea. It's usually fickle until the south swells hit in summer.

Kihei is mostly flat. It's found along the southwest coast of Maui, which only receives west swell when it's very big elsewhere. This is a beginner's surf spot for the most basic of lessons.

Kalama Park. A good beginner's spot to play in small, soft sandy beaches and learn the basics. It's not a popular surf spot but does get waves from time to time; the lineup will then be set alight very quickly with hardcore starved surfers looking for local waves on this coast.

Dumps, Ahihi Bay, is a big dumping left barrel over coral caves found about 1.5 miles past the Maui Prince Hotel. No beach facilities. When it's flat here, the many friendly fish and clear water make snorkeling in caves the best. A beauty spot that's fun on a summer head-high swell.

La Perouse Bay. The best surf spot in the southwest, where the volcanic lava turns black, La Perouse Bay is located at the end of Makena Alanui Road. From Wailea, the road turns into Makena Alanui Road; keep going past Ahihi Bay for 2 miles. The road becomes four-wheel-drive only. You can park by the historical marker. One of the best breaks in summer, mostly a left-hand reef break, it's best as a left but it can be surfed both ways. Access isn't easy over black lava, and the paddle-out is a long one—but good. Don't miss this spot. This area is covered in rough lava from the last eruption of Haleakala in 1790.

Hamoa Beach. A great bodyboarding beach, reef break, and beauty spot 2.5 miles south of Hana. Golden sands and sea cliffs with lush vegetation; offshore is the small coconut-topped island of Alau. It ranges from a beginner's surf spot to the occasional expert's spot of rare big south swells.

Koki Beach. Fast lefts and rights off the beach and a little left-hand point get solid waves. A sandy beach with rocky shoreline into the waves pulls up some extra length of ride on this shore-dumpy beach.

Hana Beach has a large, crescent black-sand beach—the result of lava eroding and washing into the ocean from a nearby stream. Rarely big and mostly closed out, it peaks along the bay. One of the best spots, with smooth clean waves. The paddle-out over rocks is pretty mellow and no problem; rights, some lefts, and a reef break that's best at 6 to 10 feet.

Wailea River Mouth. A pebble riverbed runs into the beach cove here. The waves are usually murky with fresh water. It's spooky not seeing your hands as you paddle—and sharks have been known to be in the area. Hawaiians surf the mushy rights off the point. Localism runs strong.

Wailea Beach needs a moderate swell, but you'll find good body-surfing, bodyboarding, and longboarding on this mile-long, gold-sand beach named for Lea, the Hawaiian goddess of canoe makers. Great views of Molokini Crater, Pacific humpback whales, and the distant, uninhabited island of Kaho`olawe.

**Ke`anae Beach** is a dark tan beach with a left-hander and beach-break peaks. Ke`anae Stream flows onto the beach area, creating a pool surrounded by boulders. Murky water and sharky. Rarely good.

Honomanu Bay is a remote bay located about 19.1 miles east of the intersection of the Hana and Haleakala Highways, between Haiku and Ke`anae. The highway runs close to the coast and is about 100 feet above sea level; you'll see the large, rocky, gray-sand beach. Turn off onto the dirt access road.

Jaws

Known as Peahi by the locals, this is a big-wave spot—surf only if you dare. Jaws is where world-class daredevils risk their lives on the biggest waves in the world—up to 70 feet. Mere mortals watch from the cliff as tow teams of surfers and Jet Skiers tackle this giant spot.

Best Tides: Medium.

Best Swell Direction: North.

Best Wave Size: Triple overhead to ten times overhead.

Bottom: Reef.

Type of Break: Right-hand reef break.

Skill Level: Advanced to big-wave riders.

Best Boards: Tow-in boards to rhino guns, 10 to 12 feet.

Best Seasons: Fall and winter.

Crowds: Only a few brave these waves.

Water Quality: Clean.

Hazards: Big waves, currents, rips, and rocks.

Fees and Permits: A small fee is charged when the surf's up.

Schedule: This area is found on privately owned pineapple fields.

Jaws, Maui. PHOTO ROD SUMPTER

Finding the Break

Leaving the airport, drive straight to the second stoplight, the one after the Kmart plaza. This is the Hana Highway (Hawaii Route 36). Turn left, heading toward the big volcano. After 1 mile you reach another stoplight, this one on the Haleakala Highway (Hawaii Route 37). Continue straight through this intersection. The road will follow the coast, with the ocean on your left, passing through the towns of Spreckelsville, Paia, and Haiku, and the world-famous surf spot Ho`okipa.

From Ho'okipa, Jaws is another 2.3 miles east. Access is difficult through privately owned pineapple fields, which are open to the public when the surf is up; for a fee you are driven to the clifftop to view the awesome sight. If you're allowed to drive in, be warned: This is four-wheel-drive territory, especially if it's wet. You can also walk in. It's 1.5 miles from the main road—and take a compass, because the trails are many.

Surf Description

At Jaws, surf as big as anywhere in the world happens two or three times a year. Dropping into a goliath of a wave with all the power the ocean can muster is the ultimate thrill for those who dare. The huge peak towers in with wedge-shaped ears and hooting shoulders as Mother Ocean blows and trumpets the arrival of the king of waves. The barrel is three stories round and one of Hawaii's biggest waves, if not the biggest.

Jaws is situated 4 miles east of the Kahului Airport and 20 miles from Haleakala, the 10,023-foot-tall volcano whose flanks form the whole of East Maui's "body." Nicknamed "House of the Sun," it is the largest dormant volcano in the world. Not yet extinct, it's expected to erupt sometime in the next 200 years (it last erupted in 1790). Big waves and big epic scenery abound.

This big-wave spot allows tow-in surfing for advanced big-wave riders and expert Jet Skiers, who launch from the nearby Maliko Bay in smaller calm waters and travel the short 1 to 2 miles to Jaws. Here some do-or-die moments are experienced, as each new big Jaws swell is different, demanding courage and skill to survive. The biggest waves in the world are surfed here on rare big north swells with a right angle to work and south-easterly winds. Known for its 40- to 60-foot wave faces, the break ends up on a shallow reef shelf where your teammate plucks you out of danger in a personal watercraft.

Peahi is one of the most respected surf spots in the world.

Local Events/Attractions

Haleakala National Park
P.O. Box 369
Makawao, Maui 96768
Visitor information: (808) 572–4400

So why are the waves at Jaws so tall?

It's due to the Jaws ridge—a large underwater ridge here that juts out from the shoreline toward the northwest. The principal effect of this ridge is to cause waves to refract. Refraction occurs when part of a wave in shallow water (over the ridge) moves more slowly than does the wave in deeper water. When the depth under a wave varies along its crest, the wave bends, and the crest tends to become parallel to the depth contours.

A dozen or so times a year, Pacific storms and the underwater topography of Maui's North Shore combine to create monster waves. Only a handful of surfers even try to ride these Hawaiian behemoths.

Ho`okipa

Ho`okipa is the windsurfing mecca of the world. Host to World Cup sailing and surfing contests, this spot rips. Jagged lava rock, exposed reefs, a gnarly shorebreak, light off-shore trade winds, and powerful rip currents combine to make this North Shore launch off-limits to most sailors and surfers when it's 40 feet. On smaller days it's the best wind-surfing wave-riding spot on Maui—maybe the world.

Best Tides: Low to medium.

Best Swell Direction: North.

Best Wave Size: Chest high to triple over-head.

Bottom: Sand, reef, and rock.

Type of Break: Left and right.

Skill Level: Experienced to expert.

Best Boards: Shortboards and guns.

Best Seasons: Fall and winter.

Crowds: Crowded.

Water Quality: Clean.

Hazards: Sharks and localism.

Fees and Permits: No fee or permits are required.

Schedule: Public access 24/7.

Finding the Break

Ho`okipa Beach Park is located 2 miles east of Paia on the Hana Highway just past Mama's Fish House Restaurant. The tiny beach, tucked in a cove below, serves as a launching spot for the premier waves in the world.

Surf Description

When you first set eyes on Ho`okipa's waves, you know you've arrived somewhere spe-cial—the panorama is that inspiring. You've been told about it and you've seen great rides at Ho`okipa, but it's not until you're there that the grandeur of the place hits home. There are white, light blue, and shades-of-turquoise barrels in a darker blue surf lineup, but it's not just the colors that stun you here; it's the expanse of the bay and wave power. With barrels thumping in from the point and swells combing the coast from east and west, you know you're at the heart of surfing and windsurfing at this epic location.

Situated 2.3 miles west of Jaws, this right point break works best in a northwest swell and south winds holding waves up to 20 feet. On small days this is a wave for long-boards, or shortboards from 3 to 10 feet. The right conditions for windsurfing are usu-ally found on the left side of the bay, while surfers go to the point for the best shortboard waves. The beach entry isn't easy, because lava rocks in the shape of pot-holed slabs cover most of the beach; there's also a heavy shorebreak. Ideal for wind-surfers with a lot of experience, this spot amazes the world windsurfing community with consistently epic rides.

Farther down the beach to the west are right and left reefs, but this is closer to shore and more hairy. Outer swells form on cloud break reefs, and a host of unnamed breaks

Ho`okipa, Maui. PHOTO ROD SUMPTER

up and down the coast toward Mama's Fish House Restaurant can be good. Experts launch into deep water from the beach park, off jagged coral ledges just downwind from the pavilion. Expect crowds, with many sailors around the outside and inside looking for a good wave to rip on the inside, as well as surfers vying for the slot at the point's great waves. It's ideal for experts and experienced wave riders.

Local Events/Attractions

- The **Ho`okipa Surf Classic** is held in early January, sponsored by the Surfrider Foundation.
- The **Local Motion Surf Contest** also takes place at Ho`okipa Beach Park. Call (808) 575–9264.
- **Aloha Classic World Wavesailing Championships.** Call (808) 575–9151.

Places to Eat

Mama's Fish House Restaurant
799 Poho Place
Paia, Maui
(808) 579–8488

Lanes. This is a big-wave spot. The paddle-out is from Ho`okipa, and there's a short paddle around to the takeoff. In wintertime waves reach 5 to 6 feet Hawaiian size or 18 to 20 feet West Coast size, with huge faces. Farther to the right is a reef break that connects to Badger Beach.

Kuau Bay (or Tavares Bay). A wide yellow-sand beach break that works off lumps of lava just offshore. The neat wave barrels on the shore; it's best in a strong northwest swell and south winds. It's found just before Paia from Ho`okipa.

Paia

Paia beach break with its outer reefs offers a host of good longboard, shortboard, and bodysurfing possibilities. It's one of the best beaches to surf—you could call it a playground of waves. From the little hill at the beach entrance, there are some awesome views that overlook the bay with a vista of peaks, takeoff areas, and shorebreaks. This is one of the all-time classic beaches and reef breaks in the Islands, and symbolizes the Hawaiian surf scene.

Best Tides: Low to medium.

Best Swell Direction: West-northwest.

Best Wave Size: Chest high to triple overhead.

Bottom: Sand and a little coral.

Type of Break: Left- and right-hand beach break.

Skill Level: Beginner to pro surfer.

Best Boards: Shortboards and longboards.

Best Seasons: Fall and winter.

Crowds: Crowded.

Water Quality: Average to clean.

Hazards: Sharks and localism.

Fees and Permits: No fee or permits are required.

Schedule: Public access 24/7.

Finding the Break

From the Kahului Airport, turn left onto Hana Highway (Hawaii Route 36). Go east toward the town of Paia; the beach park is on your left. From the crossroads lights at Hana Highway, it's 3.4 miles to Paia Beach Park.

Surf Description

The surf action comes thick and fast here at the most popular family beach in all Maui. This is where surf maneuvers get invented, like the barrel roll, aerial loop, and drop-the-knee. It's where the hot local surfers blend with weekenders to make a surfing fire of performance and competition.

Situated 3 miles east of Ho`okipa, this great beach has loads of breaks peaking up on different swell sizes and directions; it's a classic place to be on a good day—one giant ocean playground where folks from windsurfers to skimboarders all have their very own surf area to hot-dog and blaze a trail. And way out on the horizon are set waves where the length of ride can be immense, and a racetrack of sections over reefs where windsurfers rip. Closer to shore, sandbars form waves that dip and weave a little in depth, pro-viding a wide range of wave faces to surf. Closeout sets peak along the path of pre-vious waves, which boil over and re-form into classic wave faces. The white-water waves are even more sucky than the green walls of a raw swell.

Paia, Maui. PHOTO ROD SUMPTER

Windsurfing waves a mile out form as steep swells and comb in to another takeoff point 900 yards out. Here windsurfers fall off and turn out to sea, where a kind of Sunset Beach peak features bodyboarders and shortboarders dropping out of the sky, vying for position.

Places to Eat

Mama's Fish House Restaurant
799 Poho Place
Paia, Maui
(808) 579–8488

Baldwin Beach Park. This great park boasts an easy paddle-out, classic beach-break waves, good facilities, some nice reef breaks way out, and cloud breaks in big seas. It can be an epic spot—one of the best parks in the Hawaiian Islands. Lifeguards year-round. Site of some of the hottest surfing on the North Shore.

Kanaha. This beach break with an outer reef makes an ideal windsurfing spot, and there's some surfing in the right conditions. Long windsurfing rides on unbroken swells, classic on the right day. Very much a beauty spot with scenic views of the waves.

Kahului Harbor offers short hollow waves right off the rocks both ways. "Middles"—a right-hander in the middle of the harbor—holds swell up to 12 feet. For hardcore and expert surfers. Expect some localism, and don't leave valuables in your car.

Paukukalo, Hawaiian Homestead. A beach break with fun left- and right-hand waves. This is the site where tradition credits the Menehune with the construction of both heiau ("temples") in a single night, using rocks from Paukukalo Beach, during the Hawaiian precontact period. Localism is at its strongest here. The founding of the Hawaiian kingdom can be directly associated with one structure in the Hawaiian Islands: Pu`ukohola Heiau, built between 1790 and 1791 by Kamehameha I.

Waiehu Beach has a rocky reef with rights and lefts, and a break that throws out. There's paved access from Waiehu Beach Road to the sandy beach, which gets crowded on weekends. Localism runs strong.

Honokahau Point. This mellow, soft right-hand point break works in a swell of 3 to 8 feet. The black-pebble-and-stones beach makes for a rock-hopping entry into a pounding shorebreak. This fickle spot never seems to be surfed left off the west side of the bay—which always looks good but rarely breaks far enough away from the cliff. Local residents sell handmade shell jewelry and fruit in a parking-lot kiosk. This is one of the original Christian surfing sites made famous in the 1960s. Respect is a must.

Wind Mills

Two awesome reefs produce classic rights and lefts, which run into a huge center rip channel that makes for a quick and easy paddle-out. The access in is a nightmare, though: After a lot of rock-hopping from the end of a beach, you have to judge sets on a 5-foot rock, figuring out when to jump into the swirling, chaotic waters between splash-ups, then enter the river-speed ripout.

Best Tides: Mid-incoming tide.

Best Swell Direction: Northwest.

Best Wave Size: Overhead to triple overhead.

Bottom: Coral reef.

Type of Break: Left and right.

Skill Level: Expert to advanced due to the dangerous rock-hopping entry, which may well require coping with a wash off rocks. Reaching the beach requires a hike down a cliff along boulder-strewn paths.

Best Boards: Shortboards and guns.

Best Seasons: Fall and winter.

Crowds: Crowded.

Water Quality: Clean.

Hazards: Sharks and localism.

Fees and Permits: No fees or permits are required.

Schedule: Public access 24/7.

Finding the Break

From the Kahului Airport, head south out along Dairy Road (Hawaii Route 380). Pass several stoplights and continue past major shopping centers until you reach the Mokulele Highway (Hawaii Route 35C). Continue straight through this light; you'll be on a long, straight road through sugarcane fields.

After several miles, you'll reach a stoplight at the Honoapi`ilani Highway (Hawaii Route 30). Turn left and follow this road straight through the town of Ma`alaea. It will bend off to the right, passing the Maui Ocean Center. The road follows the coast, with the ocean on your left, for about 10 miles, taking you straight into Lahaina. Continue 5 miles past Lahaina and Honalula Bay; Wind Mills is 1 mile farther on your left.

Wind Mills, Maui. PHOTO ROD SUMPTER

Surf Description

Right from the start you know this wave is going to eat you, kill you, or give you the greatest pleasure a surfer could dream of. Picture two windmills side by side forming a perfect left and an equally perfect right, plus a rip in the middle where entry and exit border on the insane. The current runs faster than 10 miles an hour at times, while the sea is 80 degrees and turquoise-white—the color of milk—from the surge. The waves come in two to a set, like lonely dark blue sharks. This is epic stuff; this is Wind Mills, one of the greatest surf spots in the world, very fickle to catch working on a good day and certainly not a walk in the park given the crowds. Add to this localism with a well-defined pecking order and it's hard in the surf lineup.

The walk in begins as a trail over 10-foot slopes, winding for 100 yards under fir trees. Once you're in the break, the lefts swing wide near the 150-foot cliffs, bending to the shallows and breaking as a perfect barrel. It's easy to drop in and difficult to get out of the tube other than gung-ho straight through to the rip. Take the conveyer-belt current and paddle a little to the rights, which have a mean takeoff that causes a lot of panic, not to mention wipeouts and free falls down the faces. To view Wind Mills at an angle of 45 degrees from the cliff lying on your chest is one of surfing's rare and great wonders: From high above you're like a helicopter hovering over classic waves, spying on the fate of the next takeoff. Wind Mills' dual rip currents, pouring off the two reefs, are unique in the world. Nowhere else does a surf setup provide the perfect combination of left and right, with an outgoing middle channel fixed precisely to feather and dampen the shorebreak so rock-hopping entries are just makable.

The tail ends of both waves conclude in a powerful rip steaming out and fanning out to the prospective takeoffs. A mechanical engineer could not have designed so outrageously simple and effective a setup. At takeoff the current has gone straight out to sea, and the waiting area is calm and slack. This is a spot for the wave-hunting surfer with advanced skills and experience.

Local Events/Attractions

Whalers Village Museum
2435 Ka`anapali Parkway
Lahaina, Maui
(808) 661–5992

Maui Resources

Hawaii Activities Offices
Aloha Tower, 5th Floor
1 Aloha Tower Drive
Honolulu, Oahu 96813
(877) 877-1222 or (808) 524-0008
Fax: (808) 599-3778
www.hawaiiactivities.com

Aloha Airlines Baggage Offices
Maui
(808) 877-5614

Bus Service

www.akinatours.com/maui_shuttle.htm

General Information

Maui Chamber of Commerce
250 Alamaha Street, Unit N16A
Kahului, Maui 96732
(808) 871-7711

Maui County Online
www.co.maui.hi.us

Maui-info.com

Maui Net
www.maui.net/
Web page covering Maui for the visitor; details and links to other sites.

Maui Visitors Bureau
1727 Wili Pa Loop
Wailuku, Maui 96793
(800) 525-MAUI or (808) 244-3530
www.visit.Hawai`i.org/

National Weather Service
Daily forecasts for Maui: (808) 877-5111
Marine forecast: (808) 877-3477
or (808) 877-3949

Accommodations

Ka`anapali Beach Resort Association
2530 Keka`a Drive
Lahaina, Maui 96761
(800) 245-9229 or (808) 661-3271

Kapalua Resort
800 Kapalua Drive
Kapalua, Maui 96761
(800) KAPA-LUA
www.kapaluamaui.com

Wailea Destination Association
3750 Wailea Alanui
Kihei, Maui 96753
(808) 879-4258

Camping

Department of Land and
Natural Resources
Division of State Parks—
Camping Permits
54 South High Street, Room 101
Wailuku, Maui 96793
(808) 984-8109

Department of Parks and Recreation
Camping Permits, County of Maui
1580-C Ka`ahumanu Avenue

Wailuku, Maui 96793
(808) 270-7389
Maximum stay three nights.
Call for fee information.

Haleakala National Park
Camping Permits/Information
P.O. Box 569
Makawao, Maui 96768
(808) 572-4400

Surf Shops

Boss Frog's Dive & Surf Shop
Kahana Manor Shops
4310 Lower Honoapi`ilani
Highway, #110
Kahana, Maui
(808) 669-6700

Boss Frog's Dive & Surf Shop
2395 South Kihei Road
Kihei, Maui
(808) 875-4477

Boss Frog's Dive & Surf Shop
150 Lahainaluna Road
(off Front Street)
Lahaina, Maui
(888) 700-3764 or (808) 661-3333
www.hawaiidiscountactivities.com

Boss Frog's Dive & Surf Shop
Napili Plaza
Napili Market
Napili, Maui
(808) 669-4949

Hi-Tech Online store
425 Koloa
Kahului, Maui 96732
(808) 877-2111
Fax: (808) 871-6943
E-mail: htmaui@maui.net

Lightning Bolt Maui
55 Ka`ahumanu Avenue, Suite E
Kahului, Maui 96753
(808) 877-3484

Local Motion
1819 South Kihei Road
Kihei, Maui
(808) 879-7873

Local Motion
1295 Front Street
Lahaina, Maui

Neil Pryde
400 Hana Highway
Kahului, Maui 96732
(808) 877-7443 or (800) 321-7443
Fax: (808) 877-2149

Ole Surfboards
Bob Olsen
277 Wili Kio
Lahaina, Maui
(808) 661-3459

Second Wind Sail and Surf
111 Hana Highway
Kahului, Maui
(808) 877-7467

Surf Lessons

Hans Hedemann Surf School
(808) 924-7778
www.hhsurf.com

Kai Nalu Surf Tours
536 Kahua Place
Paia, Maui 96779
(808) 579-9937
Fax: (808) 579-9937
www.mauisurfing.com

Surfdog Maui
Highway 30
Lahaina, Maui 96767-0501
(808) 250-SURF (7873)

Nancy Emerson School of Surf
(808) 244-7873
www.mauisurfclinics.com

CHAPTER 3
Molokai

hether you arrive by ferry from Maui or fly into the Molokai airport, you'll pick up on this island's country vibe straight away. In many ways this is the jewel in the crown of Hawaiian surfing adventure. The surf spots around the island include Mo`omomi Beach, a fine reef and beach break 5 miles long; this is a protected area, and you'll need a permit from the Department of Hawaiian Home Land to surf here. Then there are the more accessible spots like Dixies, a left reef point break, and Pohakuloa near the Kauakoi Resort. The Sheraton at Kepuhi Beach offers surf rentals, a shop, and a reef and beach break on the west coast that really work well on a northwest swell. Halawa Bay in northeastern Molokai is arguably the finest surf spot; it works best on a north swell with a southwest wind. All around the island there are good waves in the right conditions. Even the Wharf where the ferry arrives can pump in a good south swell.

Anchored in the center of the eight major Hawaiian Islands, Molokai (the fifth largest) is 25 miles southeast of Oahu, 8 miles (across the Pailolo Channel) from Maui, and an hour and a half by boat from Lahaina. It boasts beautiful lush vegetation on the east coast, huge sand dunes (the biggest in Hawaii) on the North Shore, and dry, sparse landscapes to the west. Molokai has a 106-mile coastline and few roads to the North Shore's best beach-break waves. This is four-wheel-drive country, where permits and

Regional Map

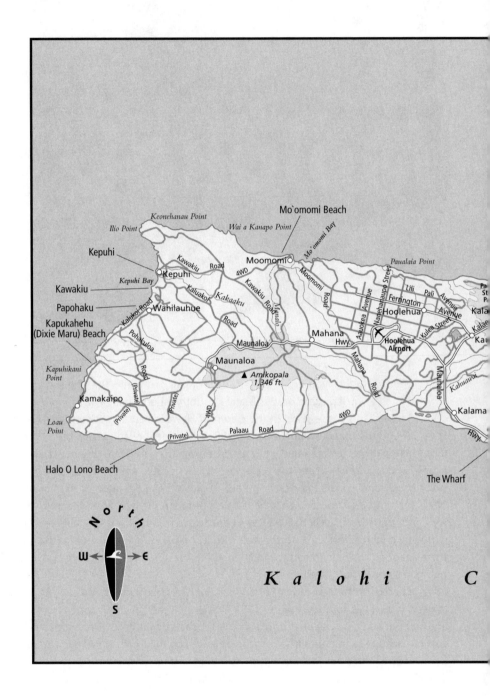

Mo`omomi Beach

Keonehanau Point

Ilio Point

Wai a Kanapo Point

Mo`omomi Bay

Kepuhi

Kawakiu Road

Moomomi

Paualaia Point

Kepuhi

4WD

Kepuhi Bay

Kaluakoi

Kawakiu Road

Moomomi Road

Kawakiu

Kakaaku

Lili

Pali   Avenue

Pa
St
P.

Papohaku

Kalukoi Road

Wahilauhue

Road

Kapuakea Avenue

Nanehahaupo Street

Farrington

Avenue

Kala

Kapukahehu
(Dixie Maru) Beach

Pohakuloa

Maunaloa

Mahana
Hwy.

Hoolehua

Airport

Hoolehua

Kulea Street

Kalae

Ka

Maunaloa

Kapuhikani
Point

Road

(Private)

Amikopala
1,346 ft.

Kaluauua

Kamakaipo

(Private)

Private

4WD

Mahana Road

Maunaloa

Loau
Point

(Private)

Palaau   Road

4WD

Kalama

Halo O Lono Beach

Hwy

The Wharf

North

W ← → E

S

K a l o h i   C

MOLOKAI

SCALE RF 1 : 300,000

```
0    Kilometers    5
0       Miles       3
```

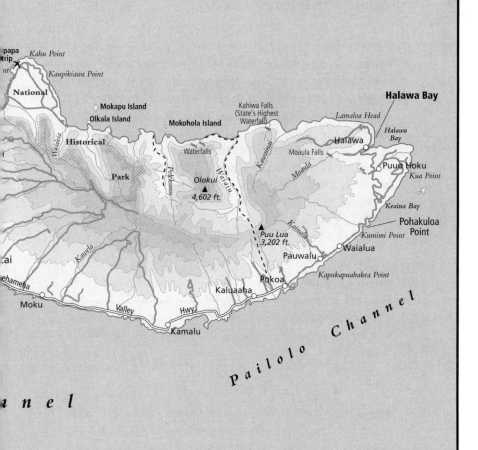

papa
trip
nt ✕ *Kahu Point*

Kaupikiawa Point

National

○ **Mokapu Island**

Olkala Island

Mokohola Island

Kahiwa Falls
(State's Highest
Waterfall)

Halawa Bay

Lamaloa Head

*Halawa
Bay*

○ Halawa

Historical

Waiakia

Waterfalls

Pelekunu

Wailau

Kawainui

Moaula Falls

Moaula

Puuo Hoku

Kua Point

Park

Olokui
▲
4,602 ft.

Keaina Bay

**Pohakuloa
Point**

ai

Kawela

Puu Lua
▲
3,202 ft.

Kainalu

Kumimi Point

○ Waialua

Pauwalu

○ Pukoa

ehameha

Valley   Hwy.

○ Kaluaaha

Kapukapuahakea Point

○
Moku

○
Kamalu

Pailolo   *Channel*

nel

private property are the rule. The emptiness of Molokai's beaches can be a blessing—no crowds and a peaceful, natural setting—but it also means there are no lifeguards or facilities.

Mo`omomi Beach is a 5-mile-long beach break with rocky outcrops and miles of waves yet to discover (like much of Molokai). Many reefs pick any northwest, north, and northeast swells, creating solid winter surf that can go very big—as well as impossible paddle-outs. Middle-size waves are the best. This is a remote location on private property and a Nature Conservancy preserve; many places require permission and/or a permit. Call Mo`omomi Preserve at (808) 553–5236.

Kepuhi, near the Sheraton hotel, a right-hand reef break, is consistent and the favorite surfing spot for experts to shred and beginners to watch, because the beach is largely rock protected and the surf and undertow can be horrendous at anything over 4 feet. Kepuhi is more or less dominated by the Kaluakoi Resort at the east end of the pristine 0.5-mile beach; the best beach breaks are in front of the resort. On the western half of the beach, coral slabs and clumps line the shore with little chance of a ride for any craft. To the west, under the brow of the cliff, a left breaks well at times.

Kawakiu is one of the northernmost accessible beaches on Molokai's west end—a white-sand beach flanked by lava outcroppings and a cliff. Many consider this the island's most beautiful beach, but it isn't easy to find. It's situated near the Kaluakoi Resort.

Papohaku. A bodysurfing and bodyboarding beach break, Papohaku Beach is the widest, longest beach on Molokai—400 feet wide, 2 miles long—and very deserted. The beach faces the open sea and has no reef, so there's high surf most of the time, but it's good for swimming and snorkeling in calm summer months. A hula festival is held here each May.

Kapukahehu Beach on Molokai's west side is also known as Dixie Maru Beach—a name it took from a 1920s Japanese fishing vessel shipwrecked off the rocky shore. It's one of the best crescent beaches, favored by locals, with good body- and shortboard surfing in the protected inlet of the cove when conditions are right. It gets a swell-window from northwest, west, and southwest swells.

Halo O Lono Beach is situated on the southwest side of Molokai— the last public beach before the private Molokai Ranch. Many reefs set at various distances out into the horseshoe-shaped white-sand beach give a wide range of bodyboarding waves, with the occasional longboard peak. Walk north from the harbor. Best in a southwest swell.

The Wharf, on the west side of the Lahaina ferry arrivals, is a magical longboarding right-hand reef break when it's 3 to 4 feet; a wedging peak with thick lips breaks onto the shallow reef for shortboards in the 6- to 8-foot range. It needs a big summer south swell. There's a left on the opposite reef that handles a head-high swell.

Pohakuloa Point has the best year-round shortboard surfing on Molokai, picking up almost any swell. The point needs a slightly bigger swell than the beach break. Pohakuloa Beach is a hot, steep short ride, fair for longboards, good for bodysurfing and bodyboards.

Halawa Bay

This right-hand reef break is a beautiful spot to see pumping ace waves; when it does, it's the best break on the island. The break has fun short peaks just past the shore edge reef and a well-lined-up point wave.

Best Tides: Low to medium.

Best Swell Direction: Northeast.

Best Wave Size: Waist high to overhead.

Bottom: Rock.

Type of Break: Right-hand point.

Skill Level: Expert.

Best Boards: Shortboards.

Best Seasons: Fall and winter.

Crowds: Rarely crowded.

Water Quality: Clean.

Hazards: Sharks and localism.

Fees and Permits: No fee or permits are required.

Schedule: Public access 24/7.

Finding the Break

From the Ho`olehua Airport, exit to the stop sign. Turn right and continue until you reach the stop sign at the main highway, Hawaii Route 450 (Kamemeha Highway). Kaunakakai is the principal town, located just a short distance from the airport. HI 450 takes you all the way down into Halawa Valley. About halfway there, the road becomes quite narrow and winds along the coastline. As it climbs up to a higher altitude, you'll see the tiny island of Mokuho`oniki—a turtle-shaped offshore rock. Halawa Bay is at the end of the road.

Surf Description

This right-hand reef break is a fickle spot to see firing ace waves, but when it pumps, it's the best break on Molokai. Situated on the northeast corner of the island, it's an hour and a half from Lahaina and forty-five minutes from the landing point at Kaunakakai Harbor. When you first see the point, the swell seems to hover as line upon line marches in on a good northeast swell. The waves wrap in around the point, splashing up on the solid dark lava cliff; spray goes 30 feet high.

The paddle-out starts with rock-hopping over 2-foot round stones all the way into the break, where the stream entrance leads in. As you wait in the lee of the small bay for the right wave, the pyramid-shaped swells that have cleared the point just to your right boom in. Then it's time to paddle in and stroke into a ride that you'll remember for a long time. The face is clean and gathers speed that hollows out, spitting like hot steam trains down the line to several cutback sections to the inside. A trail of boulders stretching 20 yards out from the black-pebble beach breaks on small days. On big days you need to take off early, hang a few turns, climb and drop, face the wall, and fire the fins to

Halawa Bay, Molokai. PHOTO ROD SUMPTER

carve—then get out quick before the reef. Ideal for experts on the right conditions, the spot can be changeable.

Set in scenic grandeur, Halawa Beach is a beauty spot with quality waves next to 300-foot-high Cape Halawa, the island's easternmost point. It needs a clean northwest-to-north swell, though; it's best in winter and during periods of little rain. It's worth the wait to see it pump.

In summer paddle around Lamaloa Head to the see the small, rocky beaches of Wailau, Pelekunu, and Haupu.

Molokai Resources

See the Introduction for information on getting to and around Molokai. There's no bus service on the island.

Hawaii Activities Offices
Aloha Tower, 5th Floor
1 Aloha Tower Drive
Honolulu, Oahu 96813
(877) 877–1222 or (808) 524–0008
Fax: (808) 599–3778
www.hawaiiactivities.com

Local Events/Attractions

- On the third Saturday in May, the Molokai Visitor's Association presents **Molokai Ka Hula Piko: A Celebration of the Birth of Hula on Molokai.** This is attended both by locals and by visitors from around the world. Besides being a tribute to the hula, it's also a day of Hawaiian music, crafts, storytelling, and food.

- In September the **Na Wahine O Ke Kai women's outrigger canoe championships** travel from Molokai to Oahu.

- In October the **Molokai Hoe men's outrigger canoe championships** are held, also from Molokai to Oahu. This famous race brings teams from many countries and requires a great deal of skill.

Places to Eat

Kanemitsu Bakery and Coffee Shop
79 Ala Malama Street
Kaunakakai (downtown)
(808) 553–5855

Kualapu`u Cookhouse
Wao Street
Kualapu`u (central Molokai)
(808) 567–6185

Molokai Pizza Café
15 Kaunakakai Place
Kaunakakai (downtown)
(808) 553–3288

Neighbourhood Store 'n Counter
Kamehameha Highway
(Hawaii Route 450)
Puko`o (east Molokai)
(808) 558–8498

Surf Shops

Molokai Surf
P.O. Box 673
Kaunakakai, Molokai
(808) 553–5093

Surf Lessons and Rentals

Molokai Outdoor Activities
P.O. Box 1236
Kaunakakai, HI 96748
(877) 553–4477 or (808) 553–4477
www.molokai-outdoors.com
Surfing and windsurfing lessons, as well as surfboards for rent. Tours and other island activities are available.

CHAPTER 4
Lanai

anai surf centers on Mount Lanaihale, with its long, sloping, sparsely vegetated sides dropping into the sea. Colored in the hues of its red rocks, green forests, and black lava, the mountain's apex is clearly seen wherever you surf on Lanai, and visible even from Maui. Bordering much of the coast are lava cliffs on the west and south shores, but the north and east favor the beach-break surfer. Named surf spots are few, although the area from Manele Point to Fishermans Shack has more ridable breaks.

Much of Lanai's western coastline plunges straight into the sea from cliffs 50 feet high. Given the absence of positive surf terrain, points, and reefs, the area is not only inaccessible but also affords the surfer only dramatic splash-ups as the swells crash in and catapult in the air. On the north and east, the coastline lays out flatter. Bays, beaches, and coves form at Keomoku Beach, Lopa Beach, Polihua Beach, and Shipwreck Beach.

Private boat charters get you into the lineup really well on the southeast shore. Another break on the south shore is Fishermans Shack, so named because from the water the only visible sign of life is the ruins of an old fisherman's shack. You can also find some rarely ridden surf spots where there's no track or access from land; you'll need a boat. Indeed, boating in is one of the last true surf adventures—though it does have its problems. Choosing the right time to go is all-important.

Regional Map

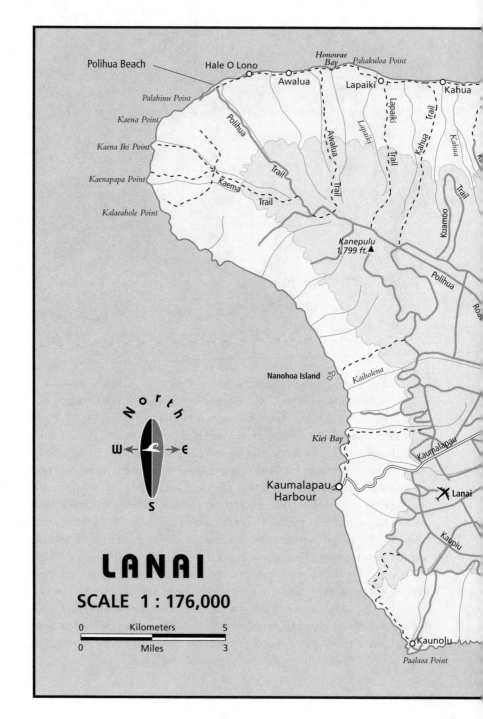

Polihua Beach — Hale O Lono

Honowae Bay

Pahakuloa Point

Awalua

Lapaiki

Kahua

Palahinu Point

Kaena Point

Kaena Iki Point

Kaenapapa Point

Kalaeahole Point

Polihua

Trail

Awalua Trail

Lapaiki

Lapaiki Trail

Kahua Trail

Kahua

Trail

Kuamoo

Kaema

Trail

Kanepulu 1,799 ft. ▲

Polihua

Road

Nanohoa Island

Kaiholena

Kiei Bay

Kaumalapau

Kaumalapau Harbour

✈ Lanai

Kaupiu

North

W ← → E

S

Kaunolu

Paalaoa Point

LANAI

SCALE 1 : 176,000

0 — Kilometers — 5

0 — Miles — 3

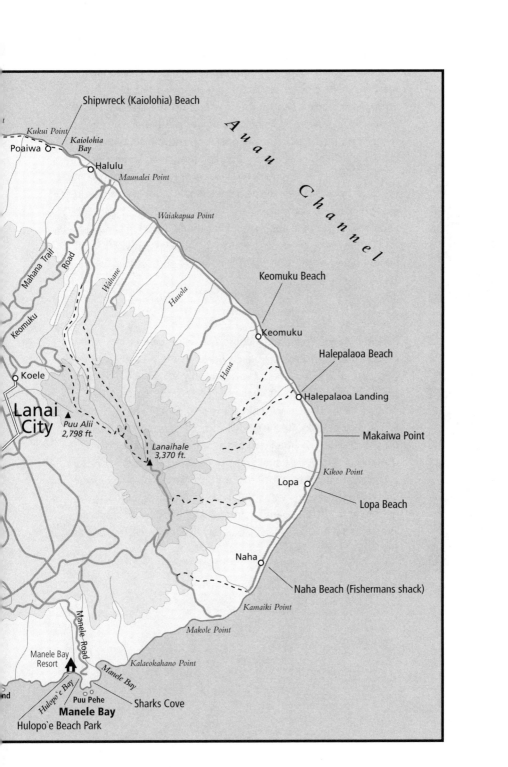

Shipwreck (Kaiolohia) Beach

Kukui Point

Poaiwa

Kaiolohia Bay

Halulu

Maunalei Point

Waiakapua Point

A u a u

C h a n n e l

Keomuku Beach

Keomuku

Halepalaoa Beach

Halepalaoa Landing

Makaiwa Point

Koele

Mahana Trail

Road

Wahane

Hauola

Haua

Keomuku

Lanai City

▲ Puu Alii 2,798 ft.

Lanaihale 3,370 ft.

Kikoo Point

Lopa

Lopa Beach

Naha

Naha Beach (Fishermans shack)

Kamaiki Point

Manele Road

Makole Point

Kalaeokahano Point

Manele Bay Resort

Manele Bay

Hulopo'e Bay

Puu Pehe

Sharks Cove

Manele Bay

Hulopo'e Beach Park

Polihua Beach, north coast. The biggest white-sand beach on Lanai is almost 2 miles long and 200 yards wide. It's mostly a pipeline barrel into the shore dump. Receiving north and north-west swells, it's best with Kona winds in spring, fall, and winter. Strong rips, current, and undertow around the left-hand reef break can all make paddling to keep your position a nightmare; this is a dangerous big-wave spot, receiving the tidal chase in the Kalohi Channel between Molokai and Lanai. Surfing when water conditions are right is for experts only. This is also one of the most famous green sea turtle nesting beaches in Hawaii and a good place to watch whales in season (December through February). It's located approximately 11 miles north of Lanai City and accessible by four-wheel-drive vehicles only. Fork off Polihua Road at the Garden of the Gods and take the Polihua Trail to the beach.

Hulopo`e Beach Park, south coast. This wide crescent of white sand is the most popular beach break in the area, with good bodysurfing and bodyboard waves. It only breaks in a big south swell, though, and is often flat. The left side of the beach is fringed by lava a few yards into the sea; some extended reefs create short peaks for fast rides into the dry coral, requiring quick kickouts. The hotel end of the beach is a sand-bottomed dump-out but does have some peel at times. Lanai's official camping area, with restrooms, outdoor showers, grills, picnic tables, and drinking water, this is a marine life sanctuary and underwater marine park. Dolphins are often seen offshore. Hulopo`e Bay is located approximately 7 miles from Lanai City at the end of Manele Road.

Manele Bay

This left-hand reef break is an amazing spot to see pumping in ace waves. When it's on, it's really on—and it doesn't take long for the word to spread. When it's not, though, you can usually still find fun short peaks just past the reef edge, as well as bodyboarding waves in the middle of the beach.

Best Tides: Low to medium.

Best Swell Direction: South.

Best Wave Size: Chest high to overhead.

Bottom: Rock and sand.

Type of Break: Left-hand point break and beach break.

Skill Level: Intermediate to expert at the point.

Best Boards: Shortboards, longboards, and bodyboards.

Best Seasons: Summer.

Crowds: Semicrowded.

Water Quality: Clean.

Hazards: Sharks, rocks, and undertow.

Fees and Permits: No fee or permits are required.

Schedule: Public access 24/7.

Finding the Break

From the Lanai airport, take Hawaii Route 440 south to New Manele Road. Turn right onto New Manele and follow the signs to Hulopo`e Beach Park.

From the Manele boat harbor, follow the coast west; it's the next bay, just over the brow over of the hill—a ten-minute walk.

Surf Description

This left-hand, coral-bottomed reef point break is a fickle spot with long, well-lined-up walls and good performance wave faces on the inside. It's situated next door to the Manele boat harbor. When you exit the ferry from Lahaina, Maui, walk northwest for 0.5 mile. There's a tiny pocket of white sand in the left corner of the bay and a reef wall fringing the beach. Manele Bay is part of the Manele-Hulopo`e Marine Life Conservation District. The beach offers good white sand and picnicking areas to wait for the best tide.

When you first see the reef point work, it's enough to get the ticker beating fast: The swell seems to hover as line upon line marches in on a good south swell. The waves wrap in around the point, splashing up on the solid dark lava cliff; spray goes 30 feet high. Wait in the lee of the small bay for the right set to pitch. When it's time to lean in, paddle, stand, and take the drop, it nearly closes out when the pyramid-shaped swells suck off the reef. Boils spout up, hitting your board, and swirling steps form on the wave face. It's not easy. On your second wave you'll have a much easier time paddling in and stroking down a ride where the face is clean and the wall gathers speed, hollowing out and spitting like a steam train as it powers down the line to several cutback sections to the inside.

Manele Bay, Lanai. PHOTO ROD SUMPTER

When conditions are 4 to 5 feet, it makes for a really long, neat ride—200 yards with loads of sections. Paddling out through a channel needs a south swell and is best in summer, April through September. If the point is flat or blown out, the beach-break reefs can also be good. Just 20 yards out, a visible barrier of coral across half the beach breaks on underwater reefs in good peaks. You need to take off early, hang a few turns, climb and drop, and get out quick before the reef dries out. Straight off the beach, breaking hard, you'll find a good left- and right-hand wave for bodyboarders and bodysurfers alike. A reef off the left side of the beach gives peaky rights and lefts, but it's the point wave that's special. The point is ideal for experts, and the beach break for intermediate surfers.

Sharks Cove, south coast, is a secluded beach next to Sharks Bay and is separated by low rocks. The rocks are colored a deep, rich red by the iron in the lava formation. The beach is sandy white— a good wave in summer.

Naha Beach (Fishermans Shack), southeast coast, is best accessed by boat when Lahaina has a good south swell. You can't miss this former fishing village and site of one of the four ancient fishponds on Lanai. The narrow beach is overhung with kiawe trees. An area frequented primarily by fishermen, the shack is the only human-made feature in sight. Offshore in north-northwest to west-southwest winds, it just needs a south swell to make it pump. Take Keomuku Road (Hawaii Route 430) from Lanai City. At the end of the pavement, a dirt road branches right along the coast, ending at Naha. You'll need a four-wheel drive to reach Naha Beach.

Lopa Beach, east coast, is a fairly long white-sand beach a couple of miles past Keomuku Village on the east coast trail. It's a summertime south-swell surfing area with a 50- to 100-yard ride offering a variety of peaks and sections. It's the location of one of four ancient fishponds in the area. The swell is blocked by Molokai and Maui, but it gets good lefts and right slide tubes on a south-to-southeast swell. It's accessible from several four-wheel-drive vehicle trails branching off Keomuku Road.

Makaiwa Point, east coast, is a hot bodyboarding spot of short closeouts with a right and left off the side reefs. A perfect small white-sand topical beach surrounded by jagged black lava and fishponds.

Halepalaoa Beach, northeast coast, picks up any swell around. Best in spring, fall, and winter, this beach is often called Kahalepalaoa, which translates into "whale house" or "whale ivory house." Good longboarding in spring, with white sands and reefs a mile long. Accessible by four-wheel-drive vehicles on the Kikoa Point Trail.

Keomuku Beach. From the long line of coconut palms, the beach turns into a reef break with good waves to be had in the middle and over the end reef. There's an eerie beauty about Keomuku, with its crumbling, deserted town. The break in front of Ka Lanakila O Ka Malamalama—the oldest church on the island, built in 1903—has a fast barrel in an east swell. Trade winds blow in and out quickly; it's best in early morning. Keomuku is an archaeological site.

Shipwreck (Kaiolohia) Beach, north coast. The escapement fringing the white-sand beach is 6 feet tall. The best access is in the middle. After an easy walk over dunes and flat rocks, you paddle out through a shallow channel that has deeper gullies farther out. Waves break on half a dozen or more reefs 500 to 600 yards out, with fast green walls and fun re-forms. Several outer reefs break in nicely as a longboarding wave in 2- to 4-foot conditions and for shortboards at 6-feet-plus; best in Kona winds. This remote bay-and-beach shoreline covers 5 miles. Waves fade in the lagoon's inshore waters to the flat-rock shoreline edge. A ship is stuck 0.25 mile out on a reef that looks haunting; there are other submerged wrecks as well. Home to some thought-provoking petroglyphs, including the Bird Man of Lanai. From Lanai City, take Hawaii Route 44 (four-wheel-drive only) northeast to the end of the road—approximately 7 miles. Turn left onto the dirt road and continue for 1.6 miles to the parking area near the lighthouse ruins.

Lanai Resources

See the Introduction for information on getting to and around Lanai. There's no bus service on the island.

Hawaii Activities Offices
Aloha Tower, 5th Floor
1 Aloha Tower Drive
Honolulu, Oahu 96813
(877) 877–1222 or (808) 524–0008
Fax: (808) 599–3778
www.hawaiiactivities.com

Surf Lessons and Rentals

Adventure Lanai Ecocentre
P.O. Box 631394
Lanai City, HI 96763
(808) 565–7373

CHAPTER 5

Oahu

To fly into the Honolulu airport during daylight hours lets you see Diamond Head and Waikiki from above. When a swell is pumping 4 to 6 feet, it's hard to stay buckled in: You'll twist your neck to watch the waves sweep in around an array of reefs where clusters of ant-size surfers are either riding the walls or waiting for sets. This is one of the all-time inspiring moments a surfer has when arriving in the islands. The daunting question, of course, is *Where's the best place to surf?* Well, this guidebook puts you in the driver's seat. Read my recommendations, and follow the weather, swell, and surf conditions on the local radio—after that, finding the best waves should be plain sailing.

Your first consideration is transportation. Unless you're just starting out or visiting Waikiki only, you have to have transport here. Buying a cheap car on the North Shore or from any of the used-car lots is ideal if you're staying for a month or more; the next best is a rental car. Public transport called The Bus runs around the island and costs just $1.00, but it doesn't carry surfboards and will take bodyboards only under 3 feet. For more information on all these options, see "Oahu Resources" at the end of this chapter.

Regional Map

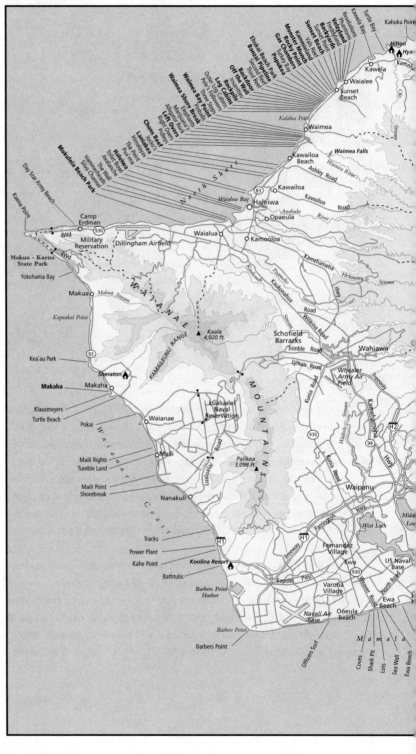

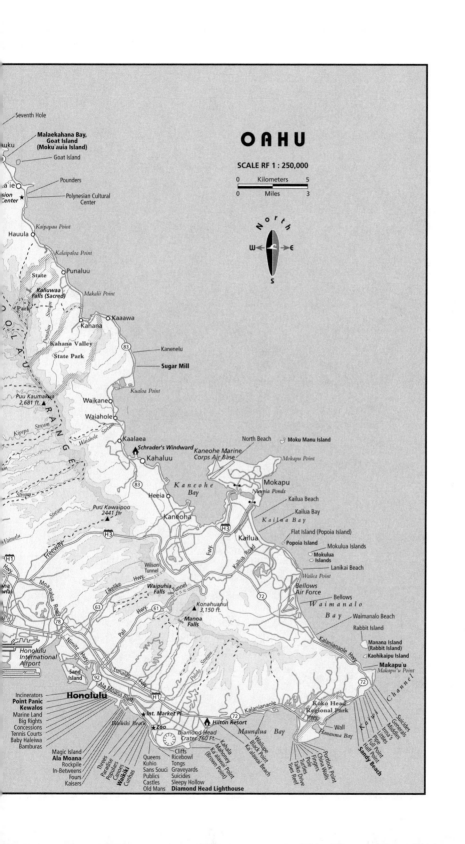

Seventh Hole

**Malaekahana Bay,
Goat Island
(Moku'auia Island)**

Goat Island

auku

Pounders

a'ie
sion
Center

Polynesian Cultural
Center

OAHU

SCALE RF 1 : 250,000

| 0 | Kilometers | 5 |
| 0 | Miles | 3 |

North

W ⟵✦⟶ E

S

Kaipapau Point

Hauula

Kalaipaloa Point

Punaluu

State

**Kaliuwaa
Falls (Sacred)**

Makalii Point

Park

Punaluu Stream

O
O
L
A
U

Kaaawa

Kahana

Kahana Valley

State Park

(83)

Kanenelu

Sugar Mill

Kualoa Point

Puu Kaumakua
2,681 ft.

Waikane

R
A
N
G
E

Waiahole

Kipepa Stream

Waiahole Stream

Kaalaea

Schrader's Windward

North Beach

Moku Manu Island

Kahaluu

Kaneohe Marine
Corps Air Base

Mokapu Point

Stream

Mokapu

Kane ohe

Nuupia Ponds

Heeia

Bay

Kailua Beach

Kailua Bay

Kaneoha

(83)

Puu Kawaipoo
2441 ft

Waimalu

(H3)

Stream

(H3)

Kailua Bay

Flat Island (Popoia Island)

Kailua

Popoia Island

Mokulua Islands

(H1)

Freeway

**Mokulua
Islands**

Hwy

Wilson
Tunnel

Kailua Road

Lanikai Beach

Wailea Point

na
arfa

Moanalua Road

Likelike Hwy

**Waipuhia
Falls**

Tunnel

Fwy

**Bellows
Air Force**

Bellows

(78)

(63)

Pali Hwy

(61)

Konahuanui
3,150 ft.

(72)

Waimanalo

Honolulu
International
Airport

**Manoa
Falls**

Bay

Waimanalo Beach

Rabbit Island

Paloto Stream

Kalanianaole Hwy

**Manana Island
(Rabbit Island)**

Sand
Island

Nimitz Hwy

Lunalilo Fwy

(92)

Ala Moana Blvd

Kaohikaipu Island

Makapu'u
Makapu'u Point

Incinerators
**Point Panic
Kewalos**

(H1)

(72)

Marine Land
Big Rights
Concessions
Tennis Courts
Baby Haleiwa
Bamburas

Honolulu

★**Int. Market Pl.**

(72)

Kalanianaole

**Koko Head
Regional Park**
Hwy

Suicides
Generals
Middles
Irma's

Waikiki Beach

★**Zoo**

Hilton Resort

Maundlua Bay

Wall

Koko

Magic Island
Ala Moana
Rockpile
In-Betweens
Fours
Kaisers

Diamond Head
Crater 760 Ft.

Cliffs
Queens Ricebowl
Kuhio Tongs
Sans Souci Graveyards
Publics Suicides
Castles Sleepy Hollow
Old Mans **Diamond Head Lighthouse**

Hanauma Bay

Kahala
Mahoney
Kawaihoa Point
(Brown Point)

Wailupe
Black Point
Ka'alawa Point

Portlock Point
China Walls
Fingers
Turtles
Taiko Drive
Toes Reef

Pipe Little
Full Point
Pipe
Big Pipe

Sandy Beach

Threes
Paradise
Populars
Canoes
Waikiki
Cunhas

Channel

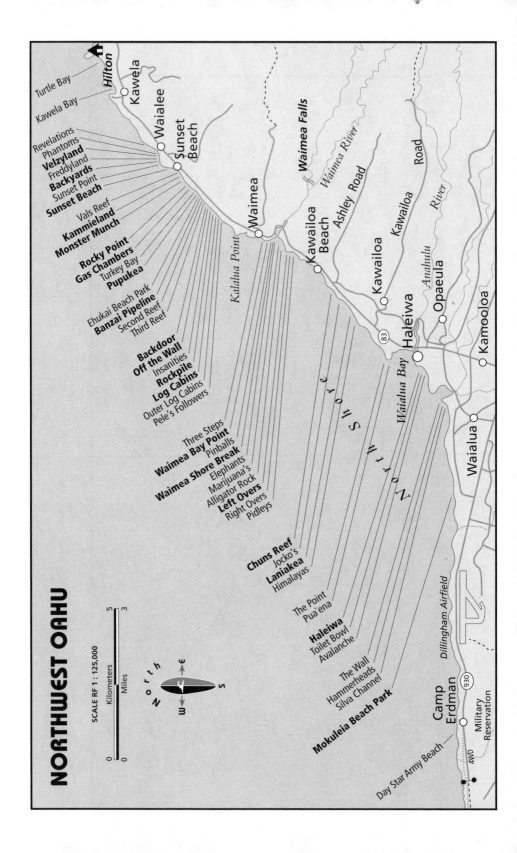

NORTHWEST OAHU

SCALE RF 1 : 125,000

Kilometers
Miles

Turtle Bay
Kawela Bay

Hilton
Kawela

Waialee
Sunset
Beach

Revelations
Phantoms
Velzyland
Freddyland
Backyards
Sunset Point
Sunset Beach

Waimea Falls

Waimea River

Ashley Road

Kawailoa Road

Anahulu River

Vals Reef
Kammieland
Monster Munch

Rocky Point
Gas Chambers
Turkey Bay
Pupukea

Waimea

Kawailoa Beach

Kawailoa

Opaeula

Kamooloa

Ehukai Beach Park
Banzai Pipeline
Second Reef
Third Reef

Kalalua Point

Haleiwa

83

Backdoor
Off the Wall
Insanities
Rockpile
Log Cabins
Outer Log Cabins
Pele's Followers

Waialua Bay

North Shore

Three Steps
Waimea Bay Point
Pinballs
Waimea Shore Break
Elephants
Marijuana's
Alligator Rock
Left Overs
Right Overs
Pidleys

Chuns Reef
Jocko's
Laniakea
Himalayas

The Point
Pua'ena

Haleiwa
Toilet Bowl
Avalanche

Waialua

Dillingham Airfield

The Wall
Hammerheads
Silva Channel

Mokuleia Beach Park

Camp
Erdman

930

Military
Reservation

4WD

Day Star Army Beach

North

N
W E
S

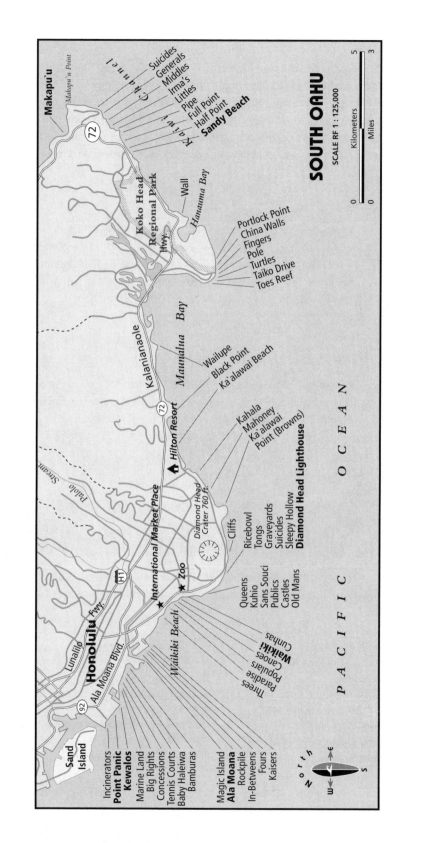

SOUTH OAHU

SCALE RF 1 : 125,000

Makapu'u

Makapu'u Point

Kaiwi Channel

Suicides
Generals
Middles
Irma's
Littles
Pipe
Full Point
Half Point
Sandy Beach

72

**Koko Head
Regional Park**

Hwy.

Wall

Hanauma Bay

Portlock Point
China Walls
Fingers
Pole
Turtles
Taiko Drive
Toes Reef

Kalanianaole

Maunalua Bay

Wailupe
Black Point
Ka'alawai Beach

72

⚓ Hilton Resort

Kahala
Mahoney
Ka'alawai
Point (Browns)
Diamond Head Lighthouse

Diamond Head
Crater 760 ft.

Cliffs

Ricebowl
Tongs
Graveyards
Suicides
Sleepy Hollow

★ Zoo

International Market Place

Queens
Kuhio
Sans Souci
Publics
Castles
Old Mans

Waikiki Beach

Waikiki
Canoes
Cunhas
Populars
Paradise
Threes

H1

Palolo Stream

Honolulu

Lunalilo Fwy.

Ala Moana Blvd.

92

Sand
Island

Incinerators
Point Panic
Kewalos
Marine Land
Big Rights
Concessions
Tennis Courts
Baby Haleiwa
Bamburas

Magic Island
Ala Moana
Rockpile
In-Betweens
Fours
Kaisers

PACIFIC   OCEAN

North

N
W   E
S

Kilometers
0   5

Miles
0   3

You'll find more surf breaks on Oahu than any of the other islands, but less between-category surfing. Conditions range from the extreme power of the North Shore at Banzai Pipeline and Sunset Beach to near flatness at Waikiki. In fall and winter (November to March), look for east, northeast, north, and northwest swells. In spring (March and April), swells are northwest, west, and southwest; in summer, southeast, south, and southwest swells overlap in-between swells. There's surfing on all four coasts of Oahu.

Revelations, a cloud break outside Velzyland, is a tow-in big-wave spot. It's surfed rarely—if ever—without a Jet Ski team and a *Let's go!* spirit. To make it out and back alive, you definitely need the right attitude. If you're prepared to surf big gnarly waves, though, you can have the ride of a lifetime here.

Phantoms, a left-hand, big-wave, tow-in spot on the outer reefs, is often the launching spot for tow-in surfing at Outer Log Cabins. Phantoms is next to Revelations and holds waves of up to 40 feet—a green wall of epic proportions.

Velzyland

This right-hander is a top-quality reef break that's hard to get to, hard to get uncrowded, and hard to surf. It's a top-to-bottom wall from a peak takeoff along the edge of shallow reef ledges.

Best Tides: Low to medium.

Best Swell Direction: Northwest.

Best Wave Size: 6 feet.

Bottom: Reef, rock, coral, and sand.

Type of Break: Right-hand break with a left peak at times.

Skill Level: Expert and experienced.

Best Boards: Shortboards.

Best Seasons: Fall and winter.

Crowds: Crowded.

Water Quality: Clean.

Hazards: Dangerous rip currents, shallow coral bottom, sharks, and localism.

Fees and Permits: No fees or permits are required.

Schedule: Public access 24/7.

Velzyland, Oahu. PHOTO ROD SUMPTER

Finding the Break

Before leaving the Honolulu International Airport, look for a road sign that reads INTER-STATE H1, HONOLULU, WAIKIKI, WAIANAE. Turn onto the exit ramp and stay left, exiting onto H1 West Waianae. Travel on H1 for 7 miles, then get into the right two lanes and look for EXIT 8A, H2 NORTH MILILANI, WAHIAWA. Take H2 for 7.6 more miles, then get off at EXIT 8 WAHIAWA. Drive straight through the town of Wahiawa. As you exit the town, you'll go down a small hill and under a bridge. Stay on this road (Interstate 99) for 8 miles until you see the brown HISTORIC HALEIWA TOWN sign. From Haleiwa Bridge, follow Kamehameha Highway (commonly called Kam Highway) east for 7.6 miles. Park where you can near the 100-yard Lava Wall and follow other surfers to the waves. *Note:* Redevelopment in this area may lead to access changes by the time you read this book.

Surf Description

Fear of flying? Heart rate up? Quickening breath and trembling hands? Chances are you're about to surf one of the most wedge-shaped breaking waves in the world, and if you mess it up you'll land on the reef, racked out like a landed fish to dry in the hot sun.

Along the North Shore from Haleiwa, there exists what is known as the "7-mile surf miracle zone," containing most of the best surf spots and waves in the world. This miracle zone ends at Velzyland.

Situated 1.5 miles east of Sunset Beach and 1 mile west of Kahuku, Velzyland is otherwise known as V-Land, its name derived from a surfer named Daly Velzy who first

Hawaii is at the root of surfing history; the sport may have been practiced for centuries before Captain James Cook first recorded it in 1778. The North Shore of Oahu is the championship surf capital of the Hawaiian Islands and is at the heart of modern-day surfing.

surfed here in the 1950s. This is one of the world's best right-hand small-wave spots, which works in surf heights of 2 to 8 feet. When it gets any bigger, the surf on the outside reef churns into a boil of white water and closes out with no shape. It's then that windsurfers, who descend like buzzards on a fresh kill, flock here and are able to put in a fantastic display, carving up strong trade winds as the swells blow out. Velzyland is also a sought-after spot for shortboards in 4- to 8-foot surf and for expert bodyboarders in even smaller waves, giving them perfect rides.

Besides the two main takeoff areas, there's a third area on the left side of the main takeoff peak. This works on a northwest swell and is a left-hand wave running into a tube section. Over the shallow reef it can be as little as a foot deep, with no channels or gullies through which to paddle back out. It is hardcore. So the left is only chosen over a right on rare occasions, and usually only by goofy-foot surfers. The right is a challenging wave to ride from the peak, having a sucky takeoff that's insanely steep. From the shoulder there's little time to drop in beside the pitching lip. Once you've dropped in, you must then trim hard across a tubing wall to a hollow outside wall and over the shallow coral reef. A flattish section that resembles a longboarder's hot-dog wave and leads to an ultratubey inside section finishes things off.

On average the length of ride here is 100 to 150 yards. The walk and paddle-out is over sharp coral at first; then a small alleyway cuts out of the coral reef and is filled with sand. This is straight out from the takeoff area and aids entry to a channel and out to the takeoff. Velzyland is the North Shore's easternmost surf break and is likely to be crowded with top-class surfers. This is a superb surf break for the expert.

Freddyland, at the west end of Velzyland, is a longboarder's slow left peak and short right-hand reef break—great fun, although it rarely produces consistent waves. It's a long walk from Velzyland's few parking spots. Expect some localism in and out of the water. It was named for the famous Californian surfer Fred Van Dyke, who pioneered much of the North Shore in the late 1950s and early '60s.

Backyards

Sand quickly turns to rock ledges and reef behind Sunset Beach to the east where huge swell produces extremely fast rights from 6 to more than 15 feet. These express-train barrels are for advanced surfers only.

Best Tides: Low to medium.

Best Swell Direction: Northwest.

Best Wave Size: Overhead to double over-head.

Bottom: Coral.

Type of Break: Right-hand reef break.

Skill Level: Expert to big-wave rider.

Best Boards: Shortboards and guns.

Best Seasons: Fall and winter.

Crowds: Rarely very crowded.

Water Quality: Clean.

Hazards: Shifting peaks and closeout sets. Difficult access over shallow coral. Watch out for rips as you paddle around and out through the channel.

Fees and Permits: No fees or permits are required.

Schedule: Public access 24/7.

Finding the Break

Before leaving the Honolulu International Airport, look for a road sign that reads INTER-STATE H1, HONOLULU, WAIKIKI, WAIANAE. Turn onto the exit ramp and stay left, exiting onto H1 West Waianae. Travel on H1 for 7 miles, then get into the right two lanes and look for EXIT 8A, H2 NORTH MILILANI, WAHIAWA. Take H2 for 7.6 more miles, then get off at EXIT 8 WAHIAWA. Drive straight through the town of Wahiawa. As you exit the town, you'll go down a small hill and under a bridge. Stay on this road (Interstate 99) for 8 miles until you see the brown HISTORIC HALEIWA TOWN sign. From Haleiwa Bridge follow Kamehameha Highway (commonly called Kam Highway) east for 7.6 miles, passing Waimea Bay and then reaching a long straight stretch of road. Keep going past a Chevron gas station (on the right), Kammies Market, and then Sunset Beach. At 0.2 mile from Sunset Beach—50 yards past Sunset Stores—park on Kam Highway. Walk north down to the alleyway that leads onto the beach. Backyards is 200 yards straight out and slightly right.

Surf Description

You can't beat a fast takeoff, and that's just what you get at Backyards. It leaves you with either a toasted grin or a hammered smile—that's *if* you make the barreling drop into the pit and pull up fast enough to tuck under the wall and zero-navigate the eye of the wave by feel. This is a great wave that packs a punch sending a lot of surfers packing.

Situated between the two great breaks of Sunset Beach and Velzyland, Backyards' only fault lies in the fact that nearly every swell on any given day breaks in a different spot. It's for surfers who know how to read sets and where to be to capitalize on the best waves; as well as being tricky, it's powerful, dangerous, and hard. When the big sneaker sets pour in, it's time for an all-out duck dive or jump and bail dive to the end of your

Backyards, Oahu. PHOTO ROD SUMPTER

leash until it passes. These waves explode, and escape is only viable if you go deep.

Backyards is also a spot for the agile surfer with the quickness of a sea snake and the strike power of a serpent to drop in and go down the line fast. There's rarely a repeat swell waiting for you when you paddle back out, so a quick turnaround and fast pushoff from the tail can see you into some vertical heaven—like flying without wings, at least until the rails and fins catch. People watching are always amazed because Sunset and Backyards look so similar from the eastern end of Sunset Point—as if they're connecting. At sunset, when the ocean turns to gold and the wave spray hangs in the air and everything seems connected, this is Backyards' best time.

Sunset Point is a classic reef point at low tide with a long, sloping peak takeoff running into a down-the-line speed wall. Epic longboarding when it's 4 to 6 feet; faster guns are needed for anything overhead. Long, fast rides are possible. Big sneaker sets call for an all-out duck dive—or you can jump and bail-dive to the end of your leash until it passes. This is a right-hand break that breaks consistently weird; it's hard to line up but easy to take what comes.

Sunset Beach

Sunset Beach may well be the most famous beach in the world. With its epic West Peak and a bowling right tube area, it breaks 15 to 30 feet or more in a northwest swell. It's hollow and very hard to make. A lot of updraft pulls you up the face, and at the top a huge lip is ready to throw you over the falls. West Peak may break if the swell switches to a northwest—if so, watch out!

Best Tides: Sunset Beach can be best at *any* tide.

Best Swell Direction: Northwest.

Best Wave Size: Head high to triple over-head and bigger.

Bottom: Reef, coral, and sand.

Type of Break: Left and mostly right.

Skill Level: Expert to advanced on all but the smallest of days.

Best Boards: Shortboards, longboards, and rhino guns.

Best Seasons: Fall and winter.

Crowds: Crowded.

Water Quality: Clean.

Hazards: When the point and outer reef-break waves start to break, the main reef rights can range from a hot-dog wave to one that spells dynamite. You'll also find a crushing bowl section, steep vertical peak, big waves, dangerous rip currents, and localism.

Fees and Permits: No fees or permits are required. There's free parking on the ocean side of Kam Highway, but no park-ing on the south side—and towing is enforced.

Schedule: Public access 24/7.

Finding the Break

Before leaving the Honolulu International Airport, look for a road sign that reads INTER-STATE H1, HONOLULU, WAIKIKI, WAIANAE. Turn onto the exit ramp and stay left, exiting onto H1 West Waianae. Travel on H1 for 7 miles, then get into the right two lanes and look for EXIT 8A, H2 NORTH MILILANI, WAHIAWA. Take H2 for 7.6 more miles, then get off at EXIT 8 WAHIAWA. Drive straight through the town of Wahiawa. As you exit the town, you'll go down a small hill and under a bridge. Stay on this road (Interstate 99) for 8 miles until you see the brown HISTORIC HALEIWA TOWN sign. From Haleiwa Bridge follow Kamehameha Highway (commonly called Kam Highway) east for 7.2 miles; you can't miss the lifeguard tower and Sunset Beach. The Bus No. 52, Circles Island, will bring you here as well.

Surf Description

Paddling out hard and looking up under the shadow of the West Peak, you'll spot a gap 20 feet wide beside the loop of the curl—just enough for you to escape and paddle to safety. Now the outer reef bears down on you, and the whole breathtaking view of ocean swells overwhelms. You could die. Like soldiers advancing on your position, you hear the waves stir your blood—time to go. You push yourself over the edge and down the face, paddling hard. It's steep to vertical before your heart, brain, and body get it together and your first turn is made.

Sunset Beach, Oahu. PHOTO ROD SUMPTER

This is Sunset Beach, on the famous strip of coastline known as Oahu's North Shore. Situated 30 miles north of Waikiki, 2 miles east of Banzai Pipeline, and a forty-minute drive from the Honolulu International Airport on Kamehameha Highway, this world-class surf spot is a long right—with the occasional left at takeoff when the wave peels off to a bowl section, hollow and very hard to make.

The Pacific Ocean's deep-water swells arrive at Sunset and break from 4 to 30 feet in winter. On big days Sunset Beach is famous for its incredibly steep peaks that seem, at first, to simply fade out, luring you into a false sense of security, only to re-form and jack up on the inside bowl. Surfers from all over the world flock to Sunset Beach to test their skills on these giant waves. Best of all, when you're done getting pounded, you can stop and enjoy the aloha spirit of beautiful sunsets, barbecues, volleyball, and beach parties.

For most surfers, the magic of Hawaii is taking off on a ride of a lifetime. This is what can happen at Sunset Beach, making it one of the most exciting places on earth to surf. Sunset is also a place of extreme variety where, on small days, you can surf on fun long-board waves, riding the nose till the sun goes down. On bigger days you can surf the main peak and get tubed in the bowl. On really huge days you can fly down the drop on takeoff and feel the roar of the wind enveloping you as you bottom-turn into a crystal wall of water. But be careful or you'll get caught in the rip and get pounded by the shorebreak while attempting to leave the water. The sheer power of the ocean is very evident here.

Danger from the Sea

As if Oahu's waves weren't enough, watch out for the Portuguese man-of-war (also known as the stinging blue jellyfish or Physalia) from June to September. And on the leeward side of the island, the box jellyfish shows up ten days after a full moon. Warning signs are posted by lifeguards.

Every year the winter season (November to April) transforms average waves at Sunset Beach into the best and biggest in the world. This famous spot is located on a curved horseshoe-shaped beach covered with pearly white sand and fringed by palm trees, lush vegetation, and tropical wooden houses—the quintessential tropical paradise. And those lucky enough to surf Sunset will leave with the same adrenaline rush they experienced after riding, upright, on their very first wave.

Towering peaks, strong offshore wind, and grinding, barreling walls make Sunset Beach the all-time great surf break, a shining star on the global surf map.

Local Events/Attractions

World-class surfing competitions are held throughout the year at Sunset Beach. Note especially the **Vans Triple Crown of Surfing Series,** the **Men's World Cup of Surfing,** and the **Women's Quiksilver Roxy Pro.** For more information, call (808) 325–7400 or (808) 638-7266.

Places to Eat

Sunset Stores and **Kammies Market** restaurant are 0.25 mile on either side of Sunset Beach on Kam Highway in Haleiwa.

Vals Reef. A patch of lava rock emerges from the sand in the middle of the beach. Not far out is Val's Reef, a short peaky wave to the shore dump named for Val Valentine. Outside Vals, a coral cloud-shaped reef gives a better, bigger peak on 6- to 8-foot days.

Kammieland

This powerful long left peak that winds across a shallow reef has a way of asking you to write your name in the wave face. There's so much turning area on the lefts that you don't feel like you're going anywhere—only straight in to the shore. The ride is about 150 yards, and in that time you can do twenty turns. If you're lucky enough to find the peak for the right-hander, you're in for a treat, because this fast-takeoff, steep, wedgy, deep-water ocean-going wave is a screaming hard-and-fast ride. You may also get the outer peak on sets with a deep-water right that hurls down the line—a masterpiece that's hard to beat. Still, it's the consistent lefts that Kammie is famous for.

Best Tides: Low to medium.

Best Swell Direction: Northwest.

Best Wave Size: Chest high to triple over-head.

Bottom: Coral and sand.

Type of Break: Left and right.

Skill Level: Intermediate to advanced; almost always an easy paddle-out.

Best Boards: Shortboards, longboards, and guns.

Best Seasons: Fall and winter.

Crowds: Crowded.

Water Quality: Clean.

Hazards: Localism.

Fees and Permits: No fees or permits are required.

Schedule: Public access 24/7.

Finding the Break

Before leaving the Honolulu International Airport, look for a road sign that reads INTER-STATE H1, HONOLULU, WAIKIKI, WAIANAE. Turn onto the exit ramp and stay left, exiting onto H1 West Waianae. Travel on H1 for 7 miles, then get into the right two lanes and look for EXIT 8A, H2 NORTH MILILANI, WAHIAWA. Take H2 for 7.6 more miles, then get off at EXIT 8 WAHIAWA. Drive straight through the town of Wahiawa. As you exit the town, you'll go down a small hill and under a bridge. Stay on this road (Interstate 99) for 8 miles until you see the brown HISTORIC HALEIWA TOWN sign. From Haleiwa Bridge follow Kamehameha Highway (commonly called Kam Highway) east for 7.1 miles; you'll pass Waimea Bay, then reach a long straight stretch of road. Keep going past a Chevron gas station (on the right) and Kammies Market, then take the next left. If you go too far, you'll reach Sunset Beach; turn around and take the first right. There's roadside parking on the edge of the beach from the bridge all the way up to the Sunset Stores. The break is straight out to sea on your left.

Surf Description

Situated between the great breaks of Sunset Beach and Monster Munch, Kammieland's distant peak breaks distinctively in a sea of blue, then it folds into a magic left that stops

Kammieland, Oahu. PHOTO ROD SUMPTER

your breath. It's a fickle wave needing just the right conditions to be perfect. Still, it offers many a day of fun and mellow, funky waves caught by the trade winds. Ideal for intermediate to expert surfers.

Monster Munch

This predominantly right-hand A-frame reef break on the North Shore is one of the great wide white-sand beaches. You wait beneath palm trees, choosing the right time of tide and swell direction to enter—either straight over a 2-foot reef or via the right-hand channel along the beach and out through some rocks.

Best Tides: Medium.

Best Swell Direction: North.

Best Wave Size: Head high to double overhead.

Bottom: Reef and sand.

Type of Break: Left and right.

Skill Level: Intermediate to advanced, due to a tricky paddle-out. The bigger the waves, the more skill you'll need.

Best Boards: Shortboards.

Best Seasons: Fall and winter.

Crowds: Fewer crowds than most spots.

Water Quality: Clean.

Hazards: Intermediate surfers will be intimidated by the expert and advanced surfers taking all the waves, and by the reef on the paddle-out.

Fees and Permits: No fees or permits are required.

Schedule: Public access 24/7.

Monster Munch, Oahu. PHOTO ROD SUMPTER

Finding the Break

Before leaving the Honolulu International Airport, look for a road sign that reads INTER-STATE H1, HONOLULU, WAIKIKI, WAIANAE. Turn onto the exit ramp and stay left, exiting onto H1 West Waianae. Travel on H1 for 7 miles, then get into the right two lanes and look for EXIT 8A, H2 NORTH MILILANI, WAHIAWA. Take H2 for 7.6 more miles, then get off at EXIT 8 WAHIAWA. Drive straight through the town of Wahiawa. As you exit the town, you'll go down a small hill and under a bridge. Stay on this road (Interstate 99) for 8 miles until you see the brown HISTORIC HALEIWA TOWN sign. From Haleiwa Bridge follow Kamehameha Highway (commonly called Kam Highway) east to the start of Sunset Beach, turning left before the bridge. (If you miss the turn and reach the Sunset Beach lifeguard tower, go back and over the bridge, turning right.) Monster Munch is 6.9 miles from Haleiwa Bridge. No parking is available near the break, so it's best to park on Kam Highway. The break is straight out.

Surf Description

You can't help but feel the downward pull of the reef as it draws the waves over your shoulder. The racing inner wall concaves deeper as the wave progresses down the line, its speed doubled in a matter of only 10 or 20 yards. This tightly packed A-frame peak starts off as a steep drop with lots of body, but turns into a completely different, hard-hitting Mach 2 barrel. The skirt and curtain are vertical and round enough to fit into, but it's set on a steep wall over shallowing coral, making you pull in tight and hold your fins in. It's a great ride that finally ends on broken lava.

Situated just 0.25 mile west of Kammieland and 0.5 mile west of Sunset Beach, Monster Munch is best with medium waves but can be good through all stages. Its main feature is the right-hand barrel with a very fast takeoff, moving out and in depending on the size. Scratching over set waves, paddling farther out to the right point, and barely making the breaking wave's face as the lip throws out toward shore is the norm at Monster Munch. It's a hard break to get down pat, creating tricky waves ideal for the expert shortboarder. There are also days when it's small and the longboard can be your best bet, moving into position easily and picking off the set waves; these days are rare, however, and don't last long in fall or winter months. The best swell here is north, but the spot will break in a fickle manner northwest and northeast. The only prediction you can make about Monster Munch is that your first fifteen seconds will feel like being munched by a monster.

The left is less consistent but may be your only option if the right closes out, peaks, or breaks too soon. You feel like you're surfing against the grain, because the swell direction favors the rights and the drift of the current heads west. The left picks up the trade winds to make it a little windy, chopping up the face. But on the right day, this can be a long performance wave, giving a lot of cutbacks and roundhouse cutbacks and maybe some longboarding at 3 to 5 feet.

Rocky Point

Rocky Point has a reputation for quality lefts and rights when the other major surf spots are missing out on the swell, or just not lined up well. Situated 0.75 mile east of Banzai Pipeline and 0.5 mile west of Sunset Beach, this rock-ledge point produces ace surf when it's 4 to 8 feet or a bit bigger.

Best Tides: **Low to medium.**

Best Swell Direction: **Northwest.**

Best Wave Size: **Chest high to triple over-head.**

Bottom: **Sand.**

Type of Break: **Left and right.**

Skill Level: **Intermediate to advanced due to a tricky paddle-out.**

Best Boards: **Shortboards and guns.**

Best Seasons: **Fall and winter.**

Crowds: **Crowded.**

Water Quality: **Average to clean.**

Hazards: **Sharks and localism.**

Fees and Permits: **No fees or permits are required.**

Schedule: **Public access 24/7.**

Finding the Break

Before leaving the Honolulu International Airport, look for a road sign that reads INTER-STATE H1, HONOLULU, WAIKIKI, WAIANAE. Turn onto the exit ramp and stay left, exiting onto H1 West Waianae. Travel on H1 for 7 miles, then get into the right two lanes and look for EXIT

Rocky Point, Oahu. PHOTO ROD SUMPTER

8A, H2 NORTH MILILANI, WAHIAWA. Take H2 for 7.6 more miles, then get off at EXIT 8 WAHIAWA. Drive straight through the town of Wahiawa. As you exit the town, you'll go down a small hill and under a bridge. Stay on this road (Interstate 99) for 8 miles until you see the brown HISTORIC HALEIWA TOWN sign. From Haleiwa Bridge follow Kamehameha Highway (commonly called Kam Highway) east to a twenty-totem-high totem pole before a Chevron gas station. Turn left and park where you can on or near Kei Nui Road. Walk to the ocean and look to your right for Rocky Point—which isn't easy to find.

Surf Description

No one walks the fine line between closeout and freight-train barrels more than Rocky Point surfers. They know that the deceptively strong lefts and rights here are like falling over a mountain pass. Jackknifing turns and hitting the anchors to go all-out is the only way out.

Rocky Point's beach is peppered by rock pools and half-submerged boulders, with palm trees fringing the point and coastline; it's a popular spot. It takes its moniker from the location and, indeed, it's aptly named; most other North Shore locations are sand. A well-lined-up performance wave, it hits hard at times, though not as hard as some heavy-weight surf spots such as Banzai Pipeline. Access to the lefts is across the beach and point, through a sandy cove to a channel in the coral that makes for an easy entry; it's a fair paddle-out to that long peeling left. Along the way you'll enjoy good view of the tube twisting past the shore. The left is far longer than the right, and is the preferred direction if both are breaking well on the same day. The right is a harder paddle-out through sets that often break wide, and there's no channel—just gaps in the reef. It's a fast walling wave with hollow sections that are makable. The shorebreak, which closes out or peels off to the coral slab shore, is often the hairiest part of the wave. This shorebreak section may continue toward Pupukea Beach if the swell has a lot of northeast direction to it. This is a must-surf spot for intermediate and above surfers on the right day.

When the North Shore's other major breaks are not at their best, Rocky seems to light up its fire. It's renowned for high-performance surfing waves in 4- to 8-foot swells—some of the best waves in the world. If the swell gets very big quickly, it will blow out Rocky Point, usually at over 12 feet. Still, this remains one of the best waves on the North Shore, a powerful, well-shaped wave that the professionals and top surfers rave about. When the trade winds are blowing a hooley and the swell is out of the northeast, you can be sure they'll be here.

Gas Chambers

The peak peels and shifts on different swell sizes and direction. This excellent right- and left-hand wave is a medium- to big-wave spot that lets you know who's in charge. Known for its heavy and aggressive takeoff, it gives nothing away easily.

Best Tides: Low to medium.

Best Swell Direction: Northwest.

Best Wave Size: Chest high to triple overhead.

Bottom: Sand.

Type of Break: Left and right.

Skill Level: Intermediate to advanced due to a tricky paddle-out.

Best Boards: Shortboards and guns.

Best Seasons: Fall and winter.

Crowds: Crowded.

Water Quality: Average to clean.

Hazards: Sharks and localism.

Fees and Permits: No fees or permits are required.

Schedule: Public access 24/7.

Finding the Break

Before leaving the Honolulu International Airport, look for a road sign that reads INTER-STATE H1, HONOLULU, WAIKIKI, WAIANAE. Turn onto the exit ramp and stay left, exiting onto H1 West Waianae. Travel on H1 for 7 miles, then get into the right two lanes and look for EXIT 8A, H2 NORTH MILILANI, WAHIAWA. Take H2 for 7.6 more miles, then get off at EXIT 8 WAHIAWA. Drive straight through the town of Wahiawa. As you exit the town, you'll go down a small hill and under a bridge. Stay on this road (Interstate 99) for 8 miles until you see the brown HISTORIC HALEIWA TOWN sign. From Haleiwa Bridge follow Kamehameha Highway (commonly called Kam Highway) east to a twenty-totem-high totem pole on the right side of the road before a Chevron gas station. Turn left and park where you can on or

Gas Chambers, Oahu. PHOTO ROD SUMPTER

near Kei Nui Road. Walk to the ocean and look right for Rocky Point; Gas Chambers is about 200 yards closer, between Pupukea and Rocky Point.

Surf Description

On big days this is the mother of all waves, big, hollow, and fast; on smaller days it's sweet perfection, a clean hot-dogging fun wave. One of the greatest facts about Gas Chambers is that the drop is straight off until you clear the trough. It's do-or-die at the impact zone, and you'll need respect, luck, and skill not to get smashed.

If you're on the North Shore, the swell is up, and the conditions have the potential, it's worth checking out Gas Chambers. Working in most swell directions, it offers a good chance of some ace waves. It's the ultimate peak takeoff and drop-down-the-face type of wave, very quick. The tube can be one of the widest in the world, pitching out a massive curl on closeouts; the takeoff has a mean lip and explosive power. When the Pacific Ocean delivers a swell and the lineup is on the increase to high seas, Gas Chambers forms a breathtaking wave on a shallow lava reef just beyond the sandbars. And the swell—which has traveled 500 miles or more—completes its underwater rotation and pitches out a curl. This is a great spot for beating the crowds, having a fun day riding demanding waves, and improving your surfing beyond its current limits. It's good from 3 to 4 feet with a first-class performance, but at 10 feet it's a challenge to make it from takeoff to kickout. This is a break for the expert surfer on all but the smallest of swells.

Peter Drouyn, a former Australian champion, was so stunned on his first trip to Gas Chambers that he likened it to a steam roller exploding. That's how crushing the curl is.

Turkey Bay. This right-hander off Gas Chambers is a beach break with superfast short sections or heavy closeouts—a palm-tree-lined beauty spot with white sand and a steep sloping low-tide shorebreak. The spot rarely produces consistent waves, but in a northeast-to-north wraparound swell, it can be better than Gas Chambers or Pupukea—it just needs the right conditions.

Pupukea

Pupukea is one of the great fun beach breaks of the North Shore, with challenging waves for the expert if it's over 6 feet and fun small performance waves at 3 feet. Walling waves are short and fast to the beach, holding up to 10 feet. Low-tide sandbars produce classic barreling waves and high-tide closeouts.

Best Tides: Low to medium.

Best Swell Direction: Northwest.

Best Wave Size: Chest high to triple overhead.

Bottom: Sand and coral.

Type of Break: Left- and right-hand reef and beach break.

Skill Level: Intermediate to expert.

Best Boards: Shortboards and bodyboards.

Best Seasons: Fall and winter.

Crowds: Crowded.

Water Quality: Clean.

Hazards: Riptides and shorebreak.

Fees and Permits: No fees or permits are required.

Schedule: Public access 24/7.

Finding the Break

Before leaving the Honolulu International Airport, look for a road sign that reads INTERSTATE H1, HONOLULU, WAIKIKI, WAIANAE. Turn onto the exit ramp and stay left, exiting onto H1 West Waianae. Travel on H1 for 7 miles, then get into the right two lanes and look for EXIT 8A, H2 NORTH MILILANI, WAHIAWA. Take H2 for 7.6 more miles, then get off at EXIT 8 WAHIAWA. Drive straight through the town of Wahiawa. As you exit the town, you'll go down a small hill and under a bridge. Stay on this road (Interstate 99) for 8 miles until you see the brown HISTORIC HALEIWA TOWN sign. From Haleiwa Bridge follow Kamehameha Highway (commonly called Kam Highway) east to the twenty-totem-high totem pole on the right side of the road, before a Chevron gas station. Turn left and park where you can on or near Kei Nui Road. Walk to the ocean and look right for Rocky Point; Pupukea is about 600 yards closer to you.

Pupukea, Oahu. PHOTO ROD SUMPTER

Surf Description

This is one of the North Shore's most unusual waves, a crescent-shaped shorebreak with a heavy dump if you wipe out or a clean tube if you don't. The takeoff is yet another do-or-die North Shore epic semi-closeout with a bowling barrel. You take off, drive down the face, turn right—and have but split seconds to make the bowl, turn left a little, and thread through a gap. Straighten up and shoot for the sun and down onto the shore dump, or be crushed like another puka shell.

Located 600 yards west of Rocky Point and 0.5 east of Banzai Pipeline, Pupukea has a steeply sloping horseshoe-shaped beach with pearly white sand and palm trees—the quintessential tropical beach break. It's famous for two things: the puka shells that wash up on every high tide (those tiny white shells with the hole in the middle, perfect for making into necklaces), and the world-class quality waves on this superb length of coastline.

One of the great fun beach breaks of the North Shore, Pupukea offers challenging waves for the expert if it's over 6 feet and fun small performance waves at 3 feet. It's best between September and April, but is also superb during the overlapping months in spring and fall. In summer months it's often flat, at which time snorkeling is ideal in its clear warm waters. In the winter season, when the short barrels start to pump, it's a magnet for hot surfers attracted by fast and challenging waves. Here it's mostly a right-hander but with some lefts.

The shifting sand bottom and lava-rock beach break pick up strong currents and undertows quickly, creating dangerous conditions on an increasing swell. An early-morning surf session in light trade winds is probably your best bet—the waves can have an eerie, glassy-smooth face to them at sunrise. For such a short length of ride—about 50 yards—the waves have impact, and it's just a short paddle out to the takeoff. In fact, you can sit on the beach and almost have enough time to see a set arriving and paddle out for it without missing it! This is an ideal wave for both beginners and experts on the right day.

When distant swells are increasing, shifting, wandering wave peaks are a feature here. Each swell moves a little to break either east or west of the last, making position-ing a challenge that changes with each breaking set, depending on tide, swell, and wave height. Considered a classic wave when it's pumping 6 to 8 feet, with a steep shorebreak *huia* (an especially high wave formed by the meeting of two crests).

Ehukai Beach Park. This beach break is best at low tide in a north-west swell of 2 to 6 feet. It's one of the all-time great parks to view Banzai Pipeline and Gas Chambers and have lunch in awe of North Shore's wave power, watching bodyboarders perform maneuvers like lip launches, aerials, and drop-knee turns in the punchy, hard-hitting waves. This is where experts go before attempting Banzai Pipeline, and it has its own mix of flash-fast vertical drops and gnarly closeouts.

Banzai Pipeline

One of the world's most challenging and epic waves, this famous steep, fast left-hand barrel reef breaks off shallow coral reefs 100 yards from shore. It's known as the most awesome left in the world.

Best Tides: Low to medium.	**Best Boards:** Shortboards and guns.
Best Swell Direction: Northwest.	**Best Seasons:** Fall and winter.
Best Wave Size: Chest high to triple over-head.	**Crowds:** Crowded.
Bottom: Sand and coral.	**Water Quality:** Clean.
Type of Break: Left.	**Hazards:** Sharks and localism.
Skill Level: Expert.	**Fees and Permits:** No fees or permits are required.
	Schedule: Public access 24/7.

Banzai Pipeline, Oahu. PHOTO ROD SUMPTER

Finding the Break

Before leaving the Honolulu International Airport, look for a road sign that reads INTER-
STATE H1, HONOLULU, WAIKIKI, WAIANAE. Turn onto the exit ramp and stay left, exiting onto H1
West Waianae. Travel on H1 for 7 miles, then get into the right two lanes and look for EXIT
8A, H2 NORTH MILILANI, WAHIAWA. Take H2 for 7.6 more miles, then get off at EXIT 8 WAHIAWA.
Drive straight through the town of Wahiawa. As you exit the town, you'll go down a
small hill and under a bridge. Stay on this road (Interstate 99) for 8 miles until you see
the brown HISTORIC HALEIWA TOWN sign. From Haleiwa Bridge follow Kamehameha Highway
(commonly called Kam Highway) east to the twenty-totem-high totem pole on the
right side of the road, before a Chevron gas station. Turn left onto Kei Nui Road and drive
150 yards; Banzai Pipeline is to your left, 6.3 miles from the Haleiwa arched bridge. The
Bus No. 52, Circles Island, will drop you off here as well.

Surf Description

You haven't fully surfed Hawaii until you've surfed the Banzai Pipeline. This is the jewel
in the crown, the one spot that always looks magical, beckoning you to come and ride—
so pretty, so taunting. Many consider riding a 12- to 15-foot wave here to be the highlight of their surfing careers. Making it down the face of a wave into a barreling wall of
pent-up Pacific power takes commitment. The way to do it is to take off by paddling

down the face, getting up before your ankles go above your head. *Don't wipe out, make the drop, get in the barrel, keep charging . . .* it's that simple if you do it right. Making that first drop is an awesome feeling. Here the world's best bodyboarders put on an amazing display while disobeying the laws of gravity.

This all-time great left-hand reef break forms close to shore from November to March, and has some of the biggest A-frame waves in the world. When the surf's up at the "Pipe," it is the mother of all dangerous surf spots, boasting a huge tubing wave, a cracking spine-chilling coral reef, and rip currents as fast as rivers. The wave can stack up a couple of stories high, throwing a white lip out over itself and making a perfect *Hawaii Five-0* circle. It's killed, injured, bruised, and made big men weep. This wave accelerates into a howling tube big enough to fit a truck in, then crushes down into spray like an imploding concrete building as it nears the shore. The reef beneath is hard and lethal, covered with spiked coral and deadly little caves, waiting to capture or trap you on wipeouts.

Historically, this is Hawaii's shortest, hollowest, steepest, and closest-to-shore wave, except for Waimea Bay Shore Break, and is the ultimate challenge to surf. This is the best place in the world for watching surfers risk it all on spectacular monster waves. No other surf spot quite matches the power of the Banzai Pipeline. For experts only.

Second Reef, Banzai Pipeline, is a cloud break 0.5 mile outside Banzai Pipeline that breaks only in 20-foot-plus surf. Mostly blown out by trade winds by midday, this is an awesome wave to see from Banzai Pipeline. It's rarely surfed, and only successfully surfed by Jet Ski.

Third Reef, Banzai Pipeline. Another cloud break, 0.5 mile farther out from Second Reef. It's a tow-in surfing spot that starts to break at 30 feet.

Backdoor

This right-hand peak concaves into a walling tube with only one way out—through the eye. Thick lips and heavy walls are common. This is a right-hand barrel with one of the best thick curling tubes in the world, breaking over shallow lava and coral. The takeoff is located just 100 yards from shore and looms up quickly, having a vertical drop followed by a curtain-lip to watch out for. Since it was first ridden in the 1980s, Backdoor has been considered the world's thickest and most dangerous right reef break.

Best Tides: Low to middle.

Best Swell Direction: Northeast to northwest.

Best Wave Size: Chest high to triple overhead.

Bottom: Sand and coral.

Type of Break: Right.

Skill Level: Expert to advanced due to a tricky and dangerous paddle-out and vertical wave faces, making over-the-falls takeoffs likely wipeouts.

Best Boards: Shortboards up to 6 feet, 10 inches and rhino guns.

Best Seasons: Fall and winter.

Crowds: Crowded, especially on smaller days.

Water Quality: Clean.

Hazards: Localism, big waves, dangerous rip currents, and shallow coral reef.

Fees and Permits: No fees or permits are required.

Schedule: Public access 24/7.

Finding the Break

Before leaving the Honolulu International Airport, look for a road sign that reads INTERSTATE H1, HONOLULU, WAIKIKI, WAIANAE. Turn onto the exit ramp and stay left, exiting onto H1 West Waianae. Travel on H1 for 7 miles, then get into the right two lanes and look for EXIT 8A, H2 NORTH MILILANI, WAHIAWA. Take H2 for 7.6 more miles, then get off at EXIT 8 WAHIAWA. Drive straight through the town of Wahiawa. As you exit the town, you'll go down a small hill and under a bridge. Stay on this road (Interstate 99) for 8 miles until you see the brown HISTORIC HALEIWA TOWN sign. From Haleiwa Bridge follow Kamehameha Highway (commonly called Kam Highway) east to the twenty-totem-high totem pole on the right side of the road, before a Chevron gas station. Turn left onto Kei Nui Road and head east till you reach Ehukai Park. Leave your vehicle here; there's free parking, but space is limited. Walk out 100 yards to the ocean. Backdoor is 200 yards on your left.

Surf Description

This is by far the world's most dangerous right-hand reef break, so awesome it defies most surfers who attempt to ride it. Backdoor Pipeline goes ballistic on a northeast groundswell from overhead to 15 feet, and then breaks in a thousandth of a second. Kelly Slater, the six-time Association of Surfing Professionals (ASP) World Surfing Champion, is known as Mr. Backdoor for surfing it so well. "I'm at the peak of my ability to surf Backdoor," he says of this awesome surf. Major ASP sponsors like Ripcurl,

Backdoor, Oahu. PHOTO ROD SUMPTER

Quiksilver, and Billabong consider this spot a guaranteed world-class surf venue, with not only the heaviest but also the fastest, deepest, and longest barrel rides on planet earth.

Riding Backdoor is a question of positioning yourself in its wedgy side and finding the right drifting peak in your face, where the whole coral reef world below you moves as the swell draws up water into the mass of the wave's face. Then it's tension-splitting, life-or-death decisions. And in a blink of an eye you're here or you're gone. It's that fast.

Backdoor is so named for its location behind Banzai Pipeline (also known as Frontdoor), which peaks and slams shut, shaking the water around you just yards away; the sound of its blast echoes across the sea's surface. The scrambling is insane as sets go wide, break out, or close. Surfers get jumped by howling, crushing Niagara Falls waves that reduce to powder-blown spray as they exit the barrel. The wave accelerates into a pipe-dream right-hand tunnel—and all the time, just inches underneath you, lies the world's meanest, nastiest coral.

Backdoor is likely to be flat during the summer months, but it picks up plenty of groundswells from November to March. This is a great surf spot for the expert surfer if it's 6 to 8 feet, and ideal for the advanced-to-experienced surfer over 8 to 10 feet in January and February.

To native Hawaiians, Backdoor is known as Lauloa, meaning "a long wave that crests and breaks from one end of the beach to the other," or Nala ha`i lala, "a wave that breaks diagonally."

Places to Eat

Kammies Market restaurant and snack bar is located on Kam Highway in Haleiwa.

Off the Wall

This famous right-hand reef break surely has one of the best tubes in the world—at least if we're to judge by the amount of Kodak film used by the lineup of photographers on the nearby wall. It works from 3 to 13 feet and is mostly a superfast tube right with the occasional cutback section.

Best Tides: Low to medium.

Best Swell Direction: Northwest.

Best Wave Size: Chest high to triple over-head.

Bottom: Sand and coral.

Type of Break: Right-hand reef break.

Skill Level: Intermediate to advanced due to a tricky paddle-out.

Best Boards: Shortboards and guns.

Best Seasons: Fall and winter.

Crowds: Crowded.

Water Quality: Clean.

Hazards: Big waves, dangerous rip currents, shallow coral, and localism.

Fees and Permits: No fees or permits are required.

Schedule: Public access 24/7.

Finding the Break

Before leaving the Honolulu International Airport, look for a road sign that reads INTERSTATE H1, HONOLULU, WAIKIKI, WAIANAE. Turn onto the exit ramp and stay left, exiting onto H1 West Waianae. Travel on H1 for 7 miles, then get into the right two lanes and look for EXIT 8A, H2 NORTH MILILANI, WAHIAWA. Take H2 for 7.6 more miles, then get off at EXIT 8 WAHIAWA. Drive straight through the town of Wahiawa. As you exit the town, you'll go down a small hill and under a bridge. Stay on this road (Interstate 99) for 8 miles until you see the brown HISTORIC HALEIWA TOWN sign. From Haleiwa Bridge follow Kamehameha Highway (commonly called Kam Highway) east to a 6-foot-tall coral wall on your left. (If you reach the Chevron gas station, you've gone about 1,000 yards too far.) Park next to or near the wall and walk the sand track to the ocean. Off the Wall is opposite another coral wall on the beach side.

Surf Description

One long walling swell hits the reef and jacks up, then breaks fast, almost closing out. Your angled takeoff is a nail-biting moment of pure adrenaline. It's wise to have a quiver of boards with you at Off the Wall, this being the best insurance policy to escape its jaws. When your ride is hooked in deep, it's getting dark, and the only way out is forward, don't worry; just keep going. Of course, praying helps.

Situated at Kewa`ena Beach between Log Cabins and Backdoor, Off the Wall is one of Hawaii's best surfing locations, an all-time great spot. (The name, by the way, is

Off the Wall, Oahu. PHOTO ROD SUMPTER

derived from the long lava wall that runs along the beachfront.) The wave's first section looks as if it's going to close out, but it doesn't, instead getting faster, tighter, and hollower. The waves then peel off in the flicker of an eye. The Hawaiians have a name for it: *lala*, meaning "diagonal surf" or "surfing diagonally to the front of a wave."

With a northeast swell of 6 to 8 feet and a light trade wind, Off the Wall will turn into the fabulous barreling wave it's best known as. This is not for the fainthearted—it can be as dangerous a surf spot as you'll find anywhere. If it's over 10 feet, it's so heavy, fast, and hard that surfboards get snapped like toothpicks. Sets can double up and you can get *ahua*—"a place close to shore where the broken waves rise and break again." This spot is ideal for the expert surfer.

The King of Off the Wall

Local surfer Larry Bertlemann became famous worldwide for riding Off the Wall better than any other in his time. He perfected 360 turns on small days at Off the Wall, making this stunt look like a smooth and relaxed circular flip between tubes. In many ways his approach gave birth to the ripping performance approach of most of today's surfers. On big days at Off the Wall, Bertlemann's performance was nothing short of outstanding. Many top surfers chose to sit out their sets and simply watch him own the surf.

Insanities is a very fast right (and sometimes left) reef break just to the left of Off the Wall. It's more of a closeout—that's why it's called Insanities. For every makable wave here, there are ten that will eat you alive.

Rockpile

This big-wave left-hander always seems impossible to ride when surfers' eyes scan up and down the beach, from Back Door or Off the Wall, in an attempt to find a peak. The black lava rocks and deep blue trench here create waves that well and break with a lot of face. Rockpile's rare small days can be good, but it's mostly a big-wave spot.

Best Tides: Low to medium.

Best Swell Direction: Northwest.

Best Wave Size: Chest high to triple overhead.

Bottom: Sand and rock.

Type of Break: Left-hand reef break with some rights.

Skill Level: Intermediate to advanced due to a tricky paddle-out.

Best Boards: Shortboards and guns.

Best Seasons: Fall and winter.

Crowds: Rarely crowded.

Water Quality: Clean.

Hazards: Dangerous rip currents, shallow coral, rocky outcrops, sharks, and localism.

Fees and Permits: No fees or permits are required.

Schedule: Public access 24/7.

Finding the Break

Before leaving the Honolulu International Airport, look for a road sign that reads INTERSTATE H1, HONOLULU, WAIKIKI, WAIANAE. Turn onto the exit ramp and stay left, exiting onto H1 West Waianae. Travel on H1 for 7 miles, then get into the right two lanes and look for EXIT 8A, H2 NORTH MILILANI, WAHIAWA. Take H2 for 7.6 more miles, then get off at EXIT 8 WAHIAWA. Drive straight through the town of Wahiawa. As you exit the town, you'll go down a small hill and under a bridge. Stay on this road (Interstate 99) for 8 miles until you see the brown HISTORIC HALEIWA TOWN sign. From Haleiwa Bridge follow Kamehameha Highway (commonly called Kam Highway) east to a long straight stretch of road where you cannot see the ocean. Look for a gap in the vegetation; this is Rockpile. Park near the lifeguard tower. The break is straight out.

Rockpile, Oahu. PHOTO ROD SUMPTER

Surf Description

First surfed in the 1970s and then on a more regular basis in the 1990s, Rockpile is a gruesome spot that few surfers can ride. It's one of the truly big, deep ocean breaks in Hawaii, an awesomely steep hooking wave that defies gravity. It takes guts and skill to surf Rockpile, and maybe a touch of madness. Clean, clear swells approach this mighty reef break then twist like muscles in a spasm around jagged rocks and turquoise seas. When the big, long sloping waves hoist up, you must drive hard to make the drop.

Named for the lava-rock formations that have piled into the sea, Rockpile is situated 6 miles east of Haleiwa and 1 mile west of Banzai Pipeline. If you're not content with Off the Wall and don't mind a strong rip current to paddle against, try this gigantic left.

Rockpile starts breaking when the swell gets over 10 feet and holds waves up to 18 feet high. Viewed through the break in the Kam Highway's vegetation, it's an impressive sight—indeed, it's sometimes called "Gap in the Road." It's at its best at 10 to 15 feet, and has a ride length of about 50 to 150 yards. There's a lifeguard tower with seasonal lifesavers who can ride Rockpile better than most, especially on

Expect the North Shore to be closed at least two or three times each winter when massive swells arrive, coming off deep low-pressure systems, traveling east across the Pacific Ocean.

their custom-made big-wave guns. Expect them to close the beach with a red flag as soon as it becomes too dangerous and when a High Sea Alert is announced. For expert and big-wave surfers only.

Log Cabins

This right-hand reef break—with a left at times—is another of the all-time great Hawaiian waves. Look for high-performance tube surfing from steep, fast A-frame peaks.

Best Tides: Low to medium.

Best Swell Direction: Northwest.

Best Wave Size: Chest high to triple over-head.

Bottom: Sand and rock bottom.

Type of Break: Left- and right-hand reef break.

Skill Level: Intermediate to advanced.

Best Boards: Shortboards up to 7 feet, 8 inches.

Best Seasons: Fall and winter.

Crowds: Crowded.

Water Quality: Average to clean.

Hazards: Big waves, rips and currents, shallow coral reef, sharks, and localism.

Fees and Permits: No fees or permits are required.

Schedule: Public access 24/7.

Finding the Break

Before leaving the Honolulu International Airport, look for a road sign that reads INTER-STATE H1, HONOLULU, WAIKIKI, WAIANAE. Turn onto the exit ramp and stay left, exiting onto H1 West Waianae. Travel on H1 for 7 miles, then get into the right two lanes and look for EXIT 8A, H2 NORTH MILILANI, WAHIAWA. Take H2 for 7.6 more miles, then get off at EXIT 8 WAHIAWA. Drive straight through the town of Wahiawa. As you exit the town, you'll go down a small hill and under a bridge. Stay on this road (Interstate 99) for 8 miles until you see the brown HISTORIC HALEIWA TOWN sign. From Haleiwa Bridge follow Kamehameha Highway (commonly called Kam Highway) east for 1.1 miles past Waimea Bay.

Surf Description

Through the leaves of lush greenery, you stare out at a blue-white reef on the North Shore. It's not just any reef, though. It's Outer Log Cabins, where the Pacific is rolling in waves the size of dinosaurs. These beauties will re-form on the inside at Log Cabins, one of the finest surf breaks on all Oahu.

Log Cabins is situated 1 mile east of Waimea Bay and 3 miles west of Sunset Beach. In the 1960s, surfers who tried to line up the surf from the water here found that they had no obvious reference point on land to use. Then log cabins were built on the side of the hill, becoming the most visible landmark from the takeoff area—hence this spot's name.

Log Cabins, Oahu. PHOTO ROD SUMPTER

Once you're out behind the waves here, the view of the surf and the mountains is magical. Log Cabins is mostly a right-hand reef break with the occasional left; the right is straight out from the cabins, which are now almost obscured by vegetation. When you're in the ideal spot, you can take off and ride for 200 yards. It's a fast drop-in and fast wall, with off-the-lip sections, a tube, as well as a hot-dog tail end to the wave if it doesn't close out too soon. Better to kick out early than be trapped on the inside during sets, because the breaking of the waves over a sharp coral bottom makes for dangerous wipeouts that could be nasty. Log Cabins is for the expert surfer on most days and the big-wave rider on huge days.

Set below the topography of craggy tropical volcanic peaks, this largely deserted stretch of coastline has a small community of locals who pride themselves on their traditional Hawaiian ways and cherish their spectacular views of mountains and surf. Coral lagoons form rock pools and shallow fishing reefs for nearly a mile. Early-morning mist regularly forms up in the tropical canopy, making for an almost prehistoric scene. The Hawaiian sun soon comes along, however, and the wave-watching resumes.

Outer Log Cabins is an outer reef that produces dynamic peak with a steep drop and lots of wave face. Mostly a right-hander with the occasional left, it's a good tow-in, big-wave spot sometimes ridden by paddle-in solo surfers and big-wave riders. Jet Ski teams generally dominate. On January 28, 1998, monster-wave surfer Ken Bradshaw was reported surfing Outer Log Cabins with waves of up to 70 to 80 feet—wave face height!

Pele's Followers breaks way out on cloud-break reefs. It's a big-wave spot for tow-in Jet Ski teams to test their mettle, and a hardcore surfer's wave when it breaks. Rare and fickle.

Three Steps is sometimes called Three Tables. The swell here breaks into short gaps between three-square blocks of lava coast; a white-sand beach is the launch spot. Almost a surfable right-hander the next break east of Waimea Bay, the last rock is a very fickle break hardly worth considering—except for the fact that it's right in Kam Highway, looking maybe ridable. A Marine Life Conservation District, the spot offers good snorkeling when it's flat.

Waimea Bay Point

A right-hand point break with some of the biggest ridable waves in the world, this famous spot was the original place to ride 30-foot-plus waves and still is one of the premier big-wave spots. It breaks two or three times in winter.

Best Tides: All stages.

Best Swell Direction: West-northwest.

Best Wave Size: Double overhead to five times overhead.

Bottom: Sand and coral.

Type of Break: Right-hand point break.

Skill Level: Expert to advanced.

Best Boards: 7-foot shortboards and guns.

Best Seasons: Fall and winter.

Crowds: Crowded.

Water Quality: Clean.

Hazards: Localism, big waves, dangerous rip currents.

Fees and Permits: No fees or permits are required.

Schedule: Open dawn till dark, year-round.

Finding the Break

Before leaving the Honolulu International Airport, look for a road sign that reads INTERSTATE H1, HONOLULU, WAIKIKI, WAIANAE. Turn onto the exit ramp and stay left, exiting onto H1 West Waianae. Travel on H1 for 7 miles, then get into the right two lanes and look for EXIT 8A, H2 NORTH MILILANI, WAHIAWA. Take H2 for 7.6 more miles, then get off at EXIT 8 WAHIAWA. Drive straight through the town of Wahiawa. As you exit the town, you'll go down a small hill and under a bridge. Stay on this road (Interstate 99) for 8 miles until you see the brown HISTORIC HALEIWA TOWN sign. From Haleiwa Bridge follow Kamehameha Highway (commonly called Kam Highway) east for 5 miles to Waimea Bay. Pull into the park and see the lifeguard for directions to the point. From Haleiwa Bridge, it's 4.3 miles.

Surf Description

For most of the year, Waimea Bay is as soft and placid as a pond. Then winter storms deep in the Arctic send waves pulsing across the blue Pacific. Waimea Bay becomes a mesmerizing, roaring fury. Surfing it is like launching off a skyscraper into a pond—it's bombs away on a vertical takeoff into a steep walling wave face. This is surfing at its most extreme.

Situated off Kamehameha Highway just 4 miles east of Haleiwa and 2 miles west of the Banzai Pipeline, next to Waimea Bay Beach Park and Waimea Bay Falls, is the famous Waimea Bay Point. Every winter viewers watch breathtaking rides and dramatic rescues at Waimea Bay on the local news. From the roadside, December through February, you can look on in amazement as the best big-wave surfers on planet earth ride 30-foot monsters. From vantage points around Waimea Bay and on the beach, without ever getting your feet wet, you can witness terrific rides and scary wipeouts on waves that'll leave you breathless and gawking.

At takeoff the drop will suck the breath from your lungs, and in a moment its massive wall lines up and breaks, throwing out its curl. The steep face falls away to the wave's trough. If you make it this far, there's only the crashing right lip to avoid, and then it's out for the shoulder and the safety of the channel. Hang on and stay trimmed, and you could outrun the roaring avalanche and make it all the way. Waimea is a great place to surf-watch—on every wave it's debatable whether a surfer will wipe out on takeoff, go over the falls, or not survive the chase across the wall to the safety of the channel.

A great place to watch the waves of Waimea Bay is from up at the Pu`uomahuka Heiau State Monument, on a 250-foot bluff above the St. Peter and Paul Church. With its stunningly huge waves, pearly white beach, and tropical surroundings, this is a view to die for.

Waimea Bay Point, Oahu. PHOTO ROD SUMPTER

Local Events/Attractions

Nestled in the gorge behind Waimea Bay is **Waimea Falls Park,** an 1,800-acre botanical garden offering historical and cultural exhibits. The highlight is a breathtaking diving exhibition from the falls, starting 55 feet above the garden. In the early 1970s the waterfall's free-fall experience was used by top wave riders as a training exercise for big-wave surfing.

Pinballs. The waves that break close to the rocky point at Waimea Bay turn into a nice right between 8 and 15 feet (Waimea Point starts to break at 15 feet). It has a great drop and a cutback kind of wall that peels down the rocky round-stone coast to the beach.

Waimea Shore Break

The ultimate big-wave beach break with pounding lefts, this is a bodyboarder's extreme wave to ride, nightmare or dream. It's a grinding left-hand beach break for only the most advanced bodyboarders.

Best Tides: Low to medium.

Best Swell Direction: West-northwest.

Best Wave Size: Overhead.

Bottom: Sand.

Type of Break: Left-hand beach break.

Skill Level: Experienced to big-wave rider.

Best Boards: Bodyboards.

Best Seasons: Fall and winter.

Crowds: Never crowded.

Water Quality: Average to clean.

Hazards: Big waves, rips and currents, pounding shorebreak, dangerous rips, undertow, and localism.

Fees and Permits: No fees or permits are required.

Schedule: Public access 24/7.

Finding the Break

Before leaving the Honolulu International Airport, look for a road sign that reads INTERSTATE H1, HONOLULU, WAIKIKI, WAIANAE. Turn onto the exit ramp and stay left, exiting onto H1 West Waianae. Travel on H1 for 7 miles, then get into the right two lanes and look for EXIT 8A, H2 NORTH MILILANI, WAHIAWA. Take H2 for 7.6 more miles, then get off at EXIT 8 WAHIAWA. Drive straight through the town of Wahiawa. As you exit the town, you'll go down a small hill and under a bridge. Stay on this road (Interstate 99) for 8 miles until you see the brown HISTORIC HALEIWA TOWN sign. From Haleiwa Bridge follow Kamehameha Highway (commonly called Kam Highway) east to Waimea Bay. Pull into the park and see the lifeguard for directions. From Haleiwa Bridge, it's 4.3 miles.

Surf Description

This wave throws, it doesn't crumble, and there are no mushy sections—just enormous artistic curves. To ride here, you need to take off with a big grin on your face and the determination of a downhill racer. It's almost impossible to make the drop, vaulting past double-up sections and vast echoing hollow tubes. So you may as well smile now, because this wave will do its best to wipe the grin right off your face.

The tropical beach park and beauty spot of Waimea Bay Shore Break is located right next to Waimea Falls, 4 miles east of Haleiwa and 2 miles west of the Banzai Pipeline. This is an epic left-hander, a surf destination for

The Waimea Bay beach-break waves are featured in many famous photographs, including those seen on the Hawaii Five-O TV series' opening credits.

Waimea Shore Break, Oahu. PHOTO ROD SUMPTER

advanced expert bodyboarders, with its multibreaking gnarly shorebreak packed with extreme power.

Surfers and big-wave riders who come here consider the destination-seeking bodyboarders crazy to surf Waimea Shore Break—they might tube just 30 yards from shore, or end in a hideous wipeout. This tubing wave is a photo call for all who love the very close-up sights and sounds of waves at their best. For the bodyboarder it's the ultimate test of courage (or madness), with its seemingly impossible heavy barrels that are makeable only on the right day. Waimea produces some classic, unforgettable rides when it's 6 to 8 feet or bigger. But watch out, because the shorebreak has a strong undertow pulling surfers back into the dangerous lineup. Lifeguards will close the beach when these powerful waves, caused by storms sometimes thousands of miles off, get too big. Expect seasonal surf alerts to occur during the winter months, from December to March, when trade winds blow in from the northwest.

From the winding road circling this beautiful bay, the view of the huge shorebreak is breathtaking—you may even see whales breaching near the point. Waimea is a dangerous shorebreak, but for a few expert bodyboarders and big-wave surfers it's ideal. And for those not willing to risk life and limb, it is a must-watch surf spot.

Elephants, a right-hand reef break best in medium to large swells, is located out from Kam Highway at the west end of Waimea Bay. Make a slow drive past, watching closely to see whether it's pumping; if so, park up toward Left Overs at your first chance. Experts only.

Marijuana's, a short reef break opposite Alligator Rock (sandwiched between Left Overs and Waimea Bay), is best at 6 feet plus. A northwest swell causes the wave to horseshoe around the reef and throw out into an A-frame that will gladly let you power-surf.

Alligator Rock, a right-hander just in front of the Alligator Rock, is a drop-off wave; the wall to the left is hollower.

Left Overs

A left-hand reef break with a soft, slow curl line and a fun hook. Other than the inside section, Left Overs offers plenty of base to the wall for both longboard and shortboard fun. It holds swell from 3 to 10 feet.

Best Tides: High.

Best Swell Direction: North.

Best Wave Size: Chest high to double overhead.

Bottom: Rock and coral.

Type of Break: Left-hand reef break with some rights.

Skill Level: Expert.

Best Boards: Shortboards and longboards.

Best Seasons: Fall and winter.

Crowds: Rarely crowded.

Water Quality: Clean.

Hazards: Sharp coral and shallow.

Fees and Permits: No fees or permits are required.

Schedule: Public access 24/7.

Left Overs, Oahu. PHOTO ROD SUMPTER

Finding the Break

Before leaving the Honolulu International Airport, look for a road sign that reads INTER-STATE H1, HONOLULU, WAIKIKI, WAIANAE. Turn onto the exit ramp and stay left, exiting onto H1 West Waianae. Travel on H1 for 7 miles, then get into the right two lanes and look for EXIT 8A, H2 NORTH MILILANI, WAHIAWA. Take H2 for 7.6 more miles, then get off at EXIT 8 WAHIAWA. Drive straight through the town of Wahiawa. As you exit the town, you'll go down a small hill and under a bridge. Stay on this road (Interstate 99) for 8 miles until you see the brown HISTORIC HALEIWA TOWN sign. From Haleiwa Bridge follow Kamehameha Highway (commonly called Kam Highway) east for 3.5 miles. Before the bend leading to Waimea Bay, look for a red-dirt pull-off on the ocean side of the road; Left Overs is between the rocky boulders 200 yards out.

Surf Description

It's a heart-stopping, thrilling moment when you paddle out to ride your first blue wave. Human-size wave trains grind by while you wonder at the hook and ledges against a jungle-covered mountain. This great left peels off and crushes everything in its path; you either ride or get wiped.

Situated 1 mile west of Waimea and 6 miles east of Haleiwa, Left Overs is one of Oahu's best secret spots, a classic left-hand reef break 0.25 mile west of Waimea's western point. The most remote and wild in appearance of all the nearby surf spots, it has days when a fine swell builds just right; it'll be clean here even if everywhere else is caught by trade winds. The paddle-out is over rock and sharp black lava as the slow left reels off toward you. Getting in is a rock-hopping exercise—awkward rather than difficult, but you'll need skill to avoid the urchins. The sunset surfing here can be the best in the world for color. Staying in the surf lineup is difficult; you'll need to paddle against the strong current. There are plenty of markers to line up with, though. When you finish the ride, the channel out is safe and easy . . . except for the inside. This wave is occasionally smaller, and then it's a soft and fun wave, uniquely protected from strong east winds slap-bang in the barrel. Ideal for and a must for expert surfers.

Right Overs, the right-hander from Left Overs, is a tricky, short peak that often closes out when least expected. On a good wave, however, the reeling wall takes you well down the bay toward Chuns Reef, while the paddle back is long and hard. The shoreline features razor-sharp lava all the way along, making walking near impossible.

Pidleys. This shallow rocky beach with little hollow waves is sheltered from strong trades. It has its days when everywhere else is windy and poor. It's quite a teaser to see little waves so good.

Chuns Reef

The reef is named for the John Chun family, who had a house inshore of the break many years ago. Native Hawaiians who fished and surfed the reef, they must have been spoiled to the core. This is a great longboarding wave—a long right-hander over coral reefs that section from a hooking neat peak into a barrel and hot-dog walls.

Best Tides: Low to medium.

Best Swell Direction: Northwest.

Best Wave Size: Overhead.

Bottom: Coral and sand.

Type of Break: Right-hand reef break.

Skill Level: Intermediate.

Best Boards: Longboards; also shortboards if it's big.

Best Seasons: Fall and winter.

Crowds: Crowded.

Water Quality: Clean.

Hazards: Dangerous rip currents, shallow sand bottom, and localism.

Fees and Permits: No fees or permits are required.

Schedule: Public access 24/7.

Chuns Reef, Oahu. PHOTO ROD SUMPTER

Finding the Break

Before leaving the Honolulu International Airport, look for a road sign that reads INTER-STATE H1, HONOLULU, WAIKIKI, WAIANAE. Turn onto the exit ramp and stay left, exiting onto H1 West Waianae. Travel on H1 for 7 miles, then get into the right two lanes and look for EXIT 8A, H2 NORTH MILILANI, WAHIAWA. Take H2 for 7.6 more miles, then get off at EXIT 8 WAHIAWA. Drive straight through the town of Wahiawa. As you exit the town, you'll go down a small hill and under a bridge. Stay on this road (Interstate 99) for 8 miles until you see the brown HISTORIC HALEIWA TOWN sign. From Haleiwa Bridge follow Kamehameha Highway (commonly called Kam Highway) east for 3.1 miles. A gap in the road allows you to see the waves and some houses and parking. A small beach with rocks leads you out to the break.

Surf Description

Take a block of wax and a longboard, rub some wax on the rails, on the deck, and a lot on the nose, then go get some of the best nose riding the world has to offer. Grab the rail and turn turtle on the outside sets, then paddle hard for the shoulder. The next wave you catch is going to have you running all over the board. By the time you've surfed four or five sets, the wax will be gone and you'll have had a ride of a lifetime.

Chuns Reef is the ideal performance right-hand reef break for longboards, and it has good days for bodyboards and shortboards as well. Half a mile west of Laniakea and 4 miles east of the Banzai Pipeline, it's famous for its classic lineup of waves. Take a look from the gap in the highway or from the small parking lot nearby, and you'll see the wave perfection awaiting you. These waves are soft compared with the heavy, gnarly barrels of other North Shore breaks. This is a perfect, laid-back classic longboarder's wave, set in a tropical coastline of reefs and surrounding coral lagoons. Its best surf conditions are in a northerly groundswell of 4 to 6 feet, with a light offshore southerly wind.

Chuns Reef is best known for high-quality waves that wall and hold up seemingly forever—ideal for maximum maneuverability and performance surfing. It has a lot to offer and, on most days, a choice of three takeoff areas. There's the outer takeoff peak that forms farthest out, especially on set waves—a good peak left and right. This then fades into the Main Peak, which re-forms as a classic takeoff—the best peak you could ever wish for. Like a mountain on the horizon slowly rising into view, the right-hand wall is a performance wave for the first 50 yards, and is ideal for either nose riding or big bottom turns and roundhouse cutbacks, then through to the inside section. The shorebreak, the third of the three takeoff areas, breaks when a swell misses the outer takeoff areas, forming a hard right and peeling off into a shallow coral reef and boulders. Which of these three takeoff areas is best depends on the swell direction and conditions of the day.

This is an ideal surf spot for intermediate surfers when it's 3 to 4 feet and great for experts when it's in the 6- to 8-foot range. In nearly all conditions, however, it's a classic longboarding wave.

Jocko's is a left-hander breaking close to surging and boiling reefs that spill over into a green combing wall, then on to a hotdog shoulder, and finally to a faded inside wave beside dead water. Can be epic.

Laniakea

Laniakea is a long right-hand reef break that resembles a point wave. It's a classic big-wave spot and fun inner reef on 4- to 6-foot days. Rides of 300 to 500 yards are possible.

Best Tides: Midtide.

Best Swell Direction: Northwest.

Best Wave Size: 6 to 8 feet.

Bottom: Coral reef.

Type of Break: Right-hand reef break.

Skill Level: Expert.

Best Boards: Shortboards and longboards on small days; on big days (over 15 feet), you'll want a rhino gun of 11 feet or more.

Best Seasons: November to March.

Crowds: Crowded on most good days.

Water Quality: Clean.

Hazards: There's a long paddle-out through coral gullies and pools over coral spikes, into and against a channel rip that doubles the distance out to the takeoff area. Except after high tide, an outgoing undertow and offshore wind will aid paddling. On big days (over 12 feet), heavy set waves clean up and break all but the toughest leg ropes. A nightmare swim in.

Fees and Permits: No fees or permits are required.

Schedule: Open 24/7.

Finding the Break

Known as the gateway to the North Shore, Laniakea is the first surf spot you reach when you leave Haleiwa. Head eastward along Kamehameha Highway (commonly called Kam Highway) over the famous arched bridge leading out to the country. The road widens as you reach a magically white sandy beach 2 miles east of town, trimmed with black lava boulders and a few wooden houses. Laniakea can be seen clearly from the road as a broad reef break—and it's a fabulous sight.

Surf Description

When the ancient sea gods planned the North Shore, it's clear they wanted to make one spot very different. Set way out on a triangular coral reef, Laniakea—"the great break"—has a freight-train right-hander that grinds its wheels, then barrel-rolls along a massive channel. Blowing like a stoked furnace, these waves actually roar. This is a unique spot.

Laniakea is a big-wave break, and there can be a horrendous paddle-out to mammoth 20-foot-high right-hand walls when the trade winds are really blowing. But the surf lineup here is amazing. If the swell's up and the sun's out, look out to the horizon; the heavens appear to crash in as sets pile along in a mounting succession of waves.

The waves are a long way out, then suddenly a surfer drops in and disappears in the tube and reappears hugging the wall. More waves break closer in, and they look inviting. This is a first view of a typically awesome big day at Laniakea. You can feel alone (but never lonely) surfing here. The nearby Waimea Bay can be a dangerously crowded spot on biggish days, but at Laniakea you'll find only a handful of surfers in the water, savor-

Laniakea, Oahu. PHOTO ROD SUMPTER

ing the adventure, alone in their own world of spiritual glee. Ride length is 300 to 500 yards on a 6- to 8-foot day, and 400 to 600 on a bigger day. Small waves of quality are also offered by the sea gods here, and most people regard it as a fine performance wave on the smaller days. This is an ace surf spot for the intermediate to big-wave rider, depending on the surf size.

Himalayas, a horizon reef break and cloud break, is a big-wave spot best surfed as a tow-in team setting out from Haleiwa. It's rarely ridden, however, given the 5-mile trek from the harbor and the wild nature of the setting.

The Point is a long, fast right best at 10 to 12 feet. It needs the right conditions: a northeast swell and light south winds. Strong currents make positioning for takeoff and surfing hazardous.

Pua`ena is a fast reef break with hollow waves over shallow reefs. Dangerous closeouts and rocks make this a difficult spot, and it rarely breaks well. Consider it one of the last-resort spots to check in a big swell and strong trades.

Haleiwa

This left- and right-hand reef break is famous for the perfect right that walls and barrels, ending up as a shallow closeout that's really scary. The takeoff is two reefs 200 and 350 yards out from the beach with loads of appeal to all kinds of wave riders. Lifeguard 24/7.

Best Tides: Low to medium.

Best Swell Direction: Northwest.

Best Wave Size: Waist high to double overhead.

Bottom: Sand, rock, and coral.

Type of Break: Left- and right-hand reef break.

Skill Level: Intermediate to advanced.

Best Boards: Shortboards and longboards.

Best Seasons: Fall and winter.

Crowds: Crowded.

Water Quality: Clean.

Hazards: Big waves, dangerous rip currents, shallow coral reef, and localism.

Fees and Permits: No fees or permits are required.

Schedule: Public access 24/7.

Finding the Break

Before leaving the Honolulu International Airport, look for a road sign that reads INTERSTATE H1, HONOLULU, WAIKIKI, WAIANAE. Turn onto the exit ramp and stay left, exiting onto H1 West Waianae. Travel on H1 for 7 miles, then get into the right two lanes and look for EXIT 8A, H2 NORTH MILILANI, WAHIAWA. Take H2 for 7.6 more miles, then get off at EXIT 8 WAHIAWA. Drive straight through the town of Wahiawa. As you exit the town, you'll go down a small hill and under a bridge. Stay on this road (Interstate 99) for 8 miles until you see the brown HISTORIC HALEIWA TOWN sign. The break is just 0.5 mile from the center of Haleiwa: Head north and, just before leaving the outskirts of town, turn left toward the marina, then right when you see Ali`i Beach Park.

Surf Description

A mighty fine swell is running, and the scales are tipping 10 to 12 feet. Haleiwa is honking and hooting on the rights. The surfer on the horizon strokes into a left peak, a pitch-

Haleiwa, Oahu. PHOTO ROD SUMPTER

black takeoff monster, and zooms right across the bay. Everyone onshore stands and cheers. This is a taste of Haleiwa.

The town of Haleiwa was established in 1899, and was known then as the "Home of the Frigate Bird." Today it's known as "Haleiwa the Surf Town," with world-class surfing and more surf shops than any other place on Oahu. Situated 30 miles north of Waikiki and 7 miles west of Sunset Beach on Kamehameha Highway (commonly called Kam Highway), Haleiwa is a quaint country town that boasts surf clothing shops, arts and crafts, and a remarkable surf museum. But most relevant to you and me, it produces some of the finest surfing anywhere in the world. This right-hand sand-and-coral reef break is a long ride—up to 250 yards on a good day. Both shortboarders and longboarders excel in this paradise of optimum waves.

Haleiwa's Ali`i Beach Park is one of the finest parks on Oahu, complete with showers, changing rooms, a picnic area, restrooms, parking, and lifeguards. Many national and international surfing championships are held here, including the Vans Triple Crown of Surfing, the Roxy Pro women's event, and the Bear longboard contest.

From a surfer's viewpoint this is the trickiest surf spot on the North Shore, and for this reason it's the most sought after, especially on medium-size days. It's here at Haleiwa that the ocean puts on a disguise of soft, sweet, perfect waves. From the shore, this ruse may fool even the sharpest tack. But behind the crafty subterfuge the waves are heavy, hard hitting, and hollow, breaking hard in shallow water over coral reefs. The difference between watching from shore and tasting your first gnarly wave, up close and personal, can be shocking. The paddle-out is also difficult, avoiding the sets while still on the shallow reef. Judging the length of the lulls can be very tricky; getting caught inside is the norm until you learn to use the rip. But then there are the small-wave days perfect for the whole family. On a sunny day, with a light offshore wind, it can be a dream location of fun waves.

There are three different takeoff areas here at Haleiwa. The first is the farthest out, where only set waves break on 8-foot days and the rights are the most fantastic walling, tubing, and nose-riding performance waves of all time. Rides that will be long remembered happen here, but not before ending 250 yards down the surf line in an ultrashallow tubing closeout—a place to kick out and get huge air! The next takeoff is the inside section, which picks up all the swell that the outside passes up, breaking as a right and sometimes a left, fast and furious, hollowing out and ending up in the rip or channel. The third takeoff area is farther on the east side of the beach. A left and right from a northwest swell direction make this happen.

Local Events/Attractions

- In 1899 **Haleiwa** opened the island's first hotel. The Haleiwa Hotel is now long gone, but the town has become a tourist haven, with fine alternative clothing and many health food shops. It leads the way in the Hawaiian lifestyle—simple quality living, fresh food, and karma. The surroundings are of lush vegetation, with banana and sugarcane fields backed by the Wai`anae Mountains. These slope down to the Haleiwa marina, where diving, whale-watching, and snorkeling in the clear water make this town a paradise.

- In December the **Vans Triple Crown of Surfing Series** starts with the G-Shock Hawaiian Pro Men's and Women's Division and Longboard Championships at Ali`i Beach Park. Call (808) 638–7266 or (808) 325–7400.

Toilet Bowl, Haliewa. A right-hand wave breaking to the inside section of Haleiwa that usually ends as a breaking section onto a sucked-dry reef.

Avalanche is a huge left-hand reef break 0.5 mile off Haleiwa. This big patch of living reef surges up deep-water swells that peak and break like, well, an avalanche. It's a huge mountain of green-blue raw wave. It can be the perfect training ground for wannabe big-wave riders at 10 to 12 feet when it's just starting to break. At 15 to 25 feet, it's a hardcore big-wave rider's spot.

The Wall, right- and left-handers in front of the lava wall, has fast peeling short waves from 3 to 6 feet. The distant reefs inspire some great shorebreak surfing. Best for bodyboards.

Hammerheads is a screaming left and right reef break into Kaiaka Bay; very shallow, and a shark breeding ground. The long paddle-out is spooky, and few surfers risk it.

Silva Channel is a reef break and shark breeding ground that's uncrowded due to the sharks but has some excellent waves. Tow surfing is ideal; launching out from Haleiwa Harbor, the trip goes past Avalanche.

Mokuleia Beach Park

Mostly deserted peaks line up and roll along a 2-mile stretch of beach. Waves form on reefs 200 to 300 yards out, offering a host of challenging rights and lefts. Reefs dotted about the main reef fringe produce the start of an A-frame peak, which then runs into the fast walling sections, closes out, and re-forms on the inside reef short of the beach.

Best Tides: Low to medium.

Best Swell Direction: West-northwest and northwest.

Best Wave Size: 6 to 8 feet.

Bottom: Sand and reef.

Type of Break: Left and right.

Skill Level: Intermediate to advanced.

Best Boards: Shortboards up to 7 feet, 4 inches, round pintails, and big-wave guns.

Best Seasons: Fall and winter.

Crowds: Crowded.

Water Quality: Average to clean.

Hazards: Rip currents, shallow coral-and-sand bottom, rocky outcrops, sharks, and localism.

Fees and Permits: No fees or permits are required.

Schedule: Public access 24/7.

Mokuleia Beach Park, Oahu. PHOTO ROD SUMPTER

Finding the Break

Before leaving the Honolulu International Airport, look for a road sign that reads INTER-STATE H1, HONOLULU, WAIKIKI, WAIANAE. Turn onto the exit ramp and stay left, exiting onto H1 West Waianae. Travel on H1 for 7 miles, then get into the right two lanes and look for EXIT 8A, H2 NORTH MILILANI, WAHIAWA. Take H2 for 7.6 more miles, then get off at EXIT 8 WAHIAWA. Drive straight through the town of Wahiawa. As you exit the town, you'll go down a small hill and under a bridge. Stay on this road (Interstate 99) for 8 miles until you see the brown HISTORIC HALEIWA TOWN sign. Mokuleia is a five-minute drive west toward Kaena Point with easy parking and good views of the waves.

Surf Description

Like a bolt of lightning, waves rise up from the deep water and head for shore. Mokuleia picks up these lightning waves, then garnishes and grooms the swell into perfect peaks across the bay. The waves are wedged, and the green walls push hard. The bold forms, powerful drops, and steaming tunnels of Mokuleia are truly heady fun.

The amazing breaks of Mokuleia Beach Park are situated just 2 miles west of Haleiwa and 1 mile east of Kaena Point at the northwestern corner of the North Shore. For many years this was a secret spot, and it's still relatively uncrowded thanks to its vast choice of breaks and demanding waves.

On smaller days when the ocean enjoys light offshore conditions and calm, even swells, this is the ideal place to spend a day of surfing. At Mokuleia Beach Park every-thing seems easy; you roll up, look out, and make some decisions on whether to surf this peak or that. After a few minutes of watching, you'll know the set patterns and will have timed the lulls. Then you're ready to go. This is the quiet part of the island, the bit that's been left as nature intended: untouched, beautiful, and with plenty of waves.

Mokuleia Beach Park parallels Dillingham airfield, off Farrington Highway, and there are three main breaks to consider. The reef break off Army Beach is a tough paddle-out on a 4- to 6-foot day, unless you judge the lulls right, take advantage of the rips and currents, and paddle out through gullies and channels in the coral to the deep-water peak. Then there's the western end of Mokuleia with its slabs of lava rock covering the ocean floor and A-frame peaks providing a perfect left on the inside of Kaena Point. Mokuleia Beach Park also has breaks in the eastward directions from Dillingham. The reef toward the town of Waialua breaks farther out, peaking as a right-hand barrel with a very steep takeoff—but also with good reentry, floater, and air possibilities. On most days there are few people in the lineup. You can park up and picnic in paradise surroundings, waiting for just the right surf to suit you. The ocean seems to pump out magical waves one after another as soon as the light southerly offshore winds blow. That's when all the breaks start to turn to perfection. This is an ideal surf spot for shortboards and longboards; occasionally, in strong trade winds, there are good wave conditions for windsurfers as well.

Day Star Army Beach. Sheltered by Kaena Point from southwest winds, this spot offers several reef breaks, and the most popular—a left off the side of the point—gets amazing. Plenty of reefs to choose from line the bay 300 yards out.

Kaena Point. Half a mile offshore, this big-wave spot has waves of 50 to 60 feet that are rarely ridden. It needs a huge storm; when surf alerts are being taken down, this can be the greatest break on earth. The original big-wave spot, where some folks use helicopters to launch into the wave lineup.

Yokohama Bay. A fast left-hand beach break 50 yards from shore that holds waves of 3 to 10 feet. The beach is the last on the northwest coast of Oahu. It's sometimes known as Keawalua Beach or Puau Beach, but everybody calls it Yokohama. No bus service.

Kea`au Park offers mostly fast rights close to a reef that's 75 yards from shore. You'll get nice views of new swell here—it's one of the best spots to check out size and direction. A good picnic area. Expect some localism.

Makaha

This right-hand point wave boasts a fantastic backwash, has a good reef and beach, and is the all-around best spot on Oahu's west coast. The famous point break starts to work in swells over 15 feet. The great variety of waves from 2 to 25 feet suits all grades.

Best Tides: Low to medium.

Best Swell Direction: West-northwest.

Best Wave Size: Chest high to triple over-head.

Bottom: Sand.

Type of Break: Beach break and right-hand point break.

Skill Level: Intermediate to advanced.

Best Boards: Short- and longboards.

Best Seasons: Fall and winter.

Crowds: Crowded.

Water Quality: Clean.

Hazards: Backwash, rocky shorebreak, ledge, rips and currents, and localism.

Fees and Permits: No fees or permits are required.

Schedule: Public access 24/7.

Finding the Break

Take Interstate H1 west out of the Honolulu International Airport and stay on this road (which turns into Farrington Highway) all the way to Makaha. When the road comes to a Y, you'll see a big overhead sign directing you to Waianae; stay in the extreme left lane and continue to Makaha, with a clear view of the waves and beach.

Surf Description

If the swell's up, load up and fire your biggest wave gun. You'll need it. This is Makaha.

Makaha is the mecca of surfing on Oahu's west coast, boasting a wave range of 3 to 30 feet. It's a spectacular half-moon bay, and the fantastic point-surf wave lines up and peels off over a coral reef into a bowl area, where the wave springs up and curves in a semicircle. Then comes the beach break, with one of the biggest backwashes in the world.

Situated 20 miles northwest of Waikiki and 10 miles southwest of Haleiwa, this spot has a long surfing history. The word *makaha* in ancient Hawaiian means "fierce" or "savage," appropriately describing the area that surrounds it.

Makaha, Oahu. PHOTO ROD SUMPTER

Makaha is famous for its big right, called Makaha Point Surf, at Kepuhi Point, hold-ing surf up to 30 feet at the outer end of the bay. The ride on a big day includes the famous Bowl area halfway into the ride, which curves around to face you in a tight escape tube. Then there's the infamous Makaha Backwash just before the shorebreak, with a reputation for sending surfers sailing15 feet into the air. This hooligan wave action occurs when a wave washes up the steeply sloping beach, and then rolls quickly back down and out to sea to meet the oncoming wave. The resulting confrontation catches unsuspecting riders off-guard, catapulting them sky high. If you're clever enough, you can turn it into a huge cutback or aerial maneuver, becoming the hero instead of the victim.

Makaha is nearly the complete surfer's playground, as it breaks year-round. Its best waves, however, roll in from April to September in northwest-to-southwest swells. At the week's end, local Hawaiian families set up their barbecues and stay all day, taking advan-tage of all this beautiful beach has to offer. There's surf for just about everyone, and on small days children and beginners can ride the shorebreak while the hot-doggers get to surf the waves farther out. On bigger days longboards rule, with nose rides and bot-tom turns taking the day. Shortboarders aren't left out, spending the day tackling the outside and inside parts of each wave and shredding the Makaha Backwash if they dare.

Makaha and much of the west side of Oahu are about as close to an unspoiled Hawaiian paradise as they come. Rising high above the shoreline, the dry, rugged slopes of the Waiane Mountains stretch up to the sky, while pineapple plantations sit farther inland. If you're on the island, you must surf here.

The King of Makaha

Hawaiian surfing legend Buffalo Keaulana lifeguarded at Makaha for seventeen years and has held the popular Buffalo's Big Board Surfing Classic contest every February or March since 1977. Considered the world's greatest switch-foot surfer, his performance during the original Makaha International Surfing Championships of 1964 impressed even the great Duke Kahanamoko. Today he's retired from lifeguarding, but you may still find him setting up his barbecue and shredding the Makaha Backwash.

Local Events/Attractions

The **Quiksilver-Roxy Wahine Bash,** a women's surf competition, is held in Makaha Beach Park each March.

Klausmeyers. This offshore left-hand reef can go off in good southwest to northwest swells; it starts breaking when Makaha is overhead. Great scenery with clear blue water and quality snorkeling when it's flat.

Turtle Beach is a bodyboarding beach break nestled between the majestic Waianae Mountains and the ocean, and between Makaha and Waianae. Short, fast lefts and rights peel off. Expect some localism.

Pokai. The most visited beach on the leeward coast, Pokai Beach County Park's sands are spotless, with good surfing and snorkeling conditions. A replica of a Polynesian double-hulled canoe is often docked at the boat ramp. Localism.

Maili Rights. This is the famous right-hander from the 1960s film *Surfing Hollow Days*—the one where Phil Edwards arches and gets tubed in wafer-thin waves. It's a fickle spot that needs just the right conditions.

Tumble Land, Ulehawa Beach County Park. Good bodysurfing conditions as well as good bodyboarding with short rides and some fine sections. Just north of Nanakuli, along Farrington Highway. Restrooms and lifeguards; camping is allowed with a permit.

Maili Point. At 6 to 8 feet, this left wave swings in and down the coast, giving classic shape. A good longboard, shortboard, and bodyboard spot, but it's fickle and needs a big west swell.

Shorebreak. Fun short rides, often dumping—but there are some class barrels here on the right day. The wave can wedge up and be very sucky. It's famous for heavy closeouts and wipeouts.

Tracks, Upper Kahe just north of Kahe Point—you can see it from Interstate H1. A fun small beach break that breaks year-round. It's crowded most of the time; don't leave valuables in your car. Localism runs high.

Power Plant is a right-hand reef break 30 yards form the rocks. Near the roadside are short rides close to rocks often seen from Farrington Highway and considered the surf indicator spot for the whole west coast. If a pumping swell is in existence, it could show here. Fickle.

Kahe Point, Kahana Valley State Park. A bodysurfing and body-boarding beach break with neat waves on a southwest swell and light trade winds. Great scenic valley and beach, camping, picnicking in a coconut grove, and pig hunting in a public hunting area. The park is open during daylight hours.

Bathtubs is a right-hander just 20 yards from shore that offers fun short, sharp bodyboarding and shortboarding waves when it's low tide and a good 4 to 5 feet from either a wraparound north-west swell or a summer southwest swell. Crowded on weekends; expect localism.

Barbers Point beach and reef break is best in the early morning before trades blow it out. There's a long paddle-out, but it's still easy to reach on a longboard. Also called Swabiland or the Jetty, it's found near the Coast Guard hangar.

Officers Surf. A fun bodyboarding and longboarding beach break with weak, easy waves most of the time. Once restricted to navy personnel, it's been open since 1999.

Coves is a fickle right- and left-hand reef break where sharks are often seen; it blows out on most afternoons for trade winds. This can be a good small wave of 2 to 3 feet—and occasionally bigger on a positive strong south swell.

Shark Pit reef break has left- and right-hand peaks. It's mostly a mushy longboard wave, but it can be a cruise-to-the-nose-and-hang-five type of wave. Prevailing trade winds blow it out regularly around midday.

Lots features various A-frame peaks along a reef that's the best spot in an area of generally poor small-surf conditions. But it can be groomed into nice tube and fast wall. Usually fickle.

Sea Wall. This sharky right- and left-hand reef break has several peaks to choose from. It blows out as soon as the trade winds pick up in midmorning; it needs a light northwest wind. Fickle and rarely big, Sea Wall is best in the early morning.

Ewa Beach, a 0.5-mile beach break, blows out in trades. Early mornings here are best—2 to 4 feet. This famous beach break is found off an area holding fun waves and big crowds.

Sand Trails, Sand Island State Recreation Area, is a beach and reef break with a small sand beach, boat ramp, sharks, and camping. It needs a south swell.

Incinerators offers hollow rights of 4 to 6 feet, perfect with light trades. Sharky, fickle, and shallow, it also gets a tube worth its weight in gold.

Point Panic

This is a great bodysurfing right-hand A-frame peak into a channel. The channel break-water and natural reef make this an outstanding bodysurfing spot—and indeed, it's posted BODY SURFING ONLY. You'll find fast rights into a bowl section with the occasional left.

Best Tides: Low to medium.

Best Swell Direction: South.

Best Wave Size: 3 to 9 feet (3 feet Hawaiian).

Bottom: Lava.

Type of Break: Rights and occasional lefts.

Skill Level: Intermediate to advanced due to a tricky paddle-out.

Best Boards: Open-heel swim fins.

Best Seasons: April to September.

Crowds: Crowded.

Water Quality: Average to clean.

Hazards: Sharks and localism. No life-guards.

Fees and Permits: No fees or permits are required.

Schedule: Public access 24/7, but parking is limited; get here before 10:00 A.M.

Finding the Break

From Ala Moana Boulevard in Ala Moana, turn left (west) onto Cooke Street and continue 1.04 miles to the Ala Moana Shopping Center, then 0.4 mile to Kaka`ako Waterfront Park. A short walk along the boardwalk will lead you to a short flight of railed steps down to the channel called Kewalo Basin. It's 60 yards to the First Peak.

The parking lot in the Point Panic Park is free, but no parking is allowed between 10:00 P.M. and 6:00 A.M.; offending vehicles will be towed at the owner's expense. There's metered parking along several streets at $1.00 per hour for a maximum of two hours.

Point Panic, Oahu. PHOTO ROD SUMPTER

Surf Description

The barrel hangs in the air, balancing, as you slot into the vertical slope and feel the rise of the swell push you out into the clean green-blue face of a perfect right. (Some folks liken this launch to being fired from a gun.) Then the wall slips away as you try to hold high in the face while the wave fades. This is a short, intense wave. The next one sucks your fins and positions you into a rollover to the right . . . and then it happens—you free-fall 3 feet down the face of the wave, where the push catapults you out from the barrel. It's caused by the outgoing channel rip at 10 miles an hour, while more water holds back the incoming ocean swell at 8 mph or so. This forms an awesome wave that's perfect for bodysurfers, and so the local authorities designated this a bodysurfing-only spot. Put down that gun, longboard, shortboard, or bodyboard and experience surf the way it was first enjoyed—making the drop and hugging the shoulder with only a pair of swim fins. A boardwalk borders the sea here, and flat rocks slope down to lava reefs and out to other breaks. These are fickle but worthy of watching out for—a low tide and new swell can produce classic waves at this South Shore surf corner.

Local Events/Attractions

- The **University of Hawaii Oceanographic Center** is 0.5 mile west of the Point Panic break.

- Sampans and other fishing boats moor in the small-boat harbor of **Kewalo Basin,** which is also the departure point for Pearl Harbor cruises.

- **Bodysurfing contests** are held between April and September. For more information, call (808) 638–8825.

Kewalos

This right and left-hand reef break set out from a large lagoon has several takeoff points. From the beach, the basin has reefs 300 yards offshore with a variety of peaks and sections. Mostly good rights.

Best Tides: Medium.	**Best Seasons: Summer.**
Best Swell Direction: South.	**Crowds: Crowded.**
Best Wave Size: Chest high to overhead.	**Water Quality: Clean.**
Bottom: Coral.	**Hazards: Sharks and localism.**
Type of Break: Left- and right-hand reef break.	**Fees and Permits: No fees or permits are required.**
Skill Level: Intermediate.	**Schedule: Open from dawn till dark, year-round.**
Best Boards: Short- and longboards.	

Finding the Break

From the Honolulu International Airport, drive along the Ala Wai Canal on Ala Wai Boulevard. Turn left onto Niu Street; it's marked with an AIRPORT sign on the corner. Turn right onto Ala Moana Boulevard.

When you see Ala Moana Beach Park on the left-hand side, you're getting close! Turn left onto Ward Avenue two traffic lights after the park. There is metered parking available for $.50 hour (quarters only) directly in front of the Fisherman's Wharf Restaurant and on the opposite end of the harbor (west side), past the fishing charter boats.

Surf Description

There's nothing better than paddling out over flat-calm shallow reefs while watching a pumping wave display of barrels, tubes, and curls right and left. This A-frame, diamond-studded, crystal-clear wave walls up on outer reefs; the green and blue swells hover, pass over coral, and then burst into reeling rights. Sets on the intermediate reefs barely break or fade out into the lagoon.

Situated 100 yards southwest of Point Panic and 2 miles northwest of Waikiki, this reef break stretches across the sandy bay of Kewalo Beach to the break called Tennis Courts. There isn't much to distinguish the takeoff area, but the favorite spot to go in is out front of the aquarium, so it's called the Aquarium. With hard, bold rights and lefts in a 6-foot swell, it feathers and sections as one of the longest rides in Kewalo Basin—a fantastically consistent peeling wave. There is rarely a closeout in offshore conditions. In onshore winds it's a peaky, mushy fun wave with lots of closeout sections—very unpre-

Kewalos, Oahu. PHOTO ROD SUMPTER

dictable. Home to many of Honolulu's most talented surfers, this is a hard spot to surf uncrowded. Ideal for the intermediate surfer when it's 2 to 3 feet, and for the experienced when it's over 4 feet.

Local Events/Attractions

Sampans and other fishing boats moor in the small-boat harbor of **Kewalo Basin,** which is also the departure point for Pearl Harbor cruises.

Marine Land is mostly a right-hand reef break straight out from the aquarium—a reef ledge that peels best from low to medium tide. Paddle out across a 200-yard lagoon, then thread through the reef to get to the takeoff.

Big Rights is an A-frame peak on bigger days (around 6 feet) on a south swell. A classic drop puts you into a fast wall and tube that favors the rights all the time. Some of the best waves in the area when it's 4 to 8 feet.

Concessions. Left- and right-hand peaks here rarely disappoint. The wave stands up with a lot of face. Easy power turning under fast-breaking sections 200 yards from shore. Easy access—it's straight out from the ice cream stand at the beach. More than 3 feet deep, this coral lagoon offers a great peak.

Tennis Courts. Green walling waves off black lava-rock outcrops give short clear-water barrels with light trade winds. Early mornings are best in spring and summer.

Baby Haleiwa is a right-hand peak that breaks and peels from deep water; the wave walls well. It's located just outside Magic Island's west breakwater entrance. There's easy access from the beach—paddle over the lagoon out through the gap in the rocks and straight into the fading end of the break.

Bamburas, a left- and right-hand reef 200 yards from shore, is frequently good at dawn on a 4- to 6-foot south swell. It's best, however, with a swell of 6 feet and light offshore northeast winds. Easy parking in Ala Moana Beach Park.

Magic Island. Rarely good, this fickle spot is best on a big south swell. Walk through Ala Moana Beach Park and out to Magic Island; there's a breakwall paddle-through. You'll see some hot waves on the left toward Ala Moana. Easy parking in Ala Mona Beach Park.

Ala Moana

This left-hand reef break is the symbol of great South Shore waves. Packed and very competitive, it's virtually reserved for locals who know how to surf inside the bowl. The bowl is just that—an inside-out section halfway in that forms between the Ala Moana boating channel and the Pacific Ocean. It holds waves of 4 to 12 feet. The takeoff is steep and fast; getting caught behind is a risk. The wave goes to the bowl superfast.

Best Tides: Low to medium.

Best Swell Direction: South.

Best Wave Size: Head high to overhead.

Bottom: Coral.

Type of Break: Left-hand reef break.

Skill Level: Advanced due to a tricky paddle-out.

Best Boards: Shortboard.

Best Seasons: Summer.

Crowds: Crowded.

Water Quality: Clean.

Hazards: Sharks and strong localism.

Fees and Permits: No fees or permits are required.

Schedule: Public access 24/7.

Finding the Break

From the Honolulu International Airport, go east on Nimitz Highway toward Waikiki for 7 miles, then turn left onto Atkinson Drive. Continue to Ala Moana Beach Park and walk out to Magic Island. There's a breakwall; the break is just off to the right. You can enter off either the boulder rocks or the little sand path into the channel. Watch out for boats.

Surf Description

Jumping into the channel at dawn and facing the bowl while boats, a strong undertow, and possibly sharks surround you sharpens the senses and really motivates precise surfing. This left-hand reef break epitomizes great South Shore waves.

Situated 2 miles northeast of Waikiki, opposite Ala Moana Shopping Center, this break is packed with crowds whenever it's good. The ultracompetitive surfing means that the spot is fiercely guarded by locals, who know how to surf it inside out. So watch out. Rides are intense with a curl factor of 50 percent, which means a lot of surfers flailing in the channel. Rides can measure 200 yards but are usually 50 to 100.

Ala Moana has some of the best scenery on Oahu: bright blue water teeming with fish, a large yachting community set against the backdrop of Diamond Head, and the splendid Honolulu skyline. This is a city break in a country environment with strong marine traditions of canoes, markets, and weekend festivals. Surfers hang out here on weekends, and when it's pumping, you can watch some amazing maneuvers, aerials, and wipeouts performed by the heroes of Honolulu's surf.

Ala Moana, Oahu. PHOTO ROD SUMPTER

Rockpile claims many injuries at low tide, but offers good high-tide lefts and rights. Classic tubes and fast sections over razor-sharp reefs make this a dangerous break. Access is over coral—not easy.

In-Betweens is a lava reef with lots of ledges that features hollow rights and lefts breaking over shallow coral. It's found to the right of Rockpiles. Park near the Halekolani Hotel and paddle out.

Fours. Mostly lefts with the odd right, this reef (located 300 yards out from Fort De Russy Park) is crowded most of the time. Paddle out over flat water 4 feet deep to reefs that become too shallow. Several gullies are deep enough to pass out to the break.

Kaisers, a right- and left-hand reef break, is famous for its consistent, quality waves and steaming tubes and barrels. To get there, paddle out by the boat channel for the *Atlantis* submarine. Expect localism to be strong.

Threes, a right- and left-hand reef break 300 yards out from Fort De Russy parking lot, is south of Fours and very similar. These outer reefs pick up a good south swell and are visible from all the high-rise hotels as part of the Waikiki vista. The break is out past the Halekoa Hotel.

Paradise, an ace A-frame peak that's way out there, has some classic walls; it's one of the best spots in Waikiki, and ideal for the intermediate surfer. This is one of the waves that made Waikiki famous.

Populars. A long paddle from the beach out over a lagoon will bring you out and around to the takeoff area for this break, which is mostly a right-hand wave with some lefts. Classic Hawaiian spot with magical waves.

Canoes. This easygoing beginner's break is one of the best places in the world to learn to surf. Rarely head high, it's a mellow, friendly wave with good karma and the right spirit of aloha.

Waikiki

The beachfront of Honolulu, the capital city of Oahu, is the most famous surf beach anywhere—period. Duke Kahanamoku Beach, in front of his statue, generally has small, quality waves for beginners as well as access to outer reefs; a great learn-to-surf spot.

Best Tides: Low tide if it's 2 feet, high tide if it's over 3 feet.

Best Swell Direction: South to southwest.

Best Wave Size: Hip to head high.

Bottom: Sand and coral.

Type of Break: Left- and right-hand reef break.

Skill Level: Beginner to intermediate.

Best Boards: Longboards and shortboards.

Best Seasons: Summer, fall, and winter.

Crowds: Crowded.

Water Quality: Clean.

Hazards: Shallow coral-reef-and-sand bottom, localism.

Fees and Permits: No fees or permits are required.

Schedule: Public access 24/7.

Finding the Break

From the Honolulu International Airport, take Interstate H1 east. Get off at the Punahou exit and turn right onto Punahou Street. At the first intersection, turn right onto Beretania Street. Get into the far left lane to turn left onto Kalakaua Avenue. Continue on Kalakaua for approximately 1.5 miles, then turn left onto Lili`uokalani; look for parking lots after the third stoplight past the International Marketplace. Ask for break directions from the lifeguards in front of the police station on the beach.

Surf Description

There's no better place to learn to surf the Hawaiian way than at Waikiki. This is where the great Duke Kahanamoko mastered the surf. Paddle into the beautiful lines of swell out on the reefs, under the awe-inspiring view of Diamond Head. Slide into waves that lift, rise, and break gracefully, ride with style, and carve off spinning curls toward the most famous beachfront on the planet.

There's no other wave that has taught more surfers to surf, seen more surfers stand up for their first time, or symbolized the idea of surfing to more people than Waikiki. Its fantastic soft, feathering reef-break waves offer some of the longest rides in the Hawaiian Islands.

Waikiki, Oahu. PHOTO ROD SUMPTER

Local Events/Attractions

- At the **T&C Keiki Surf Contest,** June, kids under fourteen vie in long-, short-, and bodyboard competitions on Queen's Surf Beach, Waikiki. Call Town and Country Surf at (808) 483–8383.

- The **Rubber Ducky Race,** a cerebral palsy fund-raiser, is held in March at the Ala Wai Canal; (808) 532–6744; www.ucpahi.org.

- The **World of Pageantry Festival** includes drill teams, marching bands, and ROTC units performing at Royal Hawaiian Shop Center, as well as a Salute to Youth Parade along Kalakaua Avenue, all in March. Call (808) 922–2299.

- **Kapiolani Park,** Kalakaua Avenue, between Kapahulu and Paki Avenues in Waikiki, is a hundred-acre public park. One of the most popular recreation areas in Waikiki, it's the site of many local events. Home of the Kapiolani bandstand, Honolulu Zoo, an aquarium, and the Kodak Hula Show.

- **Submarine Museum and Park,** Pearl Harbor, adjacent to the USS *Arizona* Memorial Visitor Center. A 1,500-ton submarine is open to the public daily, 8:00 A.M.–5:00 P.M. Admission is $7.00 adults, $2.00 children. Contact (808) 423–1341.

- **USS *Arizona* Memorial,** Arizona Place and Hawaii Route 90, Pearl Harbor. The memorial is directly over the battleship *Arizona,* which sank during the December 7, 1941, Japanese attack on Pearl Harbor, entombing 1,102 servicemen on board. It's open 7:30 A.M.–5:00 P.M. daily, with a video shown 8:00 A.M.–3:00 P.M. Call (808) 422–2771.

Cunhas reef break offers a long paddle and good longboarding in swells of 3 to 6 feet—but when the surf is overhead, this break becomes a fiery freight train closing out, and the outer breaks take over and run through. It needs a south swell.

Queens is a perfect right-hand reef for carving on a longboard and shortboard on 6-foot days. In the lee of all the hotels, it handles winds well. A very consistent break with some lefts.

Kuhio, next to the Sheraton Moana Surfrider, provides the quickest access to the Waikiki shoreline. The stretch in front of the Royal Hawaiian Hotel has a straight-off outer reef that peels at times. A good, fun spot

Sans Souci. Youngsters bodysurf on big summer swells at this popular beach in front of the New Otani Kaimana beach, best known for its sheltered position and neat shorebreak.

Publics is a longboarder's smooth, easy cruising-type wave from several reefs; with long rides, it's best in a big south swell, when it really honks. An all-time great Hawaiian break, mellow but crowded.

Castles. This outer reef is a long way out—the farthest breaking waves. Long lines of waves peel in an armada of round-shouldered walls along straight-edge swell. Made famous in black-and-white photos from the 1950s, this left-hand reef break needs a big south swell to fire. One of the all-time great Hawaiian breaks.

Old Mans, beside the Outrigger Canoe Club, is a long tidy left and a short walling right, ideal for longboards and easy surfing for outrigger canoes. On a big south swell, the reefs farther out break, and the possibilities as a classic break come alive. Where the rich and famous now hang out.

Ricebowl. Long, graceful longboarding waves that get gnarly quickly with a drop in the tide. On the south side of the Outrigger Canoe Club, Ricebowl has good shortboard and occasional canoe waves. Neat spot to surf 4 to 6 feet.

Tongs. On most swells between 2 and 4 feet, this is a soft-breaking right and left reef break, but on bigger swells it turns into a steaming, piping barrel with shifting peaks and a heavy wall. It's found straight out from Kapiolani Park; access is between houses at the east end of the park.

Graveyards. A left-hand coral reef with a long wall, Graveyards needs a 4- to 6-foot swell to start working properly—and then it's insane. Paddle out for easy access from Diamond Head Beach Park.

Suicides is an outer left reef break with a barrel straight out from Diamond Head Beach; it's known for its closeout takeout onto a shallow reef and unmakable sections. Can be a good bodyboarding wave.

Sleepy Hollow is a quality reef break and fun shortboarding over 6 feet; under head high it's best as a longboard wave. Long, even lines comb into this section of Diamond Head and separate, leaving the west end isolated and uncrowded. Good waves in small swells make this a busy spot on 2- to 3-foot days.

Diamond Head Lighthouse

This left- and right-hand reef picks up most south swells and is often the best spot on the South Shore. Protected from trade winds by Diamond Head, it's a great surfing venue. Classic 4- to 6-foot waves peel right, and the view is awesome: Waves stack up to the horizon, where Diamond Head rises 600 feet, while surfers take off and power across three reefs.

Best Tides: Low to medium.

Best Swell Direction: South.

Best Wave Size: Chest high to overhead.

Bottom: Sand and reef.

Type of Break: Left- and right-hand reef break.

Skill Level: Intermediate to experienced.

Best Boards: Shortboards and longboards.

Best Seasons: Summer, fall, and winter.

Crowds: Crowded.

Water Quality: Clean.

Hazards: Sharks.

Fees and Permits: No fees or permits are required.

Schedule: Public access 24/7.

Finding the Break

From the Honolulu International Airport, take Interstate H1 east. Pass Waikiki, take the Koko Head off-ramp, then take any road toward the water. Once you're on the waterside, head toward Diamond Head. As you near the landmark, take Kalakaua Avenue to Beach Road to the roadside parking area. At the right of the parking area, walk down the paved trail to the beach, then straight out into the waves.

Diamond Head Lighthouse, Oahu. PHOTO ROD SUMPTER

Surf Description

Drop in late, turn hard, gun around the curl up into the pocket, and head for the blue space of freedom. This fast left- and right-hander below Diamond Head is a semi-A-frame reef break 300 feet below the parking area. If it's a pumping swell, takeoffs are excellent for experienced surfers who can tuck into the barrel; for intermediates there's room to cruise long, soft walls, staying out of the hook. The waves bend and blend into reefs, forming peaks all the way from Cliffs to Lighthouse and taking on all kinds of swell directions. You never ride two waves the same here, and you don't end up in the same paddle-out spot, either.

Situated 3 miles south of Waikiki, this is the all-time great place for high-up views of surfing. All kinds of things happen when you surf this great break. One of the first things that impresses you as you wax up on a 6-foot day with light offshore winds is how clean and clear the water is. And from atop the cliffs, the swells appear in patterns, emphasizing the depth or shallowness of the ocean floor and making it easy to read what the swell will be doing next. Just off the Lunalilo Freeway, this is a first-choice break in south and west swells. There aren't many surf spots around the world with such a fabulous view from 300-foot cliffs next to an extinct volcano crater, overlooking crystal-clear surfing reefs. Ideal for the intermediate to expert surfer.

Local Events/Attractions

Each December, participants in the **Honolulu Marathon** run from Waikiki to Diamond Head. Contact (808) 734–7200.

Cliffs. Three lookouts make up this stretch of coastline from Lighthouse to Black Point. Only keen surfers pick their way down to surf these reef breaks and get away from the crowds. Ranging from 600 yards to 50 yards, from shallow to deep, this slip of ocean has a lot to offer. Difficult access.

Ka`alawai Point, also known as Browns, is a big-wave spot off the west side of Black Point. It's a classic ride on the right swell, and a big swell can be epic. It's also a dangerous spot if you break a leash and have to swim—sharky.

Mahoney, a left- and right-hand reef break, is difficult to access, requiring a long walk and paddle-out through reefs. The fun waves hold up well, however, and if it's not too big, this can be a good session midweek. It's crowded on weekends.

Kahala is a reef break 150 yards out that gives mostly short lefts. Easy access near the hotels. Good bodyboarding waves; hollow and fast on any southeast-to-south swells.

Ka`alawai Beach is a fickle bodyboarding beach break located at the end of Kulumanu Place. It's a narrow patch of white sand beside Black Point—Oahu's southernmost point—where lava flowing from Diamond Head entered into the sea.

Black Point is a left-hand reef break. The hollow, shallow reef provides low-tide surfing for longboards, shortboards, and bodyboards, but it needs south swell. Rock-hopping entry. It lies opposite some million-dollar houses.

Wailupe. This left- and right-hand reef break needs a summer south swell to happen. The paddle-out is in front of the Aina Haina Hotel, where a beach break and the reef start in Maunalua Bay. Early morning is best here, with clean, fast lefts and rights. Long paddle-out. Located along Kalaniana`ole Highway.

Toes Reef, Koko Beach Park. Left- and right-hand peaks, with lots of reef-hopping into some seriously thick, chunky waves that do throw out on a southeast-to-south swell. You'll largely find short barrels; at low tide the urchins present further problems. For experienced surfers only.

Taiko Drive is a left-hand reef break with short, fickle waves and difficult access that's rarely crowded except on weekends. Not known for consistency, it's flat much of the year.

Turtles breaks way out. It's a long, difficult paddle to this mostly left reef, but in a small swell it can be fun overhead. A bit dangerous due to the sucking reef.

Pole is a beginner to intermediate surfer's spot with fun waves of 2 to 3 feet—and rarely any bigger.

Fingers. Lefts and rights off a finger of reef makes for short walls; the shape can be good. It's also dangerous here: Intense surfing is required to escape the reef and a possible trip to the doctor.

China Walls. This left-hand point break, riding close to boulder rocks, can get good on a southeast swell. Like the Great Wall of China, this walling wave is a classic when it's 6 to 8 feet and pumping. Experts only.

Portlock Point is a right-hand reef break with difficult access between pieces of private property. There are also many hazards in the water, including a sharp reef, murky water, and sharks. It's mostly surfed by locals.

Wall. Left- and right-hand waves break up against the cliff face to create backwash conditions and very short rides over a shallow reef.

Sandy Beach

This is a seriously hardcore surf spot, one of the world's ultimate bodysurfing and body-boarding sites. It's a bone-crushing left- and right-hand beach break with a pounding shorebreak. Lifeguards make more rescues in a year here than on any other beach in the state.

Best Tides: Low to medium.

Best Swell Direction: South.

Best Wave Size: Chest high to triple over-head.

Bottom: Sand.

Type of Break: Left- and right-hand beach break.

Skill Level: Intermediate to advanced.

Best Boards: Bodyboards.

Best Seasons: Fall and winter.

Crowds: Crowded.

Water Quality: Clean.

Hazards: Dangerous rip currents, shallow sand bottom, localism.

Fees and Permits: No fees or permits are required.

Schedule: Public access 24/7.

Finding the Break

From Waikiki, take Interstate H1 east; it becomes Hawaii Route 72. Continue east through a residential area, then along the coast past Hanauma Bay. Sandy Beach is on the left side of the road. Look for a large sign by the entrance.

Surf Description

There are few places in the world where the waves actually make a *crack* sound as they break on the beach. Sandy Beach is one of them. The waves slam down on the shore in an incredible display of Pacific power. Amazingly, there's still room enough for vertical pocket turns, rolls, loops, and disappearing tunnel rides.

A local favorite, this extreme surf spot lies southeast of Waikiki and 2 miles east of Hanauma Bay on the Kalaniana`ole Highway. Sandy Beach is the ultimate left and right beach-break spot, with some of the hardest, angriest small waves on the planet. It's a shorebreak second to none, with more neck injuries and broken arms occurring here than anywhere else in Hawaii. (Local surfers and international experts here make body-surfing look so easy that many tourists give it a try, which results in even more acci-dents.) This is where short, fast, hollow tube rides might last only seconds and run only 20 yards on a good wave, but may still produce the most exciting bodysurfing or body-boarding ride of your life.

Nestled below volcanic mountains and lava hills, this is the first out-of-town spot on the South Shore. It's a powerful short wave that breaks very quickly and occasionally doubles up. The drag of the water as it sucks back into the ocean after a wave has bro-ken helps create an even more powerful wave. All the waves are close to shore, very

Sandy Beach, Oahu. PHOTO ROD SUMPTER

short, and fast, in knee-depth water. A left-hand reef point 100 yards on the left side of the beach is good for shortboards. The best surf is in summer, when the south swells arrive consistently from April to September, and with wave heights from 2 to 8 feet.

Although the waves are lovely to watch, even the finest surfers can be tricked during takeoff on what becomes a closeout from top to bottom or an over-the-falls wipeout. There are lifeguards on duty on weekends and during surf-alert High Sea Warnings. Sandy Beach is for experienced bodyboarders and bodysurfers and expert surfers only.

Local Events/Attractions

On the far right side of the beach, you'll find the much-photographed **Blow Hole,** which signals the arrival of swell with a jet of spray forced 20 feet in the air from a hole in the lava rock.

Half Point is a left-hander (with the occassional perfect-breaking right) inside Full Point over shallow coral. Entry is from the beach between outcrops of rocks; the paddle-out can see very hollow waves on good days. The area may be turned into a nature park and reserve.

Full Point, from Sandy Beach East Reefs. A mile and a half of ultra-fast short and shallow reef breaks stretching to Wawamalu Beach creates classic waves. It's a playground for daredevils who know how to barrel-ride and wipe out on sharp coral without getting hurt. Hardcore surfing at its best can be viewed from several trails through dunes.

Pipe, Wawamalu Beach, is a bodysurfing beach break. Heavy waves close out the small cove here, which is rocky along the shoreline and has two working breaks; the outer one is the bigger.

Littles. A reef ledge with fast, hollow waves right on sharp coral. Access is difficult via a rough road through dunes and scrubland and then a walk that's best with booties. Big and gnarly barrels.

Irma's is a classic left- and right-hand reef break that peels off farther out as the swells grow in size. It's mostly a bodyboarding spot for those who can handle steep, quick waves. Getting in requires a rock-hopping entry over sharp lava. Good viewing from the roadside gets you stoked. This is the spot that tells you the swell direction.

Middles is a hard right-hand walling wave that runs fast past rocks. Difficult access. *Note:* As this book went to press, plans were afoot to make the entire Kaiwi coastline (from Sandy Beach Park to Makapu`u) a protected area.

Generals. This fast reef break off the beaten track provides uncrowded waves in 2 to 8 feet in a south and southeast swell. For the advanced surfer, this is the spot to get away from the crowds of Sandy Beach.

Suicides is a hollow right- and occasional left-hand reef break with an insane rock-hoppy entry down a trail of difficult paths. Not far from Sea Life Park, where the view is epic. Take off below the cliffs here, carve across a 6- to 8-foot wave, and you could well hit the cliffs—the spot is suitable for expert and advanced surfers. Don't leave valuables in your car, and expect to find localism.

Makapu`u

The most famous bodysurfing spot in Hawaii is a 0.5-mile-long gold-sand beach surrounded by black Ko`olau cliffs on Oahu's easternmost point. Only bodyboards are allowed here, and those only up to 3 feet, with no fin. You'll also find restrooms, lifeguards, barbecue grills, picnic tables, and parking.

Best Tides: Low to medium.

Best Swell Direction: East.

Best Wave Size: Chest high to overhead.

Bottom: Sand.

Type of Break: Left and right.

Skill Level: Intermediate to advanced.

Best Boards: Bodysurfing and bodyboards.

Best Seasons: Fall and winter.

Crowds: Crowded.

Water Quality: Clean.

Hazards: High surf, fierce shorebreak, and strong undertow often occur during winter months. Check with the lifeguards regarding ocean conditions before entering the water. Obey all postings and warnings.

Fees and Permits: No fees or permits are required.

Schedule: Public access 24/7.

Finding the Break

From Waikiki, take Interstate H1 east; it will become Hawaii Route 72. Continue east through a residential area, then along the coast past Hanauma Bay. The break is on the left side of the road; there's a large sign by the entrance. You can also take The Bus No. 57 or 58.

Makapu`u, Oahu. PHOTO ROD SUMPTER

Surf Description

Stroke in looking over the falls, putting your right arm straight out and cupping your right hand into a fin-*cum*-handboard, keeping your left arm tight beside your body. Kick hard, judging the lineup and the barrel. This is surfing at Makapu`u, one of the most dynamic bodysurfing breaks in the world.

Famed for long, fast, sloping curl lines across crystal-clear swells and thumping closeouts into impacted white sand, this spot's bruising barrels and clear water make for mega bodysurfing. This beach break is the original bodysurfing spot—the one that made Oahu's east coast famous. It's where lifeguards are kept busy as swimmers and bodysurfers vie for position on the best waves. Days over 6 feet really separate the men from the boys—this is a seriously heavy surf spot demanding respect.

Twelve miles east of Waikiki and 3 miles south of Kailua, this beautiful beach sits below the Ko`olau Mountains catching an east swell and plenty of offshore winds. Best in winter, it's located below Makapu`u Point, a projection of land marking Hawaii's easternmost tip. (*Makapu`u,* by the way, means "bulging eyes.") Large waves and riptides can make swimming hazardous. Rabbit Island sits just offshore and makes this beach very picturesque.

Local Events/Attractions

- The **Kamehameha Canoe Regatta** is held at Kailua Bay each June.

- **Sea Life Park** at Makapu`u Point features an outstanding display of Hawaii's exotic marine life in a beautiful oceanside setting. The 300,000-gallon Hawaiian Reef Tank houses 2,000 island specimens: sharks, rays, moray eels, turtles, and exotic reef fish. You'll also find giant whales, dolphins, sea lions, penguins, and a variety of seabirds.

Rabbit Island (Manana Island) is a long right-hander that sweeps around the island to the northwest corner, creating a California type of point surf. Take a dive boat from the Makai Research Center pier (contact info@hawaiiscubadiving.com), or make the long paddle over.

Waimanalo Beach is a wide white-sand beach break with good small-wave bodysurfing and bodyboarding. It's popular on a big east swell when the hard onshores kick up some size and the barrels are tough.

Bellows beach break is a popular beach and surf spot when the swell's up. It's mostly a beginner's bodysurfing spot. It has shallow bars and a small, consistent shorebreak. Two lifeguard towers.

Lanikai Beach is good for longboards, shortboards, and body-boarding on a long strip of sand and several peaks on outside reefs. You can simply park at Ku`ulou on the side of the road and paddle out; it's deep enough that you don't have to walk on the reef. No showers; free parking. Located on the northeast side of Kailua.

The **Mokulua Islands** are two small islands situated about 0.5 mile off the shore of Lanikai Beach in Kailua. The islands are uninhabited, but are the home to native birds called `iwa. Many people visit the islands and enjoy recreational activities such as hiking, swimming, surfing, kayaking, and snorkeling.

Flat Island (Popoia Island) is a left reef break needing a northeast swell. From the beach it's a five-minute paddle out to the island. A popular picnic and surfing spot, Flat Island is a designated bird sanctuary.

Kailua Bay is a popular spot with a submerged coral reef. Exposure to steady northeast trade winds creates ideal conditions—indeed, this is considered the island's windsurfing capital. Several consistent surf areas, known collectively as Kailua surf break, occur offshore. Boating, camping, sunbathing, swimming, fishing, snorkeling, and kayaking are also important activities in this area.

Kailua Beach. Beach-break and shorebreak waves can be a fun at this 2-mile stretch of sandy shore between Alâla Point (Lanikai Point) and Kapoho Point that backs Kailua Bay. It's mostly popular for windsurfing and bodyboarding. A submerged coral reef extends across much of Kailua Bay at a depth of around 20 feet.

North Beach is a beach break with shallow reefs and neat, fun waves on an east swell. Located on a military base, it's restricted to U.S. Marines and their guests.

Sugar Mill

This left- and right-hand reef break sits 200 yards offshore over a shallow first reef that leads out to a middle and outer reef. Sugar Mill has excellent fun waves when an easterly swell direction is running with a light west wind or light air. Inside waves are soft and tricky to ride. They require skill to rip. If you progress out to the bigger and steeper outer reef, you could get a ride to remember. Ideal for longboards on small days and when the swell is waist to head high.

Best Tides: Low coming in.

Best Swell Direction: East.

Best Wave Size: Chest high to double overhead.

Bottom: Sand and reef.

Type of Break: Left- and right-hand reef break.

Skill Level: Intermediate to advanced.

Best Boards: Short- and longboards.

Best Seasons: Fall and winter.

Crowds: Crowded, especially on weekends.

Water Quality: Clean.

Hazards: Sharks.

Fees and Permits: No fees or permits are required.

Schedule: Public access 24/7.

Finding the Break

Sugar Mill is found off the Kamehameha Highway about 2 miles south of Kaaawa, a tiny town near the Crouching Lion rock formation. The Kualoa Ranch and Activity Club is about 1 mile farther south.

Surf Description

If you drive along the coast on a good day and the distant reefs blow back the spray of far-off breaking waves, you know you're in for some great waves at Sugar Mill.

Sugar Mill is situated on the east coast 14 miles south of La`ie and 1 mile south of Kaaawa Park. The first reef break, which is a left- and right-hander, sits 200 yards offshore and leads out to a middle reef. An outer reef is 1000 yards farther out. The inner reefs have excellent fun waves with a strong easterly swell direction and light wind blowing. Inside is a soft wave, which is tricky to ride and requires skill to rip as you progress across feathering walls and bigger, steeper, and uneven sections. It's fun at its best. The outer reef picks up any swell and is ideal on small days, although it will need to be 4 feet to break. Otherwise, swell passes through to the inner reefs, which makes the middle reef work. So outside is mostly a big wave type of spot, with a dynamic wave for the very experienced surfer. It's a longboarder's dream wave of sorts when the swell is head high and the numerous peaks break clean. Remember that here on the east coast it is usually only onshore winds and the consistent trade winds that produce a window of groundswell. So the type of wave is generally mushy to messy on the backs of waves with clean wave faces. Ideal for intermediate and above in the right conditions.

Sugar Mill, Oahu. PHOTO ROD SUMPTER

Kanenelu is a fun longboard wave. Some of the outer reefs—which do get big on occasion—can produce clean lines to surf with a big board. Expect a long paddle, and you're likely to be on your own if it's 8 feet. Best the day after strong east swell and west winds.

Polynesian Cultural Center is a fickle bodysurfing and bodyboarding beach and reef break that picks up a lot of east swell. It tends to break more than other local spots. Crowded when it's good.

Pounders is a great beach break at Kokololio Beach Park with some of the most fun bodysurfing and bodyboarding waves in Hawaii. Famous for the caves backwash and sidewash peaks on the right side of the beach. Can be epic shortboarding. Easy parking.

Malaekahana Bay, Goat Island (Moku`auia Island)

A short right- and long left-hand reef break with a long paddle-out. Strong currents and shifts in the reef make it a new experience to get used to—the reef plate pulls and pushes the water depth with each wave.

Best Tides: Medium.

Best Swell Direction: Northeast.

Best Wave Size: Knee high to overhead.

Bottom: Reef.

Type of Break: Left and right.

Skill Level: Experienced to advanced.

Best Boards: Shortboards; also long-boards on small days.

Best Seasons: Fall and winter.

Crowds: Sometimes crowded.

Water Quality: Clean.

Hazards: Sharks.

Fees and Permits: No fees or permits are required.

Schedule: Public access 24/7.

Finding the Break

Malaekahana Bay is found off Kamehameha Highway. It's a few miles north of La`ie in the Malaekahana Recreation Area on Oahu's Windward Coast.

Surf Description

Looking out to Goat Island's surf off Malaekahana Bay, there is no way of knowing exactly how smooth, hollow, or dangerous it is—at 800 yards, it's just too far away. This seems to always make the water look better, and so you'll find yourself paddling out and into some waves that might make you want to turn back.

Situated 1 mile north of La`ie is a pancake-shaped lava rock called Goat Island. The center of the island is a restricted refuge area for ground-dwelling seabirds raising their young. Once you're out on an average day of 3 to 5 feet, you'll encounter huge shifts in the plate of water over the reef you're paddling on. This may sound weird, but it's a very strange feeling to find the bottom only 3 feet away as a wave pulls in and sucks the reef shallower. Then it slides you sideways at 6 miles an hour as the hump of the reef drains water to the sides. It's like being on a roller coaster, and it's fine once you get used to it. The wave itself is a fast left and right peak off the center of the reef, but the lefts offer the longer ride—200 yards or more on a good day. This spot is ideal for the experienced to expert surfer.

Goat Island, Oahu. PHOTO ROD SUMPTER

Local Events/Attractions

Two miles north of the break, the **Polynesian Cultural Center** at La`ie is made up of native villages representative of those in Fiji, Tonga, New Zealand, Tahiti, Samoa, the Marquesas, and Hawaii.

Seventh Hole, off the Kahuku golf course. There are some serious big-wave reefs from 300 to 800 yards offshore. Always heavy and pounding in blown-out seas during strong trade winds, these peaks have good shape when the conditions switch. Remote location.

Kahuku Point. This extreme right-hand point surf wave with a left reef break works best in a 6- to 8-foot northwest swell and light south wind. The left into the beach on strong trade-wind days can be an epic wave. It's a fickle spot, for the advanced surfer.

Turtle Bay offers reef breaks and sharp coral lefts and rights over black lava spikes and caves. Very fickle short rides and difficult access, beside a private hotel.

Kawela Bay is mostly a right. It rarely breaks well, but when it does, it's a good longboard and bodyboard reef break with a white-sand beach and snorkeling. It's fickle, changing with the tides.

Oahu Resources

Hawaii Activities Offices
Aloha Tower, 5th Floor
1 Aloha Tower Drive
Honolulu, Oahu 96813
(877) 877–1222 or (808) 524–0008
Fax: (808) 599-3778
www.hawaiiactivities.com

Aloha Airlines Baggage Offices
Honolulu, Oahu
(808) 837–6816

Getting Around

If you stay in Waikiki—any of the beachfront hotels will do—you'll never need a car. Just rent a bike or motorbike to visit top surf spots (Ala Moana and so many more) close to Waikiki.

The Bus can take you around the island to see the South and North Shores for only $1.00:

The Bus
www.thebus.org

For information on renting a car, see the Introduction. If you plan to visit for a month or longer, you may decide to buy a car and then resell it at the end of your trip. If so, check out the following resources:

Aloha AUTO-Search
www.alohaautosearch.com

Island Auto Exchange
99-022 Kamehameha Highway
Aiea, Oahu
(808) 486–7177

JN Chevrolet Mazda Mazerati
2999 North Nimitz Highway
Honolulu, Oahu
(808) 831–2500

Reno Motors Incorporated
3103 North Nimitz Highway
Honolulu, Oahu
(808) 833–7555

Surf Shops

Classic Surfboards
451 Kapahulu Avenue
Honolulu, Oahu 96815
(808) 735–3594

Tropical Rush Surf Company
62-620A Kamehameha Highway
Haleiwa, Oahu 96712
(808) 637–8886
Fax: (808) 637–8516
www.tropicalrushhawaii.com

Surf Lessons

Hans Hedemann Surf School
(808) 924–7778
www.hhsurf.com

Hawaiian Fire Surf School
3318 Campbell Avenue
Honolulu, Oahu 96815
(888) 955–7873 or (808) 737–9473
www.hawaiianfire.com

Kai Nalu Surf Tours
536 Kahua Place
Paia, Maui 96779
(808) 579–9937
Fax: (808) 579–9937
www.mauisurfing.com

North Shore Surf Camp
Karen Gallagher
P.O. Box 172
Haleiwa, Oahu 96712
(808) 638–5914 or (808) 372–6289
www.northshoresurfcamps.com

Stan Van Voorhis III
P.O. Box 1174
Haleiwa, Oahu 96712
(808) 638–9503
www.ecosurf-hawaii.com

CHAPTER 6

Kauai

A rriving at the Lihue Airport where the mountains drape right down to the sea and the waves barrel and spit, you realize why Kauai is known as the Garden Island. From high up at Princeville, you can look down at Hanalei Bay with the Na Pali Mountains behind and measure surfers' wakes, their profile and skill, against the tropical greenery reaching for the heavens. For a moment you'll think you're in paradise. Here are challenging breaks such as Cannons with its fast-action left-hander, and the dangerous Tunnels on the North Shore. The town of Hanalei is packed with surf shops, shaved-ice parlors, cafes selling Kauai-blend coffee, and an activity center to put you in the frame of mind for other sports if the surf is flat—say, hiking the Na Pali Mountains, kayaking or snorkeling Hanalei Bay, or fishing the beach and reefs. The people of Kauai are very friendly to traveling surfers, and there are more churches of different denominations here than you'll find on any other Hawaiian island.

You cannot drive around the northwest coastline—there are no roads over the spots where the ribbed volcanic cliffs plunge into the ocean. But you can reach the dead-end road on the lower northwest side of the island and surf a 7-mile beach called Polihale before returning to the south coast.

Regional Map

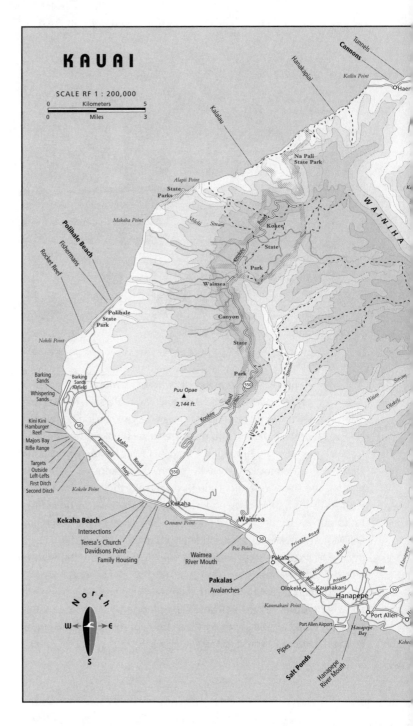

KAUAI

SCALE RF 1 : 200,000

| 0 | Kilometers | 5 |

| 0 | Miles | 3 |

Tunnels

Cannons

Hanakapiai

Kailiu Point

Haer

Kalalau

Na Pali
State Park

W A I N I H A

Alapii Point

State
Parks

Makaha Point

Mllolii   Stream   Road

Kokee

Polihale Beach

Fishermans

Kokee   State

Rocket Reef

Park

Waimea

Nohili Point

Polihale
State
Park

Canyon

State

Barking
Sands

Barking
Sands
Airfield

Park

Stream

Whispering
Sands

Kini Kini
Hamburger
Reef

Puu Opae
▲
2,144 ft.

550

Waiua   Stream

Kokee   Road

Majors Bay
Rifle Range

Okdele

Waipa

Targets
Outside
Left-Lefts

550

First Ditch
Second Ditch

Kokole Point

Kekaha

50

Kaumualii   Hwy

Maha   Road

Kekaha Beach

Oonano Point

Waimea

Intersections

50

Private   Road

Teresa's Church

Davidsons Point

Poe Point

Road

Family Housing

Waimea
River Mouth

Pakala

Kaumualii Hwy

Private   Road

Hanapepe

Pakalas

Private

Avalanches

Olokele

Kaumakani

50

North

Kaumakani Point

Hanapepe

W ← ✦ → E

Port Allen Airport

Port Allen

S

Hanapepe
Bay

Koheo

Pipes

Salt Ponds

Hanapepe
River Mouth

Hideaways

Kalihiwai Beach

MOKUAEAE Island

Kilauea Point

Hanalei Bay

The Bowl
Middle Break

Cliffs

Anini Road

Kalihiwai Bay

Kalihiwai

Mokolea Point

Kilauea Bay

Kilauea Point

Kepuhi Point

Princeville

Princeville
Airport

56

Kilauea

Hanalei

Kuhio

Rock Bay

Moloaa Bay

Kaloko
Res.

Hwy.

Papaa Bay

56

Anahola Bay

Mamalahoa
3,745 ft.

Kalihiwai River

Hanalei River

Pui Ka Ele

Anahola

Kuaehu Point

Gas
Chambers

Kahala Point

Anahola Stream

Opana Point

Wekiu
3,255 ft.

Kealia Stream

Pohakuloa Point

Crack 14

Donkey
Beach

Kealia

River

Kumukumu

Wailua

Kuamoo

Road

Kapaa

56

Pono Kai

Waipouli

Kamala
Reservoir

Wailua River

Wailua

Coconut Beach

Kauai Sands

Horners

Wailua Bay

Coco Palms

Kitchens

Kilohana
Crater

1,133 ft.

Cemeteries

Kaiwaloa

Outrigger

Hanamaulu

Ahukini Point

Maluhia Road

56

Ahukini Road

Lihue

Lihue
Airport

Puhi

Nawiliwili Road

Huleia Road

Ninini Point

Private

Kupu

Nuimalu

Nawiliwili Lihue

Kauai Point

Amonia's

Nohiu Bay

Hoary Dead Range

Lawai

50

Omao

Koloa

Kaumualii Hwy

Waita
Res.

Kuahnu Point

530

520

Road

Koloa

Kawelikao Point

Private Road

Maluhia

Kamala Point

Last Volcanic
Eruption

Lawai Bay

Sheraton

Poipu

Hyatt Regency

Acid Drop

Centers

Longhouse

Cow's
Head

First Break

Waiohai

Brennecke
Beach

Shipwreck

In fact, Kauai is the only island where you can surf on all four coasts in one day (excluding the northwest tip). It's an inspiring surf destination that expands your surfing skills beyond belief. Respect the locals and the rewards are great. With 143 miles of coastline, Kauai boasts surfing, longboarding bodyboarding, windsurfing, snorkeling, hiking, and kayaking.

Hanalei Bay

Hanalei Bay is Kauai's most famous break, known for its long sweeping, pumping right-hand reef break with glassy waves sheltered by the surrounding mountains. The beauty here is beyond belief—one of Hawaii's most scenic surf spots.

Best Tides: Medium to high.

Best Swell Direction: North.

Best Wave Size: Chest high to double overhead.

Bottom: Reef.

Type of Break: Right-hand reef break.

Skill Level: Intermediate to expert.

Best Boards: Short- and longboards.

Best Seasons: Fall and winter.

Crowds: Crowded when the word gets out that the swell is up.

Water Quality: Average to clean.

Hazards: Sharks.

Fees and Permits: No fees or permits are required.

Schedule: Public access 24/7.

Finding the Break

From the Lihue Airport exit, go north for 1.2 miles. Turn left onto Hawaii Route 570 (Ahukini Road) and go southwest for 0.5 mile. Turn right onto the private road and go west for 0.5 mile. Turn hard right onto Kapule Highway and go north for 1.3 miles. Turn right onto Hawaii Route 56 (Kuhio Highway) and go northwest for 25 miles. From Princeville, go northwest on Ka Haku Road for 1.6 miles. Fifty yards before the town of Hanalei, take a right turn down Aku Road, then turn right again down Weke Road, which leads to the beach parking areas. From the airport to Hanalei is a total of 35.5 miles.

Surf Description

With its picturesque top-quality right-hand reef waves set below the beautiful Na Pali Mountains, many consider this the most beautiful surf spot in the world. The ride consists of sweeping, even lines of swell that swing, bend, and catch the Princeville coast at Hanalei Bay to form great waves. You feel as if you're surfing in the presence of ancient kings as you carve around sections and sneak a peak at the grandeur of the mountains ahead, then drop into a barrel and reappear facing a fast walling bowl, then a shoulder and a big cutback situation. The refraction and bending nature of the swell, the clear water, and the very special scenery make this the ride of a lifetime and a wonderful place to be.

Hanalei Bay, Kauai. PHOTO ROD SUMPTER

The paddle-out is easy from either the pier or the beach; the only difficulty—and what makes Hanalei unique—is the very long, slow-sloping depth of water. The 600-yard ride ends in a fadeout fizzle when it's small, and a closeout section when it's big.

Local Events/Attractions

A **farmer's market,** including the Hawaiian Farmers of Hanalei, is held on Tuesday morning in Waipa (just past Hanalei town, driving toward Ha`ena). Contact (808) 241–6390.

Camping

For information on camping in Ha`ena, contact County of Kauai Parks and Recreation, Permit Section, Offices of Community Assistance, Recreation Agency, 4444 Rice Street, Pi`ikoi Building, Suite 330, Lihue, Kauai, Hawaii 96766; (808) 241–4460; www.kauai.hawaii .gov. Permits are required to stay in Kauai County parks.

Places to Eat

Hanalei Dolphin Restaurant
5144 Kuhio Highway (Highway 56)
Hanalei, Kauai
(808) 826-6113

La Cascata
Princeville Resort
5520 Ka Haku Road
Princeville, Kauai
(808) 826–9644

The Bowl is a right-hand outer reef break inside Hanalei Bay that needs a big swell to make it work. The bowl section is a classic—the swell is bent into a U shape that's hard and fast and at times unmakable.

Middle Break is a fickle, long left-hand reef break on the west side of Hanalei Bay, away from the spotlight of the pier and campsite of Hanalei. This side of the bay is sharky but suited for locals who know what they're doing.

Pinetrees is Hanalei Bay's beach break near the pier; it runs west around the horseshoe bay toward Wai Coco's, and it's a fantastic bodyboard wave. On the right day this can be a very fast right- and left-hand slide peeling to a nothing shorebreak or dry sand.

Wai Coco's—the point that lies opposite Hanalei's main point break—is a left-hander off a rocky black-lava-spiked seabed. It breaks close to the point and next to the winding Ha`ena Road. A good longboard wave with roadside access and some parking zones.

Tunnels. You'll have a long paddle-out over sharky waters to this predominantly right-hand peak. Good from 5 to 15 feet, it's a serious wave—a hardcore surfer's wave. Young surfer Bethany Hamilton was attacked by a shark and lost her arm while paddling out through the channel here.

Cannons

This long left-hand reef break fires a surfer like a cannon—hence the name. It's a dangerous reef, and strong rips make this an experts-only wave.

Best Tides: Low to medium.

Best Swell Direction: Northwest.

Best Wave Size: Chest high to double or triple overhead.

Bottom: Coral reef and sand.

Type of Break: Left-hand reef break.

Skill Level: Expert to advanced.

Best Boards: Shortboards and guns.

Best Seasons: Fall and winter.

Crowds: Crowded.

Water Quality: Average to clean.

Hazards: Sharks and localism.

Fees and Permits: No fees or permits are required.

Schedule: Public access 24/7.

Finding the Break

From the Lihue Airport exit, go north for 1.2 miles. Turn left onto Hawaii Route 570 (Ahukini Road) and go southwest for 0.5 mile. Turn right onto the private road and go west for 0.5 mile. Turn hard right onto Kapule Highway and go north for 1.3 miles. Turn right onto Hawaii Route 56 (Kuhio Highway) and go northwest for 25 miles. From Princeville go northwest on Ka Haku Road for 1.6 miles to Hanalei, then proceed through town. You must park at Ha`ena State Park; Cannons is 200 yards left of the lifeguard tower.

Surf Description

One of the fastest and hairiest lefts on Kauai, this fantastic break is a long walling wave with a steep drop-in, a U-shaped face, and a uniquely long, straight barrel. It has a kick-blow action like a cannon going off, forcing you out and down the line. The takeoff here is very close to bare dry coral reefs—a hair-raising speed wall down through a pipe that blasts right next to the rocks and ends in a sand-and-coral-bottomed barrel or at times a continuous barrel to the beach. You need to tuck under the lip and out through the hole to survive.

Cannons is situated 2 miles west of Hanalai Bay, 0.5 mile before the coast road stops at the foot of the Na Pali Mountains. It's a three-minute paddle-out from land beside the lifeguard tower. Surfing here is a question of guts: The reef and rocks are right up front, and the danger increases with the wave height. The bigger it gets, the thicker and heavier the lip, and the scarier and heavier it is to surf. You'll also find a smaller beach break here, which gets dangerous very easily. Cannons is ideal for advanced to expert surfers and bodyboarders.

Cannons, Kauai. PHOTO ROD SUMPTER

Local Events/Attractions

- **Ha`ena to Hanalei Run and Pancake Breakfast,** sponsored by the Hanalei Canoe Club. Call (808) 826–4619 or visit www.hanaleicanoeclub.com.
- **Ha`ena State Park.** At the end of Kuhio Highway (HI 56) in Ha`ena is a scenic sixty-six-acre wildland park. View the Waikapalae and Waikanaloa Wet Caves, sea caves formed about 4,000 years ago, or the nearby Maniniholo Dry Cave. Good for beach-related activities and swimming at Ke`e Beach, with a view of the Na Pali Coast.

Camping

For information on camping in Ha`ena, contact County of Kauai Parks and Recreation, Permit Section, Offices of Community Assistance, Recreation Agency, 4444 Rice Street, Pi`ikoi Building, Suite 330, Lihue, Kauai, Hawaii 96766; (808) 241–4460; www.kauai .hawaii.gov. Permits are required to stay in Kauai County parks.

Hanakapiai. Part of the Na Pali Mountain range, these beaches are cut off and surrounded by peaks. Boat access is your best option, although there are a few trails in for professional climbers-*cum*-surfers who enjoy a bodyboard session that might as well be on another planet.

Kalalau. Part of the beautiful Kalalau Valley, this beach break has the best white-sand beach in the valley, as well as great small-surf conditions for bodysurfing and bodyboarding. Access is by boat if the swell is under 6 feet; expert climbers can hike in. The area picks up a swell when everywhere else is flat.

Polihale Beach

This 7-mile-long beach at the southwest end of the Na Pali Mountains is a boon to those who love deserted beaches and good waves. Getting here involves a trek over red-dirt tracks and dunes to one long beach break of waves.

Best Tides: Low to medium.

Best Swell Direction: Northwest.

Best Wave Size: Chest high to triple over-head.

Bottom: Sand.

Type of Break: Left and right beach break.

Skill Level: Expert to advanced due to the remote location and heavy waves high overhead.

Best Boards: Shortboards.

Best Seasons: Fall and winter.

Crowds: Uncrowded.

Water Quality: Average to clean.

Hazards: No water, no facilities.

Fees and Permits: No fees or permits are required.

Schedule: Public access 24/7.

Finding the Break

Polihale State Park is reached by driving almost to the end of Hawaii Route 50 (Kaumuali`i Highway). Just before HI 50 ends, after the 32-mile mark, a state park sign will mark a left turn onto a dirt sugarcane road. Follow the signs for approximately 5 miles, parking near the waves. Be aware that cars can easily get stuck in the sandy dunes. The beach is 17.1 miles from Kekaha—approximately a forty-five-minute drive, depending on the traffic and time of day.

Polihale Beach, Kauai. PHOTO ROD SUMPTER

Surf Description

Polihale Beach has powerful waves that sweep down from the remote Na Pali beaches. Predominantly rights, they can be groomed by a south swell and trade winds into some of the heaviest, gnarliest short lefts you've ever seen. With needlelike precision you surf explosive power pockets, dodging crests of the superthick waves.

Situated below the southwest end of the Na Pali Mountains, this 7-mile-long beach is remote and crowdless. Here in the still of an evening glass-off surf session, you can be alone with just the waves and the mountain peaks. Many breaks lie along the long beach; only the difficult access keeps you from surfing the lot. Tide, wind, and currents shape some sandbars better than others. Best conditions are in summer south swells or big north winter swells—both can be magic.

Sandbars are best when tiers stick out from rip gullies, forcing the swell to break fast and low, giving perfect walling peaks that are continually shaped by rips and currents. The peak nearest the parking lot is a great indicator for the size and strength of swell you'll find on the rest of the beach; still, it's by no means a definitive sign as to what you'll find just out of sight over the hill, north or south.

At Polihale you can experience some of your best surfing moments, carving down raw swells that drift you away from the parking lot till you're surfing totally alone on a deserted beach. Ideal for the expert to advanced surfer.

Camping

For information about camping in Kauai County parks, contact County of Kauai Parks and Recreation, Permit Section, Offices of Community Assistance, Recreation Agency, 4444 Rice Street, Pi`ikoi Building, Suite 330, Lihue, Kauai, Hawaii 96766; (808) 241–4460; www.kauai.hawaii.gov. Permits are required to stay in Kauai County parks.

For information about camping in state campsites, contact the Department of Land and Natural Resources, Parks Division, State of Hawaii, Kauai District, 3060 Eiwa Street, #306, Lihue, Hawaii, 96766; (808) 274–3444.

Koke`e State Park
Fifteen miles north of Kekaha on Koke`e Road (Hawaii Route 550).

> This spiritually significant area was believed by ancient Hawaiians to be a departure point for souls leaving this earth for the spirit world.

Polihale State Park
Here at Polihale you'll find campsites among sand dunes on the beach, as well as picnic tables, showers, and restroom facilities. Beautiful, long sandy beach. Swimming in summer. Fishing. Check the weather report before heading out by calling (808) 245–6001.

Fishermans. A channel leads out through rips to a left-hander that's mean in winter and sweet in summer. Best in the prevailing northwest swell, it can also offer some fun small summertime wraparound swell that makes for neat longboarding.

Rocket Reef is part of a missile range (hence the name). Access is barred to the public for much of this naval area; below the high-tide mark, however, a long walk will take you to this left-hand reef break.

Barking Sands. Big sand dunes and beach-break waves, with nice left- and right-hand peaks that fold up neatly. When you walk on the sand here, it makes a sound like barking—or, put another way, the sand squeaks when you're dripping wet. It's a nifty experience.

Whispering Sands is a neat reef and beach break, but a fickle one. It offers mostly right-hand waves. The strong rips can make keeping in position a headache; a walkaround after a wave is your best option. A winter west swell is the worst here, but it's a testing wave.

Kini Kini. Good fun summer waves that pick up a summer south swell; still, the best time here is winter, when long rights helped by the sweep push down on a northwest swell. Easy parking; crowds are limited to summer and weekends on a good swell.

Hamburger Reef is a short right-hand reef break close to shore. Heavy tubing waves with thick lips grind the shorebreak and break only 50 to 75 yards out. Best at high tide, and reserved for the expert surfer.

Majors Bay. The Pacific Missile Range Facility (PMRF) located on the shoreline here is one of the foremost centers in the world for the detection of aircraft or vessels in the Pacific. Majors Bay is a well-known windsurfing site, named for one the base's former commanders, a major.

Rifle Range. A walk or four-wheel-drive trek will take you to this fast right-hand beach and coral-bottomed break. It's rarely crowded near the military base, which is surrounded by nice wilderness for 0.25 to 0.5 mile (depending on which public access point you enter).

Targets. You'll need a four-wheel drive to get here. Winter currents are really strong, with a side sweep from the Rifle Range point down toward the lifeguard tower. The waves can be great, though—worth the effort.

Outside Left-Lefts beach and reef break. Distant cloud breaks never seem to be surfed because of their long lulls and fickle nature. Left-Lefts is the exception, with an excellent steep peak and wall. Long paddle.

First Ditch has fast right-handers in a big north swell. Beside the beach shorebreak are ditches that'll help you spot the best place to jump back in as you walk the loop to avoid strong currents after each wave.

Second Ditch is another fast right-hand beach break with long walls located alongside a second ditch that you don't want to fall into. The wave is similar to First Ditch. Think about drift-surfing through to Kekaha.

Kekaha Beach

Kekaha is a mile-long beach break that offers up many classic short, fast rides. It's best in summer with a south swell. The outer reefs always look tempting but are rarely surfed because they break over very shallow reef spurs. In winter a wraparound north swell can produce some good waves.

Best Tides: The tides fluctuate only a foot, and there are two or three per day.

Best Swell Direction: North.

Best Wave Size: Waist to head high.

Bottom: Reef and sand.

Type of Break: Left- and right-hand beach break.

Skill Level: Beginner to expert.

Best Boards: Shortboards and guns.

Best Seasons: Fall and winter.

Crowds: Crowded.

Water Quality: Average to clean.

Hazards: Localism.

Fees and Permits: No fees or permits are required.

Schedule: Public access 24/7. Lifeguard year-round.

Finding the Break

From the Lihue Airport, stay on Hawaii Route 570 (Ahukini Road), which dead-ends at a stoplight approximately 1 mile from the airport. Turn left here onto Hawaii Route 56 and continue through Lihue. HI 56 turns into Hawaii Route 50, which you follow toward Waimea. The beach is located exactly 3 miles northwest of Waimea town, with easy roadside parking. It's 29.8 miles total from Lihue Airport.

Surf Description

Situated 10 miles north of Waimea, 4 miles south of Missile Beach, and not far from Waimea Canyon, this mile-long beach break is very tidal with two and three tides a day. From the lifeguard tower you can see small groups of surfers riding sharp toothpick sticks up and down the coast, but about the best beach break is straight out in front (to the left or to the right) of the lifeguard tower. Just outside the swimming zone are some of the hardest-breaking waves for bodysurfers and bodyboarders. Left and right peaks fold and push over a kind of wedge slab, giving a very short 20-yard blast of barreling fun, right across from a church and homes.

On a 6-foot-plus day, riverlike rips expose lumps of rocks in the shorebreak, adding to Kekaha's hardcore quality. When waves reach double overhead—which is rare—this spot is almost impossible. In straightforward surf, however, it may be the ultimate drift-surfing experience, with a steam-train rip running north–south at 6 miles an hour (experts only). On most regular 2- to 4-foot days, it's only a little hairy; what with the slabs of rock lurching close by, and all the disappearing tubes, you'll be begging for more.

Kekaha Beach, Kauai. PHOTO ROD SUMPTER

Locals like to hang out here watching the talent of the day. And there's a bit of security in knowing that the lifeguard can save you if you get whacked by a blunt shore-break slab of rock swept up and out by the rip.

Local Events/Attractions

A twenty-minute trip up into the mountains behind Waimea town leads to **Waimea Canyon State Park,** which world traveler Mark Twain called "the Grand Canyon of the Pacific." Here the great 3,400-foot-deep gorge takes on the colors of the rainbow, changing like a kaleidoscope as the day progresses. One mile across and 10 miles long, the canyon is nature's tribute to the elements.

Places to Eat

The Shrimp Station
9652 Kaumualii Highway
Waimea, Kauai
(808) 338–1242

Wrangler's Steakhouse
9852 Kaumualii Highway
Waimea, Kauai
(808) 338–1218

Intersections beach break has good right-handers on either side of a lifeguard tower that's staffed year-round. It breaks 50 yards from shore. Beware: Fast sections and rocky outcrops hidden in the shorebreak cause many leg injuries. A wedgy fast left on a south swell.

Teresa's Church is the best break in the area, working as a longer right and left depending on swell direction. It's a long paddle-out through flat rocks and coral alleys, through oncoming white water and swells. Once you're out at the peak, the swells line up toward you perfectly; it's obvious which direction to go on the next wave with your name on it.

Davidsons Point. The last break at the end of the beach of Kekaha is a classic left-hander breaking over flat coral with a small sand beach. The best longboarding waves come when it's 2 to 4 feet with a shortboard over 6 feet. Parking is easy right in front of the break.

Family Housing beach break offers top-to-bottom barrels in a big swell—fun waves, but crowded much of the time. Hot locals perform and compete as a ritual of breaking the barriers down. One of the last really good spots for several miles.

Waimea River Mouth. This break is where a huge amount of fresh water enters the ocean beside Lucy Wright County Park. Always crowded, this works best in a southwest swell, with solid surfing at the river mouth. Mostly left-hand peaks; you'll find more sections along the beach.

Pakalas

This fantastic left reef break is one of the longest on Kauai and is regarded as the perfect wave in small conditions. A superb long left reef break with perfect walls, it's definitely one of the best breaks in the islands. You'll take a 0.3-mile walk through sugarcane fields to reach it—but it's a wave not to be missed.

Best Tides: Low.

Best Swell Direction: South.

Best Wave Size: Knee high to overhead.

Bottom: Reef, coral, and sand.

Type of Break: Left-hand reef break.

Skill Level: Intermediate to advanced.

Best Boards: Shortboards and long-boards.

Best Seasons: Fall and winter.

Crowds: Crowded.

Water Quality: Average to clean.

Hazards: Sharks and localism.

Fees and Permits: No fees or permits are required.

Schedule: Open 24/7.

Finding the Break

From the Lihue Airport, stay on Hawaii Route 570 (Ahukini Road), which dead-ends at a stoplight approximately 1 mile from the airport. Turn left here onto Hawaii Route 56 and continue through Lihue. HI 56 turns into Hawaii Route 50, which you follow toward Waimea. You may see surfers' cars parked 2 miles before Waimea; if so, they're sure to be at Pakalas or from Waimea town. From the big Waimea Bridge, go 2 miles south (counting the bridges). Park on the soft shoulder of the roadside just before the third bridge (look for surf stickers on the side; it's near mile marker 21) and take the track beside the bridge through sugarcane fields for 500 yards to the beach. Pakalas is 25.9 miles total from the airport.

Surf Description

This classic left-hand reef-point break, located 2 miles south of Waimea, is Kauai's best west coast break. It's the most remote and wild in appearance of all the nearby surf spots, but it has days when a fine swell builds just right when elsewhere is flat—days that really pump. On these big days, staying in the surf lineup is difficult; you'll need to paddle against the strong current. Still, there are plenty of markers to line up with, and on small waist- to head-high days, it's easy and a dream wave.

The best waves swing in from around the south point. Because it's too wide to break there, they pick up on the steeply shelving coral bottom at Pakalas to produce a fabulous long, clean left-hand takeoff; with light trade winds and walls edging over for 300 yards, they really peel. At times it looks like a California break here—Trestles in reverse. This soft wave is fun when it's small. A unique feature is a shallow inside that peels off

Pakalas, Kauai. PHOTO ROD SUMPTER

to nothing or only a foot deep. But it's really at its peak at head high with a strong swell. The best swell is a south, but it's also good in a wintertime north swell. Pakalas is a must for intermediate to expert surfers. Not to be missed.

Local Events/Attractions

Cook's Landing. Located in Waimea, one of the oldest communities in Hawaii, this is the site where British explorer Captain James Cook first set foot in Hawaii in 1778.

Places to Eat

The Shrimp Station
9652 Kaumualii Highway
Waimea, Kauai
(808) 338–1242

Wrangler's Steakhouse
9852 Kaumualii Highway
Waimea, Kauai
(808) 338–1218

Avalanches. This cloud break working in 18- to 20-foot swells is an ideal tow-in spot for the big-wave rider. You have to be a big-wave surfer to even think about surfing here, however, and the specialist equipment will set you back thousands of dollars. Classic wave-watching from shore.

Pipes is a shallow reef break piping hot barrels, short rides, and a riptide strong enough to break a leg. Not for the fainthearted. The access is a long way from the main Kaumuali`i Highway.

Salt Ponds

An all-time great wave setup with lefts and rights peeling off a deep-water reef 1,000 yards from shore.

Best Tides: Low to medium.

Best Swell Direction: South.

Best Wave Size: Head high to 10 feet.

Bottom: Coral reef.

Type of Break: Left- and right-hand reef break.

Skill Level: Expert to advanced.

Best Boards: Short- and longboards on small days.

Best Seasons: Spring and summer.

Crowds: Crowded.

Water Quality: Clean.

Hazards: Localism.

Fees and Permits: No fees or permits are required.

Schedule: Public access 24/7.

Finding the Break

From the Lihue Airport, stay on Hawaii Route 570 (Ahukini Road), which dead-ends at a stoplight approximately 1 mile from the airport. Turn left here onto Hawaii Route 56 and continue through Lihue. HI 56 turns into Hawaii Route 50, which you follow toward Waimea until you reach mile marker 17 and a sign that reads PORT ALLEN/SALT POND BEACH PARK. It's a total of 22.8 miles—approximately a thirty-five-minute drive—from the airport. Park under the palm trees and view the distant reef waves.

Surf Description

As you gaze out between the palm trees, sets break and form a perfect A-frame peak. Just behind, hidden in the offshore spray of light trade winds, a surfer clings to the face; beyond that the third wave in the set towers up to 12 feet high as surfers scramble to safety. This is where native Hawaiians surf so fantastically—a very proud place to ride, and one of the nicest surfing spots in the entire Hawaiian Island chain.

Situated 5 miles south of the town of Waimea and 10 miles east of Poipu, Salt Ponds takes its name from the ponds that form behind the beach during the summer months. You can still see Hawaiians making salt here in the only natural salt pond left in the

Salt Ponds, Kauai. PHOTO ROD SUMPTER

state. This is a classic wave setup, with lefts and rights peeling off a deep-water reef 800 yards from shore.

The paddle-out is a long one that leads off a wide sand beach, into a lagoon, and out through a narrow shallow gap in the reefs to deeper waters and a channel. Paddle hard and look up under the shadow of the 12-foot cresting A-frames, then scrabble for the sky beside the loop of the curl, with just enough time to escape and paddle to safety. Now the outer reef waves bear down on you like marching soldiers advancing on your position. A long lull arrives in the wave zone at last, and a set comes exactly the size of the last waves—and you're in perfect position. It's now showtime or humble pie, though somehow it doesn't matter much which—this world is bigger than your ego.

After a long session, you notice a distant break just around the corner at Shark Bay, an easy paddle from Salt Ponds. This is an expert's peak off a rock ledge just around from the little lighthouse on Salt Ponds Point. The break is called Caves because of all the caves up in the cliff; lose your board and that's where it'll end up.

Salt Ponds is ideal for the expert to advanced surfer.

Local Events/Attractions

The **Waimea Town Festival,** held each February, includes sporting events, continuous entertainment, delectable food, games, a Lappert's Ice Cream eating contest, and a ukulele contest. Call (808) 335–2824 for more details.

Camping

Salt Pond Park, at Kaumanali`i Highway and Lele Road southwest of Hanapepe, offers grassy campsites on the beach as well as picnic tables, showers, restrooms, and swimming (with a year-round lifeguard). A permit is required to stay at any Kauai County park. For information, contact County of Kauai Parks and Recreation, Permit Section, Offices of Community Assistance, Recreation Agency, 4444 Rice Street, Pi`ikoi Building, Suite 330, Lihue, Kauai, Hawaii 96766; (808) 241–4460; www.kauai.hawaii.gov.

Hanapepe River Mouth is a fickle reef break down from the famous swing bridge; muddy waters create a wave in summer. It's sharky and spooky to surf here—best in the heat of summer, when there's less murk and more reason to surf.

Acid Drop is a mean reef break with death-defying lefts and rights; it's for the tough and experienced surfer only. Access is dangerous over sharp coral, and spike heads in the lineup make for an extreme surf session.

Centers. A popular right-hand break with the occasional left A-frame takeoffs. Usually crowded with locals, at times this is a fun wave in summer. Best on a south swell with light offshore northerly winds.

Longhouse is a consistent left-hand quality wave from 3 to 10 feet—a short right that fades. Excellent on the right day; it can be the performance wave of the South Shore. It needs a fresh northeast trade wind to blow it out.

Cow's Head. One of the best boarding breaks on the South Shore, with hollow, pounding, short peaks and steep drops. The short barrel is a marvel to look at—like a pipeline. Experts only. It's found at the western end of the Sheraton Kauai Resort, at the intersection of Ho`onani and Kapili Roads.

First Break. This longish right-hander gets crowded in summer. A mellow walling wave with just the right speed to make it fun. It's a good spot for intermediate surfers, but localism is likely on weekends.

Waiohai

This predominantly right-hand reef break is a classic Makaha type of wave: long and peely, yet the hooky curls don't quite tube. Still, the clean wave face and beautiful shoulders are worth their weight in gold.

Best Tides: Low.	**Best Seasons:** Summer.
Best Swell Direction: South.	**Crowds:** Crowded.
Best Wave Size: Chest high to overhead.	**Water Quality:** Clean.
Bottom: Reef.	**Hazards:** Localism and cleanup sets.
Type of Break: Left and right.	**Fees and Permits:** No fees or permits are
Skill Level: Intermediate to advanced.	required.
Best Boards: Shortboards.	**Schedule:** Public access 24/7.

Finding the Break

Turn left from the Lihue Airport and follow Kapule Highway (Hawaii Route 51), passing through Lihue and Nawiliwili. Turning onto Nawiliwili Road (Hawaii Route 58) will bring you to the intersection of Kaumuali`i Highway (Hawaii Route 50), which will take you to the south and southwest sections of the island. This road doesn't follow the coast, however. To reach Poipu, take Maluhia Road (Hawaii Route 520) south. When you come to the intersection marked POIPU ROAD, turn right. At the Waiohai Hotel, turn left and park in the public parking lot. Walk 80 yards following BEACH signs and look out on the reef. It's a total of 18.4 miles from the airport to Waiohai.

Waiohai, Kauai. PHOTO ROD SUMPTER

Surf Description

If you're looking for magical point surf, look no farther than Waiohai Hotel—probably the best point wave on Kauai's South Shore. The waves swing in from behind the points and perform a hot, steamy tribal dance into several reefs.

Waiohai is situated 2 miles west of Poipu and 16 miles south of Lihue, the capital of Kauai. From the parking lot—which is screened from the waves—it's something of a drama to walk around the curved path and glimpse the first reef pumping. Stop right here and wax up. A strip of reef stretches out to sea southward; sections break to form great hot-dog waves and a wave setup consisting of three reefs and a beach break.

First Reef brings up a huge wall of swell breaking over deep water holding big surf—up to 10 feet. Then comes Second Reef, which almost connects to the first; it becomes a re-forming takeoff peak, best at 4 to 6 feet. This hot-dog wall has a mighty wave face that lines up well, and you often fly past turtles returning home from fishing forays. Third Reef offers long lines of sweeping swell that works on small days from 2 to 3 feet. It's best to paddle wide in between sets, and go for the rights—the lefts tend to take you into permanent oncoming white-water slipstreams that are hard to avoid.

If you do go for the lefts, though, the reefs produce fast, nearly vertical down-the-line waves, with several sections ending in a high-performance hollow.

Brennecke Beach

This right- and left-hand beach break works best in a southwest to southeast swell. Brennecke Beach has a reputation as a solid beach-break wave that peaks like spires off multiple sandbars, and is best in summer. These wedgy waves tread their way over a seascape or reefs before breaking across little Brennecke Beach.

Best Tides: Low to medium.

Best Swell Direction: Southeast.

Best Wave Size: Chest high to overhead.

Bottom: Sand.

Type of Break: Left and right beach break.

Skill Level: Beginner to expert.

Best Boards: Bodyboards.

Best Seasons: Summer, fall, and winter.

Crowds: Crowded.

Water Quality: Clean.

Hazards: Localism.

Fees and Permits: No fees or permits are required.

Schedule: Public access 24/7.

Finding the Break

From the Lihue Airport, turn left onto Kapule Highway (Hawaii Route 51), passing through Lihue and Nawiliwili. Turning on Nawiliwili Road (Hawaii Route 58) will bring you to the intersection of Kaumuali`i Highway (Hawaii Route 50), which will take you to the south and southwest sections of the island. This road doesn't follow the coast, however. To reach Poipu, take Maluhia Road (Hawaii Route 520) south. When you come to an intersection marked POIPU ROAD, go straight over; the coast road passes the beach 1 mile on. The speed limit is 20 miles an hour along the seafront, and there's limited free parking. The total distance from the airport is 17.2 miles.

Surf Description

Dropping in, you go straight to the bottom under the hammering black shade of sunset, maybe getting the last wave of the day. Or you could wake early on this southernmost tip of Kauai to the bright light of a morning swell firing crystal waves.

Brennecke Beach breaks are blessed with sunrise and sunset surfing. Like the local turtles that surf, spin, and hunt in the bays and coves, the waves stream in, creating a 360-turn spot on a good peaky slow day. Usually set waves suddenly appear after long lulls, finally breaking as heavy shorebreak barrels that drain dry on the sandbanks close to shore. It's a hot spot for local talent to perform radical maneuvers. At low tide the fast walling sections join up to a neat right-hand reef break 200 yards west of the beach.

Situated 1 mile to the west of Poipu and 12 miles south of Lihue, this right- and left-hand beach break works best in a southwest-to-southeast swell. Brennecke Beach is where most of the Poipu area's barrel riding is done; there are good sandbars produc-

Brennecke Beach, Kauai. PHOTO ROD SUMPTER

ing quality lefts and rights off three short peaks. One is a good bodysurfing and hand-board peak, while the two others are better for bodysurfing. Indeed, Brennecke is Kauai's most famous bodyboarding spot due to consistent south swells in summer, with frequent east wraparound swells in winter and fall. The break is suitable for the beginner on small days, and ideal for the intermediate to expert when bigger.

Places to Eat

Poipu Beach Broiler
1941 Poipu Road
Poipu, Kauai
(808) 742–6433
Seafood and steaks.

Shipwreck. One of the best beach breaks on Kauai, this is a great white-sand beach with a lava-rock right-hander off the middle and a point-break left-hander at the far east end of the bay.

Amonia's is a favorite surfing spot for locals just off the breakwall at Nawiliwili. It's an easy paddle-out from a shaded beach in pretty surroundings. It's a beauty spot except for the human-made harbor wall—which created some waves, but lost more.

Nawiliwili Lihue

A classic right-hand reef break best at 4 to 8 feet in summer, in offshore southwest Kona winds. The break has a long but easy paddle-out, and the wave is usually soft, sweet, and friendly. In the right conditions it's almost perfect.

Best Tides: Low to medium.

Best Swell Direction: Northwest.

Best Wave Size: Chest high to triple overhead.

Bottom: Sand.

Type of Break: Left and right beach and reef break.

Skill Level: All grades, depending on the size of the swell.

Best Boards: Longboards and shortboards.

Best Seasons: Summer, fall, and winter.

Crowds: Popular spot.

Water Quality: Average to clean.

Hazards: Localism.

Fees and Permits: No fees or permits are required.

Schedule: Open from dawn till dark, year-round.

Finding the Break

From the Lihue Airport, turn left onto Kapule Highway (Hawaii Route 51), passing through Lihue; Nawiliwili Beach Park is on your left. Turn into the beach and park. The waves are 400 yards straight out. The drive from the airport is 2.9 miles total.

Surf Description

Take off, slip into a well-defined wall, and hope no one will drop in on you. Either you'll find a pumping, threshing, beating, manic right-hander that pulverizes the senses, or you'll just cruise in fun waist- to chest-high waves along with all the crowds of Lihue.

This is a popular spot. It's been surfed by Duke Kahanamoku, and it has a reputation for firing. It's an easy, lazy wave at times, while at others it's a pumping, steaming, grinding, barreling 6- to 8-foot-plus beast. There's a tight section called the Ledge, with often ten lines to a set, and a 200-yard ride is the norm.

Perhaps more than any other surf spot, Nawiliwili has been described with the word *perfect*. Once conditions are right, surfers gravitate out through a pipeline-spitting

Nawiliwili Lihue, Kauai. PHOTO ROD SUMPTER

shorebreak to the point-break heavies themselves. The beach break is a bodysurfing spot, and on a big day the pounding shorebreak hampers a long paddle out to the crest-shaped reef. The break is excellent in the right swell; the best is early morning on a new south swell. It's a good spot for all grades of surfer.

Local Events/Attractions

- A **Scrimshaw Contest** is held each February at the Coconut Marketplace. For more information, call (808) 822–1401.
- In May, look for the **Kauai Polynesian Festival.** Call (808) 335–6466 or visit www.kauai-polyfest.com.

Cemeteries features fun, demanding barrels just off the Wailua Golf Course; access is off Leho Drive near Lydgate Park. Not known for consistency, it's one of the most easily accessible east coast breaks.

Kitchens, off Leho Drive. The beach has boulders and a patch of coral reef that produces some clean waves in 3- to 4-foot conditions—and on up to 6 feet. A nice spot.

Coco Palms is a good bodyboarding and bodysurfing beach break up to 6 or 8 feet. It holds onshore surf conditions incredibly well and is the performance spot for drop-knee bodyboarding and spinner bodysurfing.

Horners. This beach break has solid lefts and rights with a big east swell or light west winds—but it's fickle. A pretty spot, it gets crowded when it's good. Expect some localism.

Kealia is a powerful reef point break with fast right and lefts off the beach. The bottom is sandy and rocky. Very tough and hairy bodyboarding and shortboard surfing in strong trade winds.

Donkey Beach. Just north of Kealia Beach beyond the point, but sheltered from southeast winds, this beach used to be bathing-suit-optional. It's a bodysurfer's find. Access the beach via old cane roads or by walking from Kealia.

Crack 14 is a good beach break with zippy fast lefts and rights. It's good as an east coast spot, but it rarely pumps—prevailing trades blow apart any east groundswell by midday.

Gas Chambers is a big-wave spot with a big drop and deadly, short rides. It's a mean, gnarly break most of the time due to the prevailing trade winds blowing onshore, but early mornings can be good on a 6- to 8-foot swell.

Anahola Bay

This beach break with numerous wedge sandbars produces waves that rank high in a place where the sun shines on tubing surf and where the east wind keeps the island's most consistent swell going year-round. It's a fun surfing beach and bodyboard scene. Good waves in easterly swell and west winds.

Best Tides: Low to medium.

Best Swell Direction: East.

Best Wave Size: Waist high to overhead.

Bottom: Sand.

Type of Break: Left and right.

Skill Level: Beginner to expert, depending on size.

Best Boards: Bodyboards, shortboards, and longboards on small days.

Best Seasons: Fall and winter.

Crowds: Crowded.

Water Quality: Clean.

Hazards: Localism.

Fees and Permits: No fees or permits are required.

Schedule: Public access 24/7. Year-round lifeguard.

Finding the Break

From the Lihue Airport, go north for 1.2 miles. Turn left onto Hawaii Route 570 (Ahukini Road) and go southwest for 0.5 mile. Turn right onto a private road and go west for 0.5 mile. Turn hard right onto Kapule Highway and go north for 1.3 miles. Finally, turn right onto Hawaii Route 56 (Kuhio Highway) and drive northwest for 12 miles. Anahola is the first beach past the town of Kapa`a; you can't miss it.

Anahola Bay, Kauai. PHOTO ROD SUMPTER

Surf Description

The waves are fast and the wipeouts spectacular as you walk out on this wide expanse of white-sand beach and peer into the eyes of the ocean's treasure chest of tubing waves. This is one of the most consistent surf spots on Kauai due to the prevailing trade winds. There are many onshore days with overhead waves to fully test the skill of any surfer.

Situated 12 miles south of Hanalei Bay and 4 miles north of Kapa`a, this is a beach break with numerous wedge sandbars. When you first catch a glimpse of Anahola from the south, it looks like all the waves are barreling left; if you arrive from the north, they seem to go right. In fact, it's a point break left with a beach break predominantly of rights. Surrounded by the mountains of Kalalea and Anahola, it's protected from west winds and enjoys a short rip current and runout from a steep shorebreak that creates a dozen peaks to surf. The left point break—where waves swing around on northeast trade winds—is the head of the point surf, and can be the best break on the beach. It forms a long way out and pitches out to become a bottomless peak; the only way out is the channels toward the beach. The wave faces are often bumpy and ragged in appearance, but great to surf for maneuvers.

Bodysurfers like Anahola for its drop and short shoulders, bodyboarders for the quick short barrel ride, and shortboarders because it always has some kind of wave breaking. Longboarders enjoy the knee- to chest-high days with long, sloping, soft take-offs and performance straight through to the moment your toes touch dry sand.

Camping

Permits are required to stay in Kauai County parks. For information, contact County of Kauai Parks and Recreation, Permit Section, Offices of Community Assistance, Recreation Agency, 4444 Rice Street, Pi`ikoi Building, Suite 330, Lihue, Kauai, Hawaii 96766; (808) 241–4460; www.kauai.hawaii.gov.

Anahola Beach Park

Kuhio Highway north of Kapa`a Road to right at mile marker 1. Campsites are on the beach. Showers and restrooms are available.

Rock Bay. This heavy beach break lies 2 miles off the main road along a rough dirt road; it's rarely worth the effort. One day a paved road will open up this stretch, and the crowds will flow.

Kalihiwai Beach, at the mouth of the Kalihiwai River, is a beach break. Don't be fooled, however: There are leptospirosis warning signs all over at this beach. Leptospirosis is a bacterial disease that affects humans and animals. Not recommended.

Hideaways, just around the point from Hanalei going east. The break is wedged between cliffs and is in sight of Hanalei Point. This is a classic right-hand point break that picks up swells before Hanalei. There's access from several points, all of them rock-hopping adventures on the Princesville side.

Kauai Resources

Hawaii Activities Offices
Aloha Tower, 5th Floor
1 Aloha Tower Drive
Honolulu, Oahu 96813
(877) 877-1222 or (808) 524-0008
Fax: (808) 599-3778
www.hawaiiactivities.com

Aloha Airlines Baggage Offices
Lihue, Kauai
(808) 245-6618

Bus Service

www.kauai.hawaii.gov

Air Tours

Discount Activities and Internet
Hanalei
(808) 826-1913
www.discountactivities.com

Island Helicopters
(808) 245-8588

Jack Harter
(808) 245-3774

Safari Helicopter
(808) 246-0136

Surf Shops

Activity Warehouse
Poipu Shopping Village
(808) 742-6676
Beach gear rental. Also helicopters,
Na Pali boats, luaus, and more.

Surf Lessons

Aloha Surf Lessons
4524 Lae Road
Kalaheo, Kauai
(808) 639-8614

Garden Island Surf School, LLC
(808) 652-4841
Fax: (808) 332-0654
www.gardenislandsurfschool.com

Nukumoi Surf Company
(888) 384-8810 or (808) 742-8019
Fax: (808) 742-1325
www.nukumoisurf.com

Russell Lewis Surf Coaching
(808) 828-0339

Surf Lessons by Margo Oberg
(808) 332-6100 or (808) 639-0708
www.surfonkauai.com

About the Author

Rod Sumpter has won multiple national and international surfing championships, placed top ten in the World Surfing Championships, acted as president of the English Surfing Federation, held a starring role in the U.S. surfing film *The Endless Summer,* and captured more surfing titles in his thirty years of worldwide competition than most surfers in the world alive today. These days, Rod spends much of his time revisiting and documenting many of his favorite surf spots around the world, many of which are in Hawaii. He is also the author of *100 Best Surf Spots in the World* (Globe Pequot).

Surf Notes

Surf Notes

Surf Notes

Surf Notes

Surf Notes

Surf Notes

Surf Notes

Surf Notes

Surf Notes